KING'S COLLEGE, ABERDEEN, 1560–1641:
FROM PROTESTANT REFORMATION TO COVENANTING REVOLUTION

Quincentennial Studies Series

THE STUDENT COMMUNITY AT ABERDEEN
1860–1939 (1988)
R D Anderson
ABERDEEN UNIVERSITY 1945–1981 REGIONAL
ROLES AND NATIONAL NEEDS (1989)
edited by John D Hargreaves with Angela Forbes

Forthcoming titles include:

BAJANELLAS AND SEMILINAS: ABERDEEN
UNIVERSITY AND THE EDUCATION OF WOMEN
1860–1920
Lindy Moore

PROFESSORS, PATRONAGE AND POLITICS:
THE ABERDEEN COLLEGES IN THE
EIGHTEENTH CENTURY
Roger L Emerson

ENLIGHTENED ABERDEEN: THE ARTS
CURRICULUM IN THE EIGHTEENTH CENTURY
Paul B Wood

THE STUDENT COMMUNITY AT ABERDEEN
BEFORE 1860
Colin A Maclaren

THE UNIVERSITY AND THE STATE IN THE
TWENTIETH CENTURY: THE EXAMPLE OF
ABERDEEN
Iain G C Hutchison

QUINCENTENNIAL STUDIES
in the history of
THE UNIVERSITY OF ABERDEEN

KING'S COLLEGE, ABERDEEN, 1560–1641: FROM PROTESTANT REFORMATION TO COVENANTING REVOLUTION

David Stevenson

With a translation of the New Foundation
by
G Patrick Edwards

1495–1995

Published for the University of Aberdeen by
ABERDEEN UNIVERSITY PRESS

First published 1990
Aberdeen University Press
A member of the Pergammon Group

© University of Aberdeen 1990

British Library Cataloguing in Publication Data

Stevenson, David *1942–*
    King's College, Aberdeen, 1560–1641 : from protestant
    reformation to covenanting revolution. – (Quincentennial
    studies in the history of the University of Aberdeen).
    1. Scotland. Grampian Region. Aberdeen. Universities:
    University of Aberdeen, history
    I. Title   II. University of Aberdeen   III. Series
    378.41235

    ISBN 0-08-040919-9

PRINTED IN GREAT BRITAIN
THE UNIVERSITY PRESS
ABERDEEN

Foreword

In 1995 the University of Aberdeen celebrates five hundred years of continuous existence. Some eighty other European universities had been established before 1500, of which about fifty have survived to the later twentieth century, though not all of those with an uninterrupted history. At Aberdeen, King's College and University was founded in 1495, and Marischal College in 1593, the two combining to form a single university in 1860. Such a long institutional life invites close historical study, as well as celebration; but the 1980s were not an easy time for British universities, and it is therefore the more striking that in 1984 the governing body of the University of Aberdeen decided to commission a series of historical studies in honour of the quincentenary. The decision to commit funds to this project, and to give the Editorial Board such a free hand as we have had, makes the University Court's decision the braver and more honourable.

This third volume in our Quincentennial series tackles one of the most complex and obscure periods in Aberdeen University's long history. What exactly was the 'New Foundation' of King's College in the 1580s, and how far was it implemented? Is it true that King's remained so conservative, even Catholic, that the Earl Marischal was driven to found Marischal College as a rival and more Protestant institution in 1593? Were King's and Marischal always regarded as two separate universities, or as two colleges of one university? Why was there so much dispute at King's between upholders of the New, and of the Old Foundation— the pre-Reformation Foundation of Bishop Elphinstone, as reissued by Bishop Dunbar? What did that particular dispute contribute to other political, religious and personal rivalries to produce at King's a period of remarkable acrimony in the 1630s?

Dr David Stevenson, Reader in Scottish History at the University of Aberdeen, answers these questions, and gives us much insight into the character of college life in the period between the Scottish Reformation and the triumph of the Covenanters in Scotland. He carefully reassesses

v

the fame of the 'Second Founder', Bishop Patrick Forbes, and the reputation of the 'Aberdeen Doctors' led by the bishop's son, Professor John
Forbes. He gives us as much information as can be gleaned about the
teaching and the curriculum at King's, and tantalising small glimpses
of everyday life for staff and students—all that can be won from the
surviving evidence. Indeed, only someone with Dr Stevenson's grasp
of the tangled political and religious history of these times could have
made so much sense out of the very fragmentary evidence which remains
to us, or put the history of King's College so clearly in its Aberdeen and its
national contexts. His interpretation is supported by the first translation
from Latin into English of the text of the New Foundation, a translation
made by Dr Patrick Edwards, also of this university.

It is Dr Stevenson's rather sombre conclusion that, despite all the
problems faced by the university in the years he surveys, the period
dominated by Patrick Forbes came afterwards to seem a golden age,
by comparison with the disasters which overtook King's College in the
1640s and 1650s. No wonder that modern denizens of this university
can draw some comfort from their institution's remarkable powers of
survival.

JENNIFER CARTER
General Editor

Contents

FOREWORD   v
LIST OF ILLUSTRATIONS   viii
PREFACE   ix

PROLOGUE AND EPILOGUE   1
CHAPTER 1   A Cursed Swarm? The Coming of Reformation   7
CHAPTER 2   Detested Novelty. External Pressures and the
            New Foundation   20
CHAPTER 3   Miserable Men in Dead Times? Internal
            Responses to the New Foundation   41
CHAPTER 4   A Second Founder? Bishop Patrick Forbes   61
CHAPTER 5   The Eclipse. The Coming of the Covenanters   94

ABBREVIATIONS   124
NOTES   126
APPENDIX I   Establishments and Salaries under the
               Old and New Foundations   146
APPENDIX II   The New Foundation. An English
               Translation by G Patrick Edwards 149
APPENDIX III   Examination Silver, Chamber Mails and
               Spoon Silver in 1623–4   167
APPENDIX IV   Letter from Principal William Leslie to
               Patrick Maule of Panmure, 1638   169
BIBLIOGRAPHICAL NOTE   172
INDEX   174

List of Illustrations

1 King's College in the mid seventeenth century 3
2 Old Aberdeen c.1660 11
3 Calvin's *Opuscula* 16
4 George Hay's *Oration* 22
5 Ramus's *Commentaries* 43
6 King's College graduation theses, 1622 66
7 Patrick Forbes 84
8 Andrew Strachan's *Panegyricus Inauguralis* 86
9 Device adopted by King's College Library 89
10 James Sandilands elder, canonist 92
11 William Gordon, mediciner 98
12 Arthur Johnston, rector 101
13 David Leech's *Philosophia Illachrymans* 103
14 John Forbes's *Peaceable Warning* 109
15 The Aberdeen Doctors: the Demands, the Answers and the Replies 111
16 The Aberdeen Doctors: the Second Answers and the Duplies 113
17 King's College c.1660 121

Author's Preface

I began the research which has eventually led to this study in the mid 1970s by seeking an answer to a very limited question: why was King's College, Aberdeen, dominated by bitter factional disputes among the staff in the late 1630s? I planned to produce an article on this, but it soon became clear that the explanation lay deep in the college's past, stretching back indeed almost to the Reformation of 1560. There was too much material here to develop adequately in the scope of an article, but the topic was too limited to justify a book. I therefore laid aside my work on university history, allowing myself to be diverted into other research projects for a number of years. But with the emergence of Aberdeen University's Quincentennial History Project in the mid 1980s I blew the dust off old files, for the short monographs which it was proposed to produce seemed well suited to the sort of study my earlier work had been moving towards, and I set to work to broaden it out to provide a general history of the college through eighty tumultuous years. If much of the present study can still be seen as seeking to answer my original question, it is because answering it involves most of the central themes in the college's experience in the period under review.

Work can sometimes be improved by delay, and I think this is true in this instance. In the interval between starting and finishing my work on the college's history, research on unrelated topics covering the same time span has led to the unearthing of a good many fragments of source material relevant to the college's history in places in which I probably would not have otherwise thought of looking for them. A number of publications which have appeared in the intervening years have been most valuable in illuminating both particular developments in the college and the wider background against which its history must be set. And the opportunity for mature reflection has changed my understanding of what was going on in the college—I hope for the better.

With considerable reluctance I have modernised the spelling, and occasionally the punctuation, of quotations. The vagaries of sixteenth-and seventeenth-century Scottish spelling can be a major barrier to understanding for modern readers. My reluctance stems from the fact that the process of modernisation creates a sort of sanitised text, lacking the full flavour of the original. Moreover the process inevitably is an anglicising one, destroying the distinctive Scottishness of the originals. Still, better a translation than a text the reader finds incomprehensible.

Publication of this study takes place just as I am leaving Aberdeen after twenty years in the History Department of the university, and this gives me an opportunity to record how lucky I feel to have served on the university's staff, and how grateful I am for the opportunities I have been given to pursue my researches into early modern Scottish history over these years. More specific acknowldgements of gratitude relating to this piece of research are due to Dr Jennifer Carter, the general editor of this series, and Mr Colin McLaren, the university archivist. Both have been most helpful and supportive during research and writing. So too has Dr Patrick Edwards, who has provided the first full translation of the New Foundation of King's College for inclusion in Appendix II. He has also been most helpful with some other Latin sources when my sadly limping Latinity has needed assistance. The letter transcribed in Appendix IV is published by kind permission of the Earl of Dalhousie. Finally, I am most grateful to Dr James Kirk of the University of Glasgow for reading and commenting in detail on a draft of my text. His comments have led me to make a number of changes which improve the final product—though I should add the sad (and nonetheless sincere for being conventional) confession of authorial guilt: the faults which remain are all my own.

Prologue and Epilogue

> Nowadays in Scotland rewards for learning are few and far between, and they alone keep learning alive (for learning thrives ill on an empty stomach).
>
> Sir Thomas Craig, 1605[1]

The period covered by this study of King's College, Aberdeen, is a complicated and confusing one, with many mysteries and questions that remain unanswered through lack of evidence. There were many changes of direction, a welter of visitations of the college ordered by kings, chancellors, rectors, parliaments and general assemblies—many abortive or urging changes which were never implemented. The college repeatedly came under intense external pressures to change its ways—and sometimes actually did so—and in the latter decades of the period it was riven by bitter internal disputes. It seems therefore a courtesy to readers to provide a brief prologue as a guide to some of the main strands which run through the story and give shape to it. This may help readers to follow the more detailed analysis contained in the chapters which follow.

Some readers, however, may prefer to plunge into the detail without delay, feeling that the sort of over-view provided in these introductory pages would come more appropriately after detailed exploration of the college's history has been completed, thus providing a review and conclusion in the form of an epilogue. If so, they may now skip directly to the start of Chapter 1. Labelling these pages both epilogue and prologue will, I hope, be regarded as more than just an affectation by a lazy author.

The study which follows charts the fortunes of the college between the Reformation of 1560 in Scotland and the creation of 'King Charles's University of Aberdeen' in 1641, between the revolution represented by the coming of Protestantism and the revolution imposed by the covenanters. There is a certain overall symmetry to this period of college history. Not only does it begin and end with revolutionary changes, but in each case these were imposed from the outside, as they were unwelcome to the college and indeed to Aberdeen and the North East of Scotland in general. Radical regimes in Edinburgh imposed their wills on a conservative college. Even more striking is the symmetry of it being proposed in 1560 that Aberdeen should have a two-college university, with resources significantly increased by grants from the revenues of the bishoprics, and the final achievement of this in 1641.[1]

As this long delay of eighty years indicates, the pace of reform was slow in Aberdeen. Not until 1569 did the college even pass into Protestant hands (Chapter 1), and in the decades thereafter Aberdeen was slower than the country's other pre-Reformation universities, St Andrews and Glasgow, to implement the more radical institutional and intellectual reforms associated with the names of Andrew Melville and Pierre de la Ramée, and with the New Foundations or New Erections which were imposed on the universities. But though remaining conservative in some respects, the college was unswervingly committed to Protestantism from 1569. Suggestions that Catholic influences were still present at King's in the late sixteenth century or even the early seventeenth century are erroneous.

The Aberdeen New Foundation first proposed in the late 1570s was never fully introduced, its legal status was never entirely clear, and by the early seventeenth century the college—like Scotland's other universities—was moving intellectually towards a Protestant version of the Aristotelian scholasticism which had previously been denounced (Chapters 2 and 3). Then in 1619–35 Bishop Patrick Forbes as chancellor of the university sought with self-righteous fury to sweep away the New Foundation, claiming that it was invalid, and that the pre-Reformation foundation was therefore still in force. Undoubtedly the bishop did much to revive the college's fortunes, and usher in its one era of modest

facing page

1   King's College in the mid seventeenth century. This anonymous oil painting is the earliest surviving view of the college. It shows the crown on the tower as it was rebuilt after the older crown collapsed in a storm in 1634. The shallow pyramidal roof under the crown was soon replaced by a flat roof, as shown in James Gordon's view of c. 1660 (see plate 17 below). From an artistic viewpoint the painting has been described as a 'daub' exhibiting 'gauche, juvenile crudity and inaccuracy', but historically it is of considerable value, showing the college in the form in which it existed in the period covered by this study. (R S Walker, 'The oldest view of King's College', *AUR*, 31(1944–6), 26–7). Aberdeen University, Committee Room 2.

intellectual distinction in the period under review (Chapter 4). But the core of the college's staff was never reconciled to the abandonment of the New Foundation, and after the bishop's death the college was immediately plunged into fratricidal strife between New and Old Foundation factions.

At one level it was simply a dispute about the legal situation: which foundation was legitimate according to the law of the land? But at a more practical level it was a dispute whose basic issues are, alas, again relevant in British universities today. When resources are inadequate or declining, what academic strategies are least damaging? The New Foundationers sought to narrow the range of subjects taught, arguing that it was best to concentrate the resources available on core areas—in this case, the basic arts curriculum and theology. Bishop Forbes and the Old Foundationers replied indignantly that intellectual respectability required the maintenance of the full traditional range of subjects, and they therefore restored the medical and the two law (canon and civil) faculties by appointing nominal teachers in these subjects. But this achievement was more cosmetic than anything else, for continuing lack of the resources necessary to finance this revival added weight to the arguments of the New Foundationers. Moreover, in spite of his concern to revive the three lost faculties, Bishop Forbes had in common with all the other regimes which dominated the college in these eighty years the assumption that the basic function of the university was training parish clergy: and his most significant institutional achievement was the foundation of the chair of theology which was occupied with great distinction for twenty years by his son, John Forbes—the most distinguished scholar to hold office in the college since the Reformation. Patrick Forbes can also be seen as the inspiration behind the distinctive Aberdeen school or cast of thought, best known through the stand the 'Aberdeen Doctors' made against the covenanters in 1638. The Aberdeen theologians argued for Protestant unity: there was agreement on fundamentals, and the differences which separated the various Protestant churches were in matters in which flexibility and the acceptance of a measure of disagreement were legitimate. In the context of an age riven by rival fanaticisms this intellectual tendency is attractive, and it has been much praised by ecumenically-minded modern historians. The praise is partly misplaced, however: the Aberdeen theologians might be more tolerant than most, but their arguments about the necessity of making concessions to achieve Protestant unity were inspired by the belief that only through such unity could Protestantism survive and defeat the antichristian menace of Catholicism. Nonetheless, the relative tolerance of the Aberdeen Doctors is creditable when contrasted to the rigidity of their covenanter opponents. But the covenanters had the big battalions on their side: the college was purged, and thus the only period of notable intellectual achievement in the college since the Reformation was brought to an abrupt end by the expulsion of its greatest scholar, John Forbes (Chapter 5).

In its slowness in accepting Reformation and a New Foundation, King's College might be said to be 'backward' compared with its Scottish counterparts: but none of them could boast a distinction such as that shared by King's and Marischal Colleges in producing the Aberdeen Doctors. For the rest of the period, King's tends to appear humdrum and rather inward-looking, though this conclusion may be influenced by lack of evidence about what was going on in the college in the decades immediately before the arrival of Bishop Forbes. It seems clear, however, that the college's finances were managed incompetently, perhaps corruptly, in the decades before 1619: scholars are not necessarily the best administrators, a theme common in university history. So too is the fact that scholars may have lofty ideals, but in conflict with their colleagues they can be as petty, bitter and unscrupulous as anyone else—a point well displayed in the dispute over the two foundations. Nor was intellectual and social vitality in the college stimulated by the fact that, of the first four Protestant principals who headed it in the years 1569 to 1639, three (Alexander Arbuthnot, Walter Stuart and William Leslie) are specifically described as melancholic; and the fact that the character of David Rait, the longest-serving of the four (principal from 1592 to 1632), remains so obscure suggests that the same word may well apply to him. Respected scholars these four principals might be, but none proved an inspiring leader.

Certainly all the successive changes accepted by or imposed on the college failed to lead to the large increases in student numbers hoped for. There was a recovery from the slump in numbers in the years around 1560, but in the opening decade of the seventeenth century the college remained small even by Scottish standards—though by then the emergence of Marischal College, providing an alternative destination for northern students, can hardly have failed to affect recruitment to King's. Numbers grew somewhat in the period of Bishop Forbes's reforms—but only modestly. Still, the college was producing significant numbers of candidates for the parish ministry, and under Forbes their academic training was probably better than in previous generations. If the college consistently failed to live up to the church's high expectations of it, the same is true of Scotland's other colleges—and at least the acquisition of some of the revenues of the deposed bishops in 1641 held out some hope of solving the perennial financial problems that beset all the colleges and had contributed much to academic decline and low morale. The 1640s were to prove that optimism was unjustified.

★

Very little information survives to indicate what students made of their experiences in the college. The few fragments that do survive suggest satisfaction, but perhaps only the satisfied recorded their opinions, conventional loyalty to their college silencing the discontented. The fullest expression of student opinion comes near the end of our period, and it is perhaps appropriate to end with it—though it must be admitted that the student concerned was far from typical, being of high birth and having no intention of graduating.

Simon Fraser, Master of Lovat, decided at the age of fifteen or so to sample university life. In January 1636 he:

> well appointed with a noble retinue, goes to university, choosing the first year to study at the King's College of Aberdeen . . . and all the while he stayed there not one nobleman in both colleges was in greater esteem, beloved of all that conversed with him, the ornament of the university, as he was termed, singular at all exercises and recreations, 'ballown, cachpole, byars, bowles, the goffe, and artching'. And it is observable that at the strictest rate he carried the arching that year 'at bowmarks and rovers' gaining the silver arrow.

In 1637 the master:

> took another tour and progress south, stayed a quarter of a year in the University of St Andrews, in the Leonardine College, to try the different methods of learning there from Aberdeen, where he had spent his former course. In the spring he returned north, and passed another quarter at King's College, where, as he said, there was more profit to be had, where he best liked the grain of the students and genuine temper of the masters. By this time he is master of some philosophy and, after seeing the solemnity of the graduation, he returned home in July.[2]

This sporting young aristocrat was doubtless more interested in extra-curricular activities than anything else; but such activities have often bulked largest in student memories of their university experiences, as more profitable and formative than their academic studies (a sobering thought for their teachers down the ages), and they have always been seen as legitimate and important aspects of university life. The masters of the college would probably have been well pleased with Simon Fraser's testimony.

Chapter 1

A Cursed Swarm? The Coming of Reformation

. . . . I pray you to eject
A cursed byke [swarm] that chiefly does malign [act malignantly]
In Aberdeen, of sophists the wellspring;
And in their place put learned men of God.
                                        'Exhortation to the Regent', 1567[1]

The year 1560 saw the triumph of the Protestant Reformation in Scotland, with Catholic worship outlawed and a new reformed Confession of Faith given official approval. But it was to be another nine years before Protestantism triumphed in King's College, Aberdeen.[2] In many parts of Scotland there were considerable delays in turning the official victory of 1560 into the reality of firmly established Protestantism, and nowhere in Lowland Scotland was this more clearly seen than in the North East. In general the new church found itself hindered by what it saw as lack of full commitment by the state to supporting it—at first because Mary Queen of Scots herself remained a Catholic, and after her abdication in 1567 through the political instability of the regimes which sought to control the country during the long minority of King James VI. This lack of full commitment meant that the process of removing clerics who remained Catholics from their livings was a slow and gradual one and, as a result, the transfer of property from the old, moribund church to the new Protestant church was protracted—and indeed a process which was never completed, as the strength of lay vested interests in the property of the old church was so strong that, in the event, much of it was lost permanently to the new church.

In the North East of Scotland the new church found particular problems in addition to the general ones of lack of money and ministers. The region tended towards conservatism in both religion and politics. Some scattered evidence of support for Protestant heresy can be traced in the decades before 1560, but occasional general statements suggesting that heresy was thriving in the area seem to reflect Catholic panic rather than reality. Even when Protestantism gained official approval at the national level, no strong support for it appeared in the region.[3] The indications are that the majority who wished to retain the old faith were at first encouraged in resisting Protestantism by the fact that the two leading figures in the region in civil and ecclesiastical affairs actively resisted the revolution of 1560. George Gordon, 4th Earl of Huntly, was one of the most powerful men in all Scotland and dominated the whole North East. In the crisis of 1559–60 he vacillated, but thereafter he openly defied the new church, hindering its efforts to gain a foothold in the region, and urging Mary Queen of Scots to join him in seeking to reimpose Catholicism by force of arms. William Gordon, his uncle, was Bishop of Aberdeen—and thus, *ex officio*, chancellor of the University of Aberdeen. Though guilty of the prevailing sins of the prelates of the age (keeping concubines and alienating church property wholesale to relatives and friends),[4] Bishop Gordon not only remained loyal to the old faith but continued to reside in his palace in Old Aberdeen, thus acting as a focus for defiance of the new church. The example of the two Gordons, earl and bishop, encouraged most lesser landowners, many of the common people and significant numbers of the old Catholic clergy to attempt to hang on to their old faith. It was these local circumstances that made it possible for King's College to defy Protestantism—with both deeds and words—for nearly a decade after 1560.

Reformation came first to a reluctant Aberdeen through violence. When it became clear that Aberdeen was not going to support the revolt of the Lords of the Congregation against Catholicism voluntarily, an armed mob of reformers from Angus and the Mearns occupied the burgh in the last days of December 1599, looting three friaries. The mob then moved on to the adjacent little burgh of Old Aberdeen, the ecclesiastical centre of the diocese, containing the bishop's palace, the cathedral of St Machar and King's College. The mob evidently managed to plunder the cathedral, but a later tradition claims that the college was saved, being defended by staff and students organised by the subprincipal, Alexander Anderson.[5] Unfortunately, though the actuality of this incident has been generally accepted by historians, the evidence relating to it is confusing and uncertain. It is first mentioned in a late seventeenth-century source: the fact that it is one generally hostile to Anderson might be seen as giving it credibility in this instance, as it praises Anderson, but it fails to date the incident. Further, it specifically credits Anderson with saving the lead from the chapel roof and its bells from the reformers. But a mob out for easy loot would not have had the time or facilities to attempt to carry off the vastly heavy lead and bells. Eight years later, however, lead was stripped from the roofs of the cathedrals of Aberdeen and Elgin (see below, page 15), and it may have been resistance by Anderson at this later date to efforts to extend the pillaging of lead to the college chapel that this source refers to. To add to the confusion, there is also evidence of damage to the college in 1561.[6]

The zealous reforming mob of December 1559 soon withdrew from Aberdeen, and the fact that it had succeeded in forcing the burgh into official support for the Lords of the Congregation showed that the threat to the old religion was a real one, even in the north. But the staff of King's College were not cowed into passivity by this, hoping to retain their religion by avoiding drawing attention to themselves. On the contrary, when in January 1561 Subprincipal Anderson and John Leslie, the canonist (professor of canon law), were summoned to Edinburgh with other Aberdeen clerics to answer for their stubborn Catholicism, they not only went but were prepared to stand up publicly for their beliefs in the capital. They debated some of the central points of their faith with John Knox and other Protestant ministers. According to Knox, he wiped the floor with these ignorant and superstitious papists: when questioned on the Mass and sacraments, Anderson evaded the issue, eventually excusing himself by saying 'that he was better seen in philosophy, than in theology'. Leslie did no better, confessing 'I know nothing but the canon law'.[7] Luckily we have Leslie's own account (or rather two accounts) to balance this. In the first account he states, fairly moderately, that 'nothing was concluded, for that every one of them remained constant in their own profession'.[8] Later, however, Leslie converted a drawn debate into a Catholic victory: Anderson 'answered so cunningly, constantly and ably, that the Catholics he much confirmed, the heretics so flyted [chided or ridiculed], and abased so far'.[9] In practical terms the debate achieved nothing, but it was symptomatic of the way in which clerics and theologians associated with Aberdeen provided many of the leading Scottish Catholic apologists in the years after 1560: Catholicism in the area was stronger and more articulate than anywhere else in Scotland.[10]

According to John Leslie, the outspoken Aberdeen clerics were ordered to remain in Edinburgh after the debates, it being 'a long span' before they were allowed to return to Aberdeen. But their detention cannot have been prolonged: as Leslie himself relates, by mid April he had not only returned to Aberdeen but had been commissioned by Huntly and other Catholic nobles to go to Mary Queen of Scots and offer to help her restore Catholicism by force; had sailed to France; and had had an audience with her.[11]

Leslie now disappears from college affairs, becoming secretary to Mary Queen of Scots, and later Bishop of Ross. Anderson returned to the relative obscurity of Old Aberdeen, to continue the difficult task of running a Catholic college in a Protestant country. While Anderson had been away in Edinburgh the college had suffered an attack of some sort, perhaps taking advantage of the absence of some of the most senior and active staff. In February, while still in Edinburgh, Anderson had been instructed to produce a charter relating to a case before the Court of Session in which he was involved. His reply was that it had been in his own chamber 'when he last came from home', but that since then 'the said college and the houses thereof are broken up', so he was not sure the charter was still there for him to produce.[12] Whether the damage to the college had been the work of religiously inspired Protestants or burglars with more mundane motives remains unclear.

The fact that Queen Mary herself remained a Catholic may at first have given some hope for the future to Anderson and his colleagues, and they must have been encouraged by the fact that when, in 1561, a tax was imposed on the clergy of the old church of one-third of their revenues, the revenues due to King's College were exempted from payment. The college, it seems, was valued as an educational institution even though it was in Catholic hands. But in 1562 Queen Mary followed the advice of her Protestant advisers by leading an army north to tame the pretensions of the Gordons and punish their open support for the Catholic cause. This objective was easily achieved, with the defeat of Huntly's forces at the battle of Corrichie and the convenient death of the earl immediately afterwards. Catholics in King's College as elsewhere must have feared the consequences of this victory by a Protestant regime in the heartland of Catholic resistance, but in fact the regime knew its limitations. The Gordons had been taught a lesson, but any attempt to destroy their power completely and impose Protestantism would have led to civil war.

facing page

2   James Gordon's map of Old Aberdeen in about 1660, showing the little market town sandwiched between the two institutions which dominated it, King's College to the south and St Machar's Cathedral to the north. The bishop's palace, residence of Patrick Forbes, lay just to the east of the cathedral, but it was in ruins by this time. The following is a key to some of the numbers on the map:

11   The Musician's Manse, residence of the cantor and master of the Music School—Gilbert Ross in the 1630s.
12   The Grammar School—just to the east of the numeral, attached to the west front of the college.
13   The Humanist's or Grammarian's Manse. He also acted as master of the Grammar School.
15   Site of the Canonist's Manse.
17   The College Garden.
18   The Mediciner's Manse, home of William Gordon in the 1630s.
19   Ruins of the Civilist's Manse.
20   Professor of Divinity's Manse, residence of Professor John Forbes.
25   The Marquis of Huntly's house.

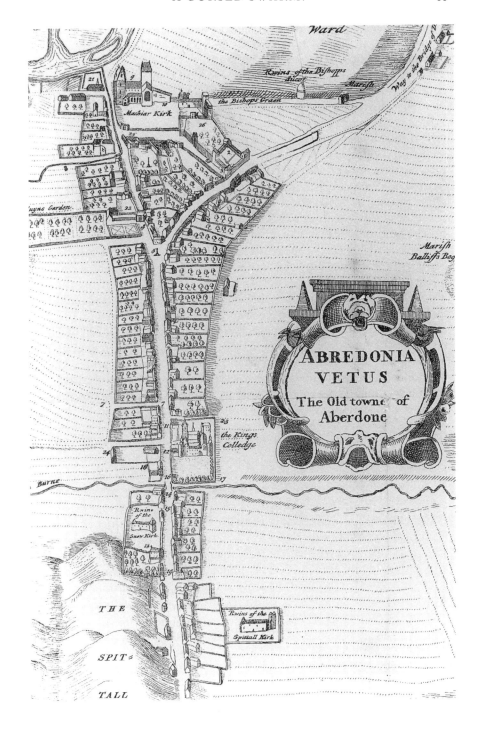

Ward

Ruins of the Bishops Pallace   Marish

the Bishops Green

Way to the Bridge of D

Muchiar Kirk

Tuyns Garden

Marish
Balliffs Bog

ABREDONIA
VETUS
The Old towne of
Aberdone

the Kings
Colledge

Burne

Ruins of the
Snow Kirk

THE

Ruins of the
Spittall Kirk

SPIT

TALL

Thus only five days after Corrichie Mary signed a letter of protection, confirming the rights of King's College: a formality perhaps, but a reassuring gesture in the circumstances.[13]

There is very little evidence as to the condition and activities of the college and its staff in these years of lingering Catholicism. On the one hand the spirited resistance of the college to Reformation, unique among Scotland's universities, suggests confidence and high morale—though one of the college's regents (Gilbert Gardyne) may have defected to the new church.[14] A generation earlier, in 1534, an Italian visitor had called Aberdeen the most celebrated university in Scotland.[15] The reputation of Aberdeen scholars was high, their academic achievements considerable, their contacts with the wider world of European learning and humanist and other trends within it close.[16] But there is also evidence of decline by 1560, not just in Aberdeen but in the universities of Glasgow and St Andrews as well. There seems to have been an increasing tendency for Scots to be sent abroad instead of to Scottish universities.[17] The records of a visitation of King's College in 1549 present a sorry picture of low student numbers, staff neglecting their duties, discipline collapsing, and buildings in disrepair[18]—though it has been argued that decline at Aberdeen was not as serious as at the other two universities.[19] When Mary Queen of Scots reached Old Aberdeen in August 1562 an English agent accompanying her was not impressed: he observed that there was a university there, but added sarcastically that it was really just one college with fifteen or sixteen students.[20] As teaching staff probably numbered about nine in the 1560s (as in the 1550s)[21] this indicates an enviable staff-student ratio, but there can have been little else to envy. We have no earlier figures for student numbers with which to compare the 1562 figure. Numbers had probably already been very low immediately before 1560, and it seems probable that further decline took place through the decade that followed: a Catholic education intended primarily to lead to the priesthood did not provide good career prospects in a Protestant country in which saying Mass repeatedly was a capital offence. Some effort may have been made to modify teaching to take account of the Reformation: but all that can be said with certainty is that teaching continued and a tiny trickle of students graduated. Theophilus Stewart, the grammarian, has left us a detailed account of the daily routines of the grammar school in which he taught outside the college,[22] but neither he nor his colleagues describe life within the college. However, one scrap of surviving evidence reveals students engaged in practical experimentation in the science of astronomy. James Cheyne of Arnage evidently graduated in 1566, and later became a professor in the Catholic college at Douai. In one of his publications when discussing the movements of the stars he refers to the 'elevation of the pole such as we ourselves have observed in Aberdeen, almost in the middle of Scotland, in order that students may more easily gain practice'. Moreover, the observation recorded was surprisingly accurate, though it has been suggested this was more due to luck than to unusually advanced methods. Activity in the medical faculty—or at least by the mediciner—is demonstrated by the publication by Gilbert Skene in 1568 of the first Scottish medical treatise to be printed.[23] The college might be in decline, the future uncertain, but clearly there were still sparks of light.

As well as being an academic institution the college was also a collegiate church, with provision for frequent and elaborate services in the chapel. Mass was probably said more often in Old Aberdeen than anywhere else in Scotland in these years—though Queen Mary herself ordered Bishop Gordon to desist in 1565[24]—and doubtless it was said from time to time in the college chapel. But services were probably irregular, as old routines collapsed. As the years passed the staff must have come to accept that it was all but inevitable that a time would come when the Protestant regime felt strong enough to destroy Scotland's last remaining Catholic university.[25] Some continued to be optimistic, however bad things seemed in worldly terms. It was evidently a student at the college who wrote, as late as 1566:

> Good Lord, how splendid and joyfull will that day be when the fear of pestilent heresy is left behind and we shall be able to frequent the normal study of letters. At present, alas, some scholars run here, some there, like vagrants, in confusion.[26]

A few new appointments to posts in the college can be traced in these years as indications of continuing activity. Three canonists held office in turn in 1560–9.[27] John Kennedy, evidently the town clerk of Aberdeen, became bursar of civil law in 1562;[28] and a few years later Subprincipal Anderson at last became principal on the death of John Bisset: the latter had been sick for many years, Anderson in effect running the college.[29]

By the mid seventeenth century assertions were being made that Anderson, foreseeing a Protestant take-over, deliberately ran down the college so that it would be of little value to the heretics.[30] Anderson, according to a rather later version of the story:

> was a great scholar, and a subtle disputant, but no great friend to the college. For the hatred he bore to the reformed religion, he alienated some of the college revenues, destroyed many of its writings and evidences [charters], whereby many lands and other rents . . . are quite lost; sold the ornaments, books and other furniture belonging to the college.[31]

The story has generally been dismissed as malicious Protestant propaganda, perhaps intended to disguise the sins of a later Protestant principal, David Rait, in alienating college property.[32] But though the story may be exaggerated, there may be some truth in it—truth not necessarily discreditable to Anderson when seen in terms of his beliefs. Friars and other Aberdeen clerics had transferred their property to individual burgesses or to the burgh itself in the hope of saving it from plundering by the reforming mob from the south in 1559, the hope being that when Catholicism was reimposed the property could be returned to the church. The treasures of St Machar's Cathedral had been entrusted to the Earl of Huntly and others to save them from the same threat.[33] Might Anderson not have acted in the same way? Indeed, especially where 'the ornaments, books and other furniture' were concerned, would this not have been positively a duty? When the Protestant take-over took place the elaborate liturgical manuscripts, the rich vestments and other embellishments of the chapel would immediately become surplus to requirements, to be destroyed or broken up and sold. Any conscientious custodian of such property would be likely to seek to preserve it from such a fate, and precedents were there for Anderson to follow in transferring it to sympathetic local Catholics. Moreover, in acting in such a way Anderson would have been following the lead of the university chancellor: Bishop Gordon was highly active after as well as before 1560 in alienating the lands of his bishopric through feuing, and other revenues through gifts of pensions, in a way which might be taken to suggest a determination to leave as little as possible to a Protestant successor.[34] Nonetheless, responsibility for the disappearance of much of the moveable property of the pre-1560 college remains obscure: Protestant sources tend to blame Anderson, Catholic ones to denounce Protestant destruction—like the imaginative early seventeenth-century priest who claimed that the furious heretics partly burnt the contents of the college library, consigning the rest to the common sewer![35] The only certain conclusion is that the claims made by the various sources tell us more about their authors' prejudices than about historical events.

That Reformation did not come to King's College until 1569 was due to political circumstances, and was certainly very much against the wishes of the new Protestant church. The First Book of Discipline, the 1560 blueprint of the reformers for their new church, had sketched elaborate plans for university reform. St Andrews was to have three colleges, while Glasgow and Aberdeen would have two each, specialising in different fields of study.[36] These great plans came to nothing, though Glasgow and St Andrews at least became Protestant institutions without the long delay experienced by Aberdeen.

In 1563 and again in 1565 the general assembly ordered that all university teachers be adherents of the new faith, those who were not being replaced,[37] but the church was powerless to implement such orders in Aberdeen without state help. Not until 1567, with the Catholic Mary Queen of Scots replaced by a Protestant regent, the Earl of Moray, did attention at the national level return to university reform, as part of a more general assault on the country's remaining Catholics. The anonymous poet quoted at the head of this chapter urged Moray to purge the Catholic stronghold of Aberdeen of the cursed swarm infesting it,[38] and on 25 July the general assembly of the kirk ruled that:

> none be admitted, nor permitted hereafter to have charge over schools, colleges, universities, or yet openly and publicly to instruct the youth, but such as have been tried by the superintendents and visitors of the kirk; such as shall be found sound, and able to teach, and as shall be admitted by them to their charges.[39]

In the same year (1567) Moray discussed his intention of reforming the universities—with an optimistic correspondent who believed that excellence in letters was 'flitting out' of the 'hot countries to refresh themselves in the cold and wholesome air of Scotland'.[40] But though the kirk was evidently spurred on by complaints from Adam Heriot, the first Protestant minister of Aberdeen, at the continued existence of a Catholic institution, King's College, virtually on his doorstep in Old Aberdeen,[41] progress in applying the act locally was slow. When in February 1568 Alexander Anderson was summoned to appear before the privy council it was as one of a group of Aberdeen Catholic clerics, not through any initiative aimed directly against King's College.[42] But in July 1568 the general assembly, doubtlessly encouraged by Heriot, urged the regent to appoint commissioners to reform the college of Aberdeen 'so that the youth may be instructed in godliness and good letters'. The Earl of Moray duly ordered a commission to be issued for placing godly and qualified masters in King's.[43] Yet again no immediate action followed this declaration of good intentions. The 5th Earl of Huntly was openly defying the regent and working to restore the dethroned Mary Queen of Scots, and the college lay firmly within his protective sphere of influence—though there was an ominous indication of the limitations of that influence in that the lead from the roofs of the cathedrals of Aberdeen and Elgin was stripped off and sold on Moray's orders,[44] and the lead of King's College Chapel may also have been threatened.[45] Many local notables made formal protests at this plundering of St Machar's Cathedral, but though many were university graduates (most of whom

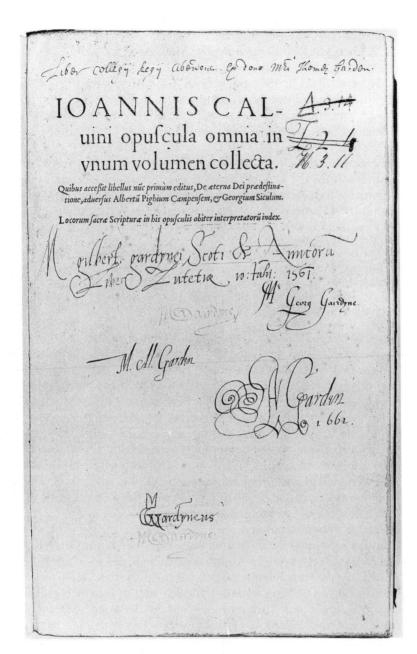

3   Title page of a copy of Calvin's *Opuscula*, published in the 1550s, bearing the signatures of Gilbert Gardyne (dated 1561) and of later members of his family. Gardyne had been a regent in King's College in the 1550s, but it is not known whether he was still a regent when he became a Protestant.

AUL, π f. 2081 Cal 1.

had probably been educated at King's), only one member of the college staff is known to have ventured to sign—the canonist.[46]

Huntly's challenge to the authority of the regime forced the regent into giving priority to the situation in the North East. In 1569 Moray's pressure forced Huntly to submit, and he followed up this success by marching an army north to receive the submission of Huntly's followers and establish the regime's authority by 'showing the flag' in the region. Having done this, the regent on his way south stopped in Aberdeen and dealt with the relatively minor problem posed by the stubborn Catholicism of King's College. The attack was a joint one by church and state, the former represented by John Erskine of Dun, Superintendent of Angus and the Mearns and also (since no superintendent for Aberdeen had been appointed) commissioner for the shires of Aberdeen and Banff, and the latter by the regent and his council.

On 29 June 1569 Principal Anderson, Subprincipal Andrew Galloway and two regents in arts (Andrew Anderson and Duncan Norie) were summoned to sign the reformed Confession of Faith. They appeared on 30 June and steadfastly refused. All of them were therefore deprived of their posts in the college by the regent and his council as 'persons dangerous and unmeet to have care of the instruction of the youth'. The college and its property was to be handed over to the provost of Aberdeen for safe-keeping until persons of sound doctrine and sufficient literature were appointed to replace them. The church then added its authority to that of the state. Erskine of Dun summoned the staff, and though only the two Andersons appeared he deprived them all and ordered publication of the sentence against them the following Sunday, 3 July. The church's deprivation names a third regent, Thomas Ogston: doubtless the sentence of the regent had been intended to include him as well, his name having been left out of the records by accident.[47]

The purge did not represent a clean sweep of the college's academic staff: the canonist (Alexander Cheyne), civilist (Nicholas Hay), mediciner (Gilbert Skene) and grammarian (Theophilus Stewart) all continued in office. So too did the sacrist (Alexander Wright).[48] There are two possible ways of interpreting this. They may have been left in office as they were (or hastily became) Protestants. Far more likely, however, is that they were ignored because no need was seen for deposing them. The sacrist was not a teacher and the others taught in higher faculties that had few if any students. The men deposed were those directly involved in teaching arts and theology. That was the minimum that would satisfy the new church. That being done, other staff were left in office, just as Catholic clergy in the parishes were still being allowed to retain their benefices—though not to say Mass.

The blow of deprivation in 1569 was softened by the fact that in the years ahead it was still possible to practise Catholicism in the area without too much difficulty: in 1572 Old Aberdeen was named as one of the few places in Scotland where Mass was still being said.[49] Andrew Galloway, the former subprincipal, was able to practise his religion locally until 1578, when he evidently went into exile in France.[50] Of the three deposed regents two disappear without trace, but Thomas Ogston emerges in the 1580s as master of Turriff grammar school, presumably after conforming at least outwardly to Protestantism—though his son is recorded as a Jesuit novice.[51] Bishop Gordon, anomalously, remained chancellor of the now Protestant university of Aberdeen. He also must have made some token submission to Protestantism in order to retain office, as under legislation of 1573 he would otherwise have been deposed: but in reality he remained a notorious Catholic until he died in 1577.[52] Alexander Anderson was not so flexible. In 1573 he was deprived of the parsonages and vicarages of Mortlach and Tyrie, and the vicarage of Kinkell and Tullynessle.[53] Moreover he was summoned to Edinburgh and ordered to accept the reformed Confession of Faith, remaining there until he did so. When he returned home in defiance of these orders he was 'put to the horn' (declared an outlaw) and his moveable goods were ordered to be confiscated.[54] But though he incurred excommunication as well as outlawry, in the Catholic stronghold of Old Aberdeen he was able to cling to his faith until his death in 1577.[55] Alexander Cheyne, the canonist, proved more ready to change with the times when the crunch came in 1573: he is recorded as conforming to the new faith.[56]

For over half a century King's College had been an institution dominated by the Catholic church and dedicated primarily to serving it by educating clerics. The 1529 charter defining its structure specified that out of a total of twenty-three adult members of staff, twenty-two must be priests or students of theology. A few graduates who remained laymen can be identified, but the 1549 visitation ordered that all masters of arts be ordained.[57] The college had always remained small, with probably never more than a few dozen students, and its faculties of canon law and medicine in particular had failed to develop, though there are indications of at least sporadic activity in them and it has to be remembered that much is obscure through lack of records and it is dangerous to equate this with lack of activity. The college may have been facing increasing problems of recruitment and morale in the decade or two before 1560, part of the wider problems being experienced by the old church. But, in spite of all this, the college had had a notable impact on the region. The way in which Protestantism failed to win widespread support in the region before, and even after, 1560 can be explained partly by geographical, social and political arguments, but appears to owe something also to the little nucleus of orthodox scholarship at the college and to the graduates it produced, men who came to hold many of the old church's benefices in the North East. The example set by Principal Anderson and his colleagues after 1560 is another symptom of the relatively high morale and religious and intellectual confidence of the college, which produced the only Catholic staff at a Scottish university willing to venture into the lion's den and undergo the bruising experience of debating theology with John Knox before a largely hostile audience. In the end the college's defiance of Reformation proved futile: its stand proved one of a few isolated examples of Catholic resistance, contrasting with the willingness of the vast majority of the Catholic clerics either to conform to the new faith or at the most adopt a low profile and hope to hang on to at least part of their revenues without converting.

The 1569 purge at King's was intended to convert it from being a servant of the old church to being a servant of the new. The job market now required reformed parish ministers, not Catholic priests. The new church was arrogantly confident that King's could be quickly turned from the rather decayed institution it had become, teaching error and superstition, to a thriving and godly reformed college. The experience of the late sixteenth and early seventeenth centuries was to demonstrate repeatedly the great practical difficulties that stood in the way of achieving this.

Chapter 2

Detested Novelty. External Pressures and the New Foundation

The very name of novelty is rightly detested by all men of wisdom
Oration by George Hay at King's College, 1569[1]

The old regime at King's College having been dismantled, the next step obviously was to erect a new one. Nothing could disguise the fact that massive change, imposed from outside, had come to the college, but some effort was made to make what was happening palatable to the remaining staff and students. On 2 July 1569 George Hay, a well-known Protestant minister who was acting as chaplain to the regent and his council on their tour of the north, delivered a Latin oration to an audience of final year (and perhaps other) students, urging them to accept change. The speech, elaborately composed in elegant classical Latin, was designed to be at once conciliatory and firm.

Rather surprisingly, perhaps, to modern readers, Hay felt it necessary to begin by denouncing change:

> The very name of novelty is rightly detested by all men of wisdom, and all who have had experience of practical affairs have the very best of reasons for dreading, shunning and fearing all changes, because the results of all changes are grievous misfortunes, ruinous losses, and disastrous political upheavals. To this all the histories of all ages bear witness.

Thus Hay, in a conservative age which sought its inspiration in the past, established his credentials as a right-thinking man with no taste for innovation. But, he continued, the issues at stake were complex, and the argument against change should not be used crudely and automatically to reject everything which seemed to involve change. Next, he tried to appeal to his audience, which was no doubt shocked and resentful at what was happening, by admitting his own feelings of inadequacy for the task the Regent Moray had set him. The earl, sent by God to cure the body politic, almost at the point of collapse through political instability, had a high regard for literary studies. He believed it important to correct defects in such matters caused by 'the carelessness of good men or even through the fault of wicked men'. Matters were well regulated in the other colleges of the kingdom, but not in Aberdeen. Moray had first 'tried a policy of complaisance and gentleness', but this failed 'because of the cunning and fraudulent pretences of crafty men', whose procrastination was aimed at avoiding reform. The obstinacy of stubborn men had therefore had to be curbed by the severity of the law. They had been deposed 'so that they should cause no further danger for the young generation', and would be replaced by men 'who had loyally served religion'. He knew that some viewed this development with bitter hostility, but asked them to listen to his explanation of why deposition was necessary if literary studies were to thrive:

> what was to be expected from those demented masters whose strength lay in the empty display, not in the discovery, of knowledge, in the reputation of virtue, not in the solid and clear-cut embodiment of it, in the semblance of earnestness, not in the living and realistic representation of it? What happened as soon as the young generation, having emerged from the grammar schools, was handed over to these men? Certain barren, jejune, and dull precepts were put before them in the dryest possible manner, not derived by a process of reasoning from the springs of Aristotle and the ancient logicians but drawn off by a process of sophistry from the stinking pools of Tartaret and utterly stupid sophists like him.

This brought Hay to the centre of his argument. His attack on the deposed staff is not, as might have been expected, being justified by references to the Bible and Calvinist theology. He had evidently decided that that sort of direct religious assault would be counter-productive, for his audience of Catholic students would react by re-affirming their faith. Instead, therefore, he made a more general intellectual attack on the old teachers. The Protestant arguments for religious and for wider intellectual change at the universities had basic similarities. In religion Protestants claimed not to be introducing novelty but to be rejecting it. They were overthrowing centuries of Catholic theology and practice in order to return to the pure religion of the early Christian church, as described in the Bible. It was the pure well-spring, but had been polluted by centuries of human interpretation and invention in the Middle Ages. Reformation meant rejecting this corrupt mediaeval heritage. Similarly in the broader field of intellectual endeavour in the arts and philosophy— what Hay calls 'literary studies'—it was claimed that generations of misguided mediaeval scholastic philosophers had buried the true wisdom and philosophy of the ancients, and above all of Aristotle, below thick layers of superstition and confusion. As in religion, the real sources of truth had come to be ignored, study being concentrated instead on

M. G. HAYI
ORATIO HABITA IN
Gymnaſio Aberdonenſi 2.
Iulij. 1 5 6 9.

EDINBVRGI
EXCVDEBAT ROBER-
tus Lekreuik. Anno. Do. 1571.

4   Title page of the only surviving copy of the published version of the *Oration* George Hay delivered in King's College in 1569, when the college ceased to be a Roman Catholic institution and became a Protestant one. NLS, F. 5. g. 35.

mediaeval commentaries and interpretations which in reality seriously
distorted the originals. Petrus Tartaretus was a scholastic commentator
on Aristotle who is known to have been studied at King's College:[2]
George Hay evidently knew this, and therefore singled him out as
symbolising the stinking pools of mediaeval scholarship which were
now to be rejected.

The intellectual trend which Hay advocated had in fact long pre-dated
Protestantism: it was central to the humanist tendency which itself was
an aspect of the Renaissance effort to revive the values and knowledge of
the classical world of Greece and Rome. But though humanist influences
can be seen at work at King's College long before 1560,[3] Hay ignored
this, because he was using the attack on scholasticism to discredit the
old regime in the college. Knowing how strong the memory of Bishop
Elphinstone, the revered founder of the college, was in Old Aberdeen,
he was careful to reject the charge that he was attacking him and his
colleagues: the purge of 1569, on the contrary, was intended to implement
'the wishes of your founders'. They had been supporters of true learning,
but the college had been corrupted by their successors. Thus on all
fronts Hay evaded the dreaded charge of supporting innovation. On
the contrary, he claimed to stand for restoration, sweeping aside the
innovations made by Catholic theologians, scholastic philosophers, and
the corrupters of good Bishop Elphinstone's worthy ambitions:

> the keen desire and intention of the founders was that the young generation,
> which is rightly termed by the ancients the seed-bed of the state, should
> be educated in good literature, should be entrusted to the care of teachers
> who are good men and outstanding in all branches of knowledge.

Not even a taste of the true liberal arts had yet reached King's College.
Literature had been studied in the past, and Hay applauded the efforts
and good intentions of those involved. But many important parts of
every field of study had been omitted. Above all 'the thing which is
the most essential of all, I mean the task of combining holiness with
learning'. Literature combined with unholiness was a poison, but again
Hay emphasised that he was not attacking learning as such. Literature was
like fire or water: of immense value if properly used, but potentially the
cause of great disasters. Thus it was essential that 'the same people should
teach literature as teach holiness', so the two could not be separated.
Thus Hay at last made the transition from discussing literary studies to
religion:

> The rest of my speech is addressed to you, young students of literature. In
> the present age a great debate is taking place concerning a very important
> subject, I mean the true worship of God, the duty of man, the salvation

which was won through Christ, the forgiveness of sins, the nature of sin, and the hope of immortality.

Debate on these matters was still raging, and:

> we urge all to listen and we challenge our opponents to debate. They stop up your ears, cover over your eyes, forbid you to listen to anyone but them, to read anything but what has been provided by themselves; so that, when they have persecuted you by the cruel butchery of your conscience they can impose upon your ingenuous minds the wretched yoke of slavery by which they bind their pupils to themselves, not to Christ.

Stirring stuff—though of course a Catholic might, in retrospect, have said that this prefigured how students were to be treated in the new, Protestant college after 1569 rather than what had happened before then.

Hay ended his oration with a plea to students to devote themselves as wholeheartedly to their work under their new masters as these masters would devote themselves to their students. They should at least listen to the new teachers and their ideas, 'and having carefully compared them with the old you embrace what proves the better': 'I guarantee that in the next twelve months you will make greater progress than in the whole of the previous three years'—a rash promise.

George Hay's speech is worth considering at some length. It emphasises quite how radical a revolution King's College experienced—or was intended to experience—in 1569. To a complete purge of the core (arts and theology) teaching staff and the change from Catholicism to Protestantism was added the change in other arts subjects from reliance on mediaeval authorities to the original texts of Aristotle and other classical authors. The college was to experience a number of further sudden upheavals in the seventeenth and early eighteenth centuries, as changes of regime in Scotland were followed by imposition of new political and religious orthodoxies and purging of staff. But none of these upheavals was to be as fundamental as that of 1569—though the shock of the change which then took place must have been lessened by the fact that it was something that had been anticipated for nearly a decade. In that decade, moreover, the college had probably declined to a very low level of activity, both academically and in the liturgical life of the chapel, and this decline was a continuation of the decay evident in the 1540s and 1550s. In one sense, indeed, it could be argued that the 1569 upheaval was intended to bring not a revolutionary change in direction, but a return to former glories, a revival of the humanistic influences which had distinguished the college in the early sixteenth century.

Nonetheless, the shock was great. There is no direct evidence as to

how the surviving members of the college—the students, the shadowy
teachers of grammar, law and medicine, and the servants—reacted,
though Hay clearly regarded the audience to whom he delivered his
oration as hostile. Perhaps some students withdrew, but the records
are silent. Almost certainly there would not have been any attempt to
impose a religious test on students and expel those who refused it, as
had happened with the staff. If students had been led astray it was the
job of the new masters to convert them, not expel them. Not until 1587
were religious tests for students introduced to Scotland's universities.[4]

Those who assembled to hear George Hay on 2 July may have been
told who their new teachers were to be, though formal appointments
did not begin to be made until the following day. The Earl of Moray
then appointed Alexander Arbuthnot (minister of Logie Buchan since
1562) to the principalship, and James Lawson (who was teaching Hebrew
at St Andrews) to the subprincipalship, and asked Erskine of Dun as
representative of the church to admit them to office.[5] At least two
Protestant regents in arts were soon added.[6]

King's College had, in Protestant eyes, been rescued from the darkness
of papist superstition and obscurantism. Yet, ironically, the half century
that followed was to be just about the most obscure in its history. No
visitation records survive; nothing is known of student numbers until
1600. What was taught, and how, is largely unknown—except through
what can be deduced from the fact that under its new management it soon
began to produce students who were accepted into the parish ministry
of the new church. To that extent the 1569 purge was a success, but
the general impression is that the college continued to be very small, to
experience severe financial and other difficulties, and therefore to fail to
live up to the expectations of the new church that it would play a leading
role in the swift destruction of Catholicism in the region. Repeated
attempts were made to bring further reform to the college, yet very
little was achieved.

Historians have sometimes attributed this failure to continuing Catholic influence in the college, but this is merely an assumption: there is no
evidence of such influence. What is more likely is that King's failed to live
up to the high hopes of the Protestant reformers because it was having to
struggle in a local environment in which Catholicism was still evident:
external, not internal, Catholicism was the problem. Further, attempts
to improve the situation of the college were repeatedly thwarted by
developments in religious and political conflict at the national level.

In the decades after 1569 King's College was unquestionably a
staunchly Protestant institution, though it is likely that the Protestant
humanist revolution in the teaching of the arts that George Hay had
hoped for was not fully realised, in spite of the fact that from the 1570s

increased emphasis was put on the importance of this type of educational reform in Scotland.

The appointment of Arbuthnot and Lawson to preside over the introduction of Protestantism to King's College brought to Old Aberdeen two men who were to achieve some distinction in Scottish intellectual circles. The new principal, subprincipal and both the new regents appointed in 1569 were graduates of St Andrews, and all had studied in St Mary's College there. Arbuthnot had studied civil law at Bourges, and was highly regarded for his learning in a wide range of disciplines. George Hay, in his *Oration*, had emphasised humanism rather than theology, and it may be that he had tailored his speech to fit the appointment about to be made: though a parish minister, Arbuthnot was not a specialist in theology (as the college principal was supposed to be). Perhaps it was hoped that a man generally respected for humanist learning (while of course also a sincere Protestant) would be more effective in Aberdeen than a firebrand Protestant theologian. Lawson had also studied in France, acting as tutor to the widowed Countess of Crawford's sons in Paris and, later, Cambridge. Brought to Aberdeen because of his skill in Hebrew, he soon became a confidant of John Knox, and was to succeed him in his ministry in Edinburgh.[7]

The difficulties faced by Alexander Arbuthnot and his colleagues after 1569 were immense. There is no evidence that the chancellor of the university, Bishop William Gordon, attempted to resist the 1569 purge; nor was there any attempt to purge him, so the newly Protestant college was faced with the problem of having a Catholic bishop as chancellor until his death in 1577. Thereafter Protestant bishops of Aberdeen acted as chancellors, but they do not appear to have displayed much interest in the college. Indeed, the 'University of Aberdeen', as opposed to King's College, was little more than an abstract concept in these decades. No rector of the university is known to have been appointed between 1563 and the 1580s, and from then until 1618 only occasional rectors are known. The first known post-Reformation dean of the faculty of arts appears in 1618.[8] So little documentation survives for the period that this may be misleading, but it certainly looks as though university offices were little more than formalities: it was the college posts that mattered.

Here too there were problems, however. The college staff frequently had their attention distracted by other responsibilities. Subprincipal Lawson became the first Protestant minister of Old Aberdeen shortly after his college appointment. Principal Arbuthnot continued to be minister of Logie Buchan, and in 1569 became, in addition, minister of Forvie and Arbuthnot. After Lawson left Aberdeen in 1572, Arbuthnot took over from him as minister of Old Aberdeen, though giving up the parishes of Arbuthnot and Forvie.[9] These multiple appointments evidently reflect lack of adequate financial provision for either college staff or parish ministers, and perhaps also shortage of men of ability prepared to serve the new church in the hostile north. In addition to his college and parish responsibilities, Arbuthnot took a leading part in ecclesiastical affairs at a national level in the 1570s, twice being moderator of the general assembly.[10]

Further problems were created by the collapse of political stability. The Regent Moray was murdered just six months after presiding over the purging of King's College, and the country disintegrated into three years of civil war during which the 5th Earl of Huntly controlled the North East and attempted to establish a Catholic regime, ruling in the name of the deposed Mary Queen of Scots, in place of the Protestant regency which ruled for the young James VI. The bid failed, but right up to the later 1590s the earls of Huntly and other conservative landowners in the North East were active in conspiring with foreign powers and doing all they could to hinder the spread of Protestantism in the region. George Hay's part in reforming the college may have helped to earn him election as moderator of the general assembly in March 1570, but when he was chosen to be commissioner for Aberdeen, responsible for supervising the spread of the faith in the region, he petitioned (unsuccessfully) to be freed from this burden, 'in respect there was no obedience in these parts, and ministers were not answered'.[11]

In this unfriendly environment it is not surprising that the progress of the newly Protestant college in Old Aberdeen was slow. It had some advantages. Its new principal was a young man (about thirty years old) of considerable ability, learning and energy, and the fact that he was a member of a landed family from the Mearns, being the brother of the laird of Arbuthnot, added to his authority. Archbishop Spottiswood was later to sum up Arbuthnot's achievements in Aberdeen as follows:

> by his diligent teaching and dextrous government, he not only revived the study of good letters, but gained many from the superstitions whereunto they were given. He was greatly loved of all men, hated of none, and in such account for his moderation with the chief men of these parts, that without his advice they could almost do nothing: which put him in a great fashery, whereof he did often complain. Pleasant and jocund in conversation, and in all sciences expert; a good poet, mathematician, philosopher, theologian, lawyer, and in medicine skilful, so as in every subject he could promptly discourse, and to good purpose.[12]

But though respected for his scholarship and judgement, Arbuthnot's effectiveness as the spearhead of reformed learning in the North East may have been diminished by other aspects of his character. He appears to have been both melancholy and pessimistic, and the fact that the same traits have been discerned in his subprincipal, James Lawson, suggest that the atmosphere of the college under their control may not have been stimulating.[13]

Nonetheless, modest progress was made. On the material side Arbuthnot was able to improve the college's position. Several grants of revenues from the old church's property were made to the college: in 1574 the rectory and vicarage of the Spital and of the parish of Forvie, two chaplaincies, and the property of a Banff friary; in 1579 the deanery of Aberdeen and the attached rectory and vicarage of Old Machar (the parish containing Old Aberdeen). In both gifts it was specifically stated that the grants were being made because of the insufficiency of the college's revenues.[14] Under his successor as principal, Walter Stuart, the rectory and vicarage of Methlick followed. Stuart had become subprincipal in 1572 and rector of Methlick ten years later, and after becoming principal (1584) he resigned the benefice in favour of the college, though retaining the liferent for himself.[15] There may have been an attempt to revive the teaching of law in these early years of Protestantism at King's. As already noted, the canonist, Alexander Cheyne, appears to have submitted to Protestantism in 1573, and he then received the gift of a chaplaincy as he could not be 'reasonably sustained' on his existing emoluments 'to discharge his office of teaching of the laws'.[16] The plural 'laws' may indicate that he was at this time entrusted with teaching both civil and canon law: but nothing further is heard of this, and in these decades King's College was if anything even more clerically dominated than in pre-Reformation times. The urgency of securing a supply of properly educated parish ministers to staff the infant Protestant church meant the neglect of all fields of study not directly relevant to this purpose, and whereas before 1560 many of the Catholic clergy had included study of law in their education this now formed no part of a minister's training.

One new branch of study that probably did emerge was the teaching of Hebrew: with the new emphasis on textual study of the Bible had come a new emphasis on the importance for students of theology of the ancient languages of the Near East, and it may well have been that one of the main reasons for Lawson's appointment was his skill in Hebrew, still a fairly rare attainment.[17] However, with Lawson's transfer to the parish ministry of Edinburgh in 1572, the ability to provide teaching of Hebrew may well have been lost—though Thomas Ogston, one of the regents appointed in 1569, is said to have known Hebrew.[18] Another fragment of evidence about change in the college under Arbuthnot reveals him reforming the graduation ceremony.[19]

Arbuthnot was also active in trying to bring reform to the structure and staffing of his college. In this work he was closely associated with Andrew Melville, who returned to Scotland from Geneva in 1574 and became principal of Glasgow University. Melville's main ambition was to bring more thorough reform to Scotland's universities than they had yet experienced, and the end result was to be new foundations for all three of Scotland's universities. His intention was not so much to change the directions of educational reform from those which had already been established in the years since 1560, as to extend and accelerate movement in these same directions by major reforms of the structures of the universities and the distribution of resources within them.[20] Melville's return to Scotland was well timed. The civil war was over, and the Protestant regimes in both church and state could now turn their attention to advancing the work of reformation instead of merely fighting to survive. The general assembly in 1574 requested the then regent, the Earl of Morton, to 'take order that doctors may be placed in the universities and stipends granted unto them'.[21] 'Doctor' was becoming the accepted term for a university teacher, and in the Second Book of Discipline, an updating of the church's 1560 reform plan which was accepted by the general assembly in 1578, the doctor was accepted as virtually a member of the reformed ministry: most university teachers were parish ministers, were training for the ministry, or had served as ministers at some stage of their careers, emphasising the point that though the stranglehold of the clergy on Scotland's universities changed with the Reformation, it remained just as strong as before.[22] The Second Book also repeated the 1574 demand for state intervention in university reform, craving that 'Doctors would be appointed in universities, colleges and other places needful and sufficiently provided for to open up the meaning of the scriptures'.[23] The state felt that the need for university reform was just as pressing: an act of parliament of 1578 concerned the reform of all the universities, describing them as being 'misused by particular persons to their own advantage, without respect to the education of the youth in virtue and good letters, regarding nothing the common wealth of this realm'.[24]

The influence of this new wave of zeal to carry university reform further was soon felt in Aberdeen, and had the full approval of the college's principal. James Melville, Andrew's nephew, records that after the 1575 general assembly he and his uncle went to Angus with Principal Arbuthnot, 'a man of singular gifts of learning, wisdom, godliness, and sweetness of nature'. Andrew Melville revealed his plans for reform in Glasgow to Arbuthnot, and the two men then 'agreed, as thereafter was set down, in the new reformation of the said colleges of Glasgow and Aberdeen'.[25]

Melville's plans for Glasgow University were embodied in the *Nova Erectio* of 1577. In 1579 reform of St Andrews University on Melvillian lines began, and the following year Melville moved there as principal of

St Mary's College. Aberdeen also got a New Foundation in these years, but exactly when, what it comprised, and how far it was implemented remain doubtful. For over half a century, the controversial question of new foundation or old was to be central to the history of King's College.

In 1578 parliament appointed commissioners to consider the foundations of the Scottish universities and colleges, with full power to reform things tending to superstition and popery, and to replace members of staff if necessary. The commissioners for Aberdeen (of whom George Hay was one) were to meet there in November and submit a report to king and privy council by 1 January 1579.[26] The commissioners failed to keep to this schedule, and in July 1579 king and council received a supplication from the general assembly urging that reform of St Andrews be proceeded with.[27] This was agreed, but where Aberdeen was concerned it was simply noted that nothing had been done under the 1578 commission.[28]

The New Foundation for St Andrews was completed by November 1579,[29] and it seems highly likely that the commissioners then proceeded to draw up a similar reform plan for Aberdeen. Certainly a plan of some sort was presented to parliament in November 1581. Commissioners were then appointed to treat and conclude on certain articles and papers, among them some concerning the reformation of the University of Aberdeen.[30] But no action appears to have followed, so a year later (October 1582) new commissioners were appointed by the assembly, with orders to meet with others appointed by king and council and visit the colleges and universities by the end of November, considering their finances, doctrine and discipline, and to report back to the next assembly.[31] The king's commission duly followed (30 November), appointing commissioners headed by the Earl Marischal and overlapping to some extent with the church's commissioners: George Hay, for example, was on both commissions. The king's commissioners, and presumably the church's, met in Aberdeen on 12 March 1583. Unfortunately the main evidence that survives of their proceedings is a document drawn up later in the king's name, and it is concerned more to explain away the commission's activities in changed political circumstances than to clarify them. The commission, it was declared, had been intended primarily to examine the accounts of the college revenues during Arbuthnot's principalship (since at that time it was thought that he was leaving to become minister of St Andrews), though it was also to see that 'the foundation of the said college is conformable in all respects' to the New Foundation at St Andrews. The king's version of events implies that in practice his commissioners merely audited the college accounts.[32] In reality they appear to have agreed, along with the college staff and the church commissioners, on a new foundation for King's College.

The contradictory versions of what had happened reflect the fact that efforts at achieving university reform were complicated by religious and political faction fighting. Melville had emerged as an important figure in more than just educational controversy: he had become the leader of the faction in the church which, in reaction to attempts by the state (in the person of the Regent Morton in the 1570s and later of the young King James VI) to extend its control over the church, proclaimed the separation of church and state, insisting that a king had no power over ecclesiastical affairs. Further, as the state was attempting to infiltrate the church by building up the power of bishops as royal agents, the 'Melvillian' faction insisted on 'parity' of ministers, bishops having no place in a true church. All ministers were to be equal, and to have a say in church government through representation on church courts. The district court in the new structure which emerged, the presbytery, gave the 'Melvillian tendency' its alternative name, 'presbyterian', while the king's supporters became known as the 'episcopalian' faction. Thus in the 1570s began the great and growing split within Scottish Protestantism which was to dominate religious and political controversy for many generations to come.

In 1582–3, with a plan for Melvillian university reform in King's College agreed, and commissioners appointed who were evidently intended to settle the details, the prospects for the New Foundation had looked highly promising, and at first political developments seemed to confirm such optimism. In 1581–2 it had been feared that the young King James VI had been falling under Catholic influence, and to prevent this an extreme Protestant noble faction virtually kidnapped the king in August 1582 in the 'Ruthven Raid'. The church had had no part in planning the coup, but the dominant Melvillian faction expressed enthusiastic approval of what had been done. The assembly which in October 1582 ordered the visitation of the universities, also praised the seizure of the king as 'good and acceptable service' to God, king and country. Political power was in the hands of men sympathetic to Melville.

When the next assembly met (April 1583) Thomas Smeaton, a sup-porter of Melville and his successor as Principal of Glasgow University, was moderator, and university reform was actively pursued. Regarding Aberdeen, it was reported that 'travail had been taken therein, and an order set down which is in the principal's hands'. Later, on the supplication of the commissioners concerned, the assembly appointed three ministers to consider the proceedings of the commissioners con-cerning the reform of Aberdeen. If they found the text of the proposed reforms acceptable they were to give it to the Earl Marischal 'that his lordship may travail for the king's majesty's confirmation thereof'. That the approval of the new erection by the three ministers was regarded as a foregone conclusion was indicated by the fact that the assembly simultaneously appointed new commissioners (including Melville and Smeaton) to meet at St Andrews on 5 September to see if the staff of King's College, Aberdeen, 'be correspondent to the order and provision of the said erection'; and the fact that Marischal was delegated to gain royal approval is clear evidence that the reform was fully supported by the commissioners, for he had been their leader.[33]

It seems all but certain that this reform plan of 1582–3 was, at least in essentials, the *Nova Fundatio* which now survives only in eighteenth- and nineteenth-century copies—though these copies must have been taken from a version dating from after 1587 as they mention the rectory and vicarage of Methlick as among college properties. It may be, indeed, that the *Nova Fundatio* essentially dates back a few years further; the 1582–3 erection may be based on the proposals of 1581, and they in turn may be based on the work of the 1578 commissioners.

The assembly had now approved a new constitution for King's College. But royal approval was still needed, and obtaining this proved impossible. The regime of the Ruthven Raiders was becoming increasingly weak and divided, and the young king, restive at his humiliating semi-captivity, was in no mood to approve reform plans for Aberdeen sponsored by a Melvillian faction which had approved the actions of the kidnappers. It seems likely that it was in hostile response to an approach from the Earl Marischal over the new erection that James wrote on 25 May 1583 to David Cunningham, the first Protestant Bishop of Aberdeen and thus chancellor of the university, and the rector and other members of King's College.[34] James stated that he was told that the general assembly 'intend to pervert the order of the foundation established by our progenitors and estates of our realm. Wherefore we will and command you to observe and keep the heads of your foundation, and in no ways to hurt the funds' until parliament met. He would then consider what in the college needed reform. Any orders to the contrary were to be ignored. James also forbade Principal Arbuthnot to accept a proposal by the assembly that he become minister of St Andrews 'where-through our said college shall be heavily damnified, and the foundation thereof prejudged'.[35]

The political situation continued to deteriorate from the point of view of reform at King's. A month after forbidding implementation of the new erection, James VI escaped from the Ruthven Raiders, and a reaction against the more extreme Protestants began. When the general assembly met in October 1583, it tried to ignore these developments and protested against the king's order to Arbuthnot to remain in Aberdeen.[36] Moreover, it proceeded with its plans for reform at King's College, ignoring the king's denunciation of them. The assembly noted that (yet again) the two commissions concerning the college appointed by the previous assembly had not carried out their tasks, various excuses being given. Therefore two new sets of commissioners were named, one 'to read and peruse the said erection and accounts, and give their judgement thereupon before the end of the assembly', the other to examine the staff of the college to see 'if they be conform to the order and provision of the new erection'. Again the staff were, for the convenience of the commissioners, to come to St Andrews to be tried, but provision was made to invalidate two excuses previously made by the staff for not appearing. Peter Blackburn, minister of Aberdeen, was ordered to convey officially the assembly's orders to the staff, so they could not plead ignorance of them; and the staff were not all to come to St Andrews at once. The subprincipal and one regent were to appear for trial on 6 March 1584, the other regents on 1 April. Principal Arbuthnot himself was not summoned, either because his suitability for his job was not questioned or because he was known to be ill—he died on 20 October 1583. Trying the staff in two groups was arranged because 'doubts are cast, if they be drawn to St Andrews, of the skailing of their whole class'. In other words, if all the staff were absent at once there would be no-one left to supervise the students, who might then scatter to their homes.[37]

Later in the same assembly the commissioners ordered to consider the new erection reported back, approving the document. The full assembly then gave it formal approval.[38] But from this time onwards there is no reference to the reform of King's College in the surviving records of the general assembly (though admittedly these are incomplete). The commissioners appointed to try the Aberdeen staff never met for, as Robert Wodrow later put it, 'we had none assemblies for some time, and the heavy change, by the king's falling under unlucky hands soon after this, I suppose, prevented any inquiry to be made at the time appointed'.[39] The presbyterian party in both church and state was routed. In December 1583 parliament declared the Ruthven Raid, which the general assembly had so rashly approved, to have been treason. Early in 1584 Andrew Melville (himself one of the commissioners for trying the Aberdeen staff) and some of his followers fled to England, and the assembly due to hear the commissioners' report in April was forbidden to meet by the king. In May the Earl of Gowrie, leader of the Raiders, was beheaded, and the 'Black Acts' (as presbyterians came to call them) were passed, asserting royal control over church as well as state, restoring the powers of bishops and condemning presbyterianism.

These political developments were accompanied by continuing evidence of the king's hostility to the proposed reform at Aberdeen. In February 1584 James confirmed the election of Walter Stuart as principal to replace Arbuthnot, this being pointedly referred to as being done 'according to the old foundation',[40] and in August of the same year James ratified the work of the commissioners he had appointed to visit King's College in November 1582 in a way which (as noted above) distorted what they had done: they had, it was now asserted, merely audited accounts, which was their chief function, and the college's members should not 'esteem themselves anyway prejudiced through the generality of the clause' about distribution of college revenues. In other words, James implicitly reassured those who might stand to lose revenues through the proposed reorganisation of the college that they need not worry: that part of his own commissioners' work was being suppressed.[41]

Some of the staff of King's, however, either failed to understand the political climate or decided to defy it in a final attempt to get the New Foundation accepted. Perhaps they calculated that, though it had been closely associated with the Melvillian cause, there was much in the New Foundation which should be acceptable to all Protestants, since it concerned rationalisation of resources and reform of teaching to make the college a more effective instrument for propagating the faith. The staff therefore submitted a supplication to parliament relating that, by consultation with learned men in the diocese of Aberdeen, they had 'conceived a form of erection' for their college. They requested that a committee of three officers of state, the Archbishop of St Andrews and the Bishop of Aberdeen consider this, and that the 'foundation' then be confirmed by parliament. It was notable that the foundation now put forward was said to have been drafted locally, in Aberdeen: no mention was made of the general assembly's leading role in its origins. It is probable that in reality the foundation being proposed was essentially the same as that approved by the assembly, but that the King's staff recognised that it would be political folly to ask parliament to confirm reforms specifically stated to have been inspired by the now discredited Melvillians. Further, asking that two bishops and three royal officials be those appointed to consider the latest new erection looks like a deliberate attempt to dissociate the change from the Melvillians.

If such political calculations were indeed present, then at first they seemed to be having the desired results. In August 1584 commissioners were appointed to 'consider and approve' the erection, reporting back to parliament so that the erection 'being found formal and in good order may be confirmed and approved'.[42] But that was as far as the reform proposals got. There is no record of the commissioners reporting back to parliament and, after nearly a decade of almost continual discussion of the reform of King's, there follows a period of eight years in which there is no mention at all of the subject. Parliament might still be ready to flirt with university reform, but the king wanted nothing to do with it.

The next references to reform that appear relate to 1592, and are more confusing than enlightening. In 1638 the supporters of the New Foundation party in King's College produced what they claimed was a copy of an act of the Privy Council signed by James VI at Aberdeen in 1592 which supported the New Foundation. Unfortunately, James VI did not visit Aberdeen in 1592, and no record of any such act exists in the council's records. An act of the general assembly dated Edinburgh 1593 was also produced, but the assembly met that year in Dundee, not Edinburgh, and its records contain no such act.[43] Yet it does seem that 1593 saw some attempt to revive the New Foundation, even if the evidence later produced to support the claim was incompetently forged. The years 1586–92 had seen the emergence of an uneasy compromise in the church between the king and the Melvillians, and this culminated in 1592 in a series of measures giving royal recognition to a presbyterian structure of church government: though bishops existed in name, they had little real power. This revival of the fortunes of the Melvillian party doubtless encouraged a new attempt to impose the originally Melvillian-sponsored New Foundation. Moreover in 1592 Arbuthnot's successor as principal of the college, Walter Stuart, had died and he had been succeeded by David Rait, who in his later career emerges as a strong supporter of the New Foundation.[44] Finally, the 1593 assembly at Dundee did pass an act relating to King's College which indicates that reform was again in the air, though without specifically mentioning the New Foundation.

On 27 April 1593 the Earl Marischal, Andrew Melville, David Cunningham (Bishop of Aberdeen, and formerly dean of the faculty of arts at Glasgow University during Melville's principalship), Peter Blackburn (minister of Aberdeen—and formerly a regent in Glasgow University when Melvillian reforms had been introduced there) and three others were commissioned to visit King's College in Old Aberdeen and 'there to try and examine the doctrine, life, and diligence of the masters thereof', the 'discipline and order used by them', and the college's finances. The visitors were to reform whatever abuses they could, and remit those they could not to the assembly. Meanwhile no new leases of college property and no new appointments to the staff were to be made.[45]

Earlier the same month there had been a major academic development just to the south, in New Aberdeen. There the Earl Marischal had founded a rival institution to King's, Marischal College; and the new college was founded very much on the lines of Melvillian reform ideas. Indeed its foundation charter was based on the King's College New Foundation, drafted over a decade before—which in turn was based on Melville's Glasgow *Nova Erectio* of 1577.[46] Historians have often seen the founding of Marischal College as a reaction to failure to reform King's College satisfactorily. The earl had been involved in attempts to reform King's in 1582 and 1584 but, it is argued, had despaired of that conservative institution ever becoming a true godly and reformed university, so he founded a new university to fulfil that role in the north.[47] But, as G D Henderson pointed out long ago, there is no real evidence to support this interpretation. Henderson concluded that though it was possible that the Earl Marischal thought King's 'obscurantist or not responsive', it was not any backward-looking intransigence of King's that led to the founding of the new Marischal College.[48] However, Henderson also believed that if the New Foundation of King's had been fully ratified and implemented, the Earl Marischal would not have founded his own college, a judgement which appears to contradict his earlier conclusion.[49] Yet as Henderson himself showed (and is discussed below in chapter 3), much of the new foundation was probably already in force at King's. And the fact that only a few days after the earl founded his own college he was placed at the head of a commission aimed at further reform at King's indicated that it certainly was not the case that all hope of reform there had been abandoned. It is true that the orders of the 1593 assembly did not specifically state that the New Foundation was to be imposed at King's, but the fact that both the Earl Marischal and Melville were members of the commission surely indicates that this was the intention.

Again, it is not entirely clear (though it is usually assumed) that Marischal College was intended to be a college in a new university, quite separate from the old one which had King's as its only college. As Henderson has demonstrated, the foundation charter leaves it in doubt whether Marischal College was to be the one college of a new university; a second college with King's in the existing university; or an independent college not within any university![50] It is quite possible that the earl deliberately left the options open. Moreover, he provided for one permanent link between the two colleges which makes nonsense of the idea that he thought King's hopelessly corrupt: the Marischal College foundation charter makes the principal of King's College *ex officio* one of those who were to examine and admit the teachers of Marischal College.[51] The clause was perhaps intended to make the foundation of Marischal College acceptable to King's. If so, it seems to have worked. According to a rather later source, Rait's lack of opposition to the emergence of Marischal aroused comment. On his:

> consenting to the building of a new college upon his own nose King James VI called him Principal Blait and so he was for suffering that which he might have hindered.[52]

'Blait' or 'blate' means timid, or even stupid. Rait soon, it would seem, changed his mind, for it was said that he refused to recognise Marischal 'for school or college'.[53] Presumably, therefore, he refused to take part, as principal of King's, in choosing the principals of Marischal College. But the fact that the Earl Marischal had offered him such a role remains significant in indicating the earl's respect for the older college.

Thus other motives need to be sought in establishing why a new college was founded. The fact that the battle against Catholicism in the north had still not been won indicated that further provision for Protestant higher education in the area was needed. The Earl Marischal, the leading Protestant noble in the north, was seeking to expand his power northwards into the sphere of influence of the Catholic earls of Huntly, and what better way to demonstrate this than by sponsoring a reformed college bearing his own name in Aberdeen, where for long periods Catholics had benefited from Huntly's influence? In this context 1593 was a most opportune time for action: Huntly's power was waning, and an associate of the Earl Marischal had been elected provost.[54] The burgh of Aberdeen itself was eager to have its own college, and the new institution which emerged was as much the town's college as the earl's: Aberdeen felt it unfair that though it was the main population and trading centre, the ecclesiastical, educational and legal capital of the region was the neighbouring bishop's burgh of Old Aberdeen. The new college would help to redress the balance. The First Book of Discipline had argued that there ought to be two colleges in Aberdeen, and the Earl Marischal may have seen himself as implementing its godly intentions.

The foundation of Marischal College is not evidence that King's was regarded as being beyond redemption; and the fact that the 1593 assembly did not refer to the New Foundation in arranging the visitation of King's probably indicates not that it had been abandoned there, but rather that it was already in force there, at least in part. There is no evidence whatever that Catholic influence was still feared to be present at King's. The visitation ordered by the general assembly in 1593 does indicate that the college still had problems, but these probably related to lack of resources, low morale, and a tendency to accept the institutional changes arising from the Melvillian New Foundation, while making little effort to introduce changes in the content and method of teaching (see chapter 3 below).

Moreover, there was lingering uncertainty as to the status of the New Foundation. It had been approved by the church in 1583, but it still lacked royal and parliamentary ratification. The matter was therefore brought before parliament again in November 1597, the church's 1593 initiative having achieved nothing. Parliament at last passed an act ratifying the New Foundation of the college, but stipulated that it was to be revised by commissioners appointed for that purpose—John Lindsay of Menmuir (the king's secretary), James Elphinstone (a lord of session) and David Cunningham (Bishop of Aberdeen). The foundation was to be given to the clerk register, who was 'to extend an act of parliament thereupon'.[55]

Interpretation of this ambiguous act was to cause endless trouble in the years to come. On the one hand it stated that parliament (and thus the king, who approved the act) had ratified the New Foundation; but then it ordered revision of the foundation. Was the foundation ever revised by the commissioners? If so, did this in itself automatically bring parliamentary ratification into force? Or was the foundation in effect ratified even if the revision was not carried out? The records of parliament have nothing further to say on the matter. Some were to argue that is was because ratification was already completed; others that it indicated that the New Foundation was not finally approved. James Gordon, minister of Rothiemay, writing nearly half a century later, is the only source to provide any explanation of what happened—or rather what did not happen—in 1597. By his account Principal Rait 'drew a draft of a foundation, wherein all the old institution was turned upside down'. He presented this to James VI and 'it went near to be ratified in parliament'. But one of the commissioners appointed to revise it, James Elphinstone, 'a great statesman' (a phrase perhaps intended to suggest cunning as much as ability) was bitterly hostile to it, for he was a kinsman of Bishop Elphinstone, the founder of the college, and was determined that his foundation should not be superseded. Therefore 'the new draft was stifled in the birth' by James Elphinstone's wiles.[56]

Elphinstone was a powerful figure, becoming the king's secretary in January 1598 and being created Lord Balmerino in 1604, and there is nothing inherently improbable in Gordon's story. But there may have been another reason for the failure to ratify the New Foundation unambiguously in 1597. In 1596 the king had won the initiative in a renewed struggle with the Melvillians for control of the church. One sign of this was an attack on Melvillian power in the universities, and in July 1597 a royal visitation deprived Melville of the office of rector of St Andrews University.[57] Moreover, there were reports that James intended to follow up this St Andrews success in other parts of the country, and that he had made his secretary, Lindsay of Menmuir, 'general chancellor' of all the colleges in Scotland.[58] Nothing more is known of this, but if James did give his secretary some temporary role in supervising universities, then that responsibility would have passed to James Elphinstone at the beginning of 1588 when he replaced Lindsay in that office, putting him in an ideal position to protect his kinsman's foundation at King's under the guise of carrying out James VI's policy of undermining Melvillian influence in the universities. In such political circumstances it is hardly surprising that an attempt to further a 'Melvillian' New Foundation at the college was quietly suppressed. Indeed what is surprising is that parliament should have supported reform there several months after the king had purged St Andrews.

So far as official action was concerned matters rested thus for twenty years, until in 1617 James VI (now also King of England) visited his native land. An act was then passed in parliament ratifying all the former privileges of King's College. Mention was made of the foundation by Bishop Elphinstone; nothing was said of the New Foundation, so the assumption evidently was that it had no validity. This was confirmed by the fact that earlier gifts by James VI to the college which were now being ratified were said to have been made because its revenues were inadequate for supporting the staff according to the first foundation.[59] Quite why this act was passed is obscure. It seems highly unlikely that (as was later argued by some) it was specifically intended to confirm the suppression of the New Foundation and restore the Old. Had that been the case, the act would surely have been far more explicit. Three other motives for the act may be suggested. First, it was common for individuals and institutions to get old rights and privileges confirmed from time to time, and this act may simply be such a routine confirmation. Second, there had been a worrying rumour that while in Scotland James intended to reduce the number of universities there, suppressing the post-Reformation foundations of Marischal College and Edinburgh University—and perhaps King's College as well.[60] The rumour was groundless, but nonetheless it may have provoked a desire for a new confirmation to prove King's still had royal support. Finally, in 1617 James was completing his long campaign to re-establish episcopacy in Scotland with the restoration of cathedral chapters, and the act concerning King's College specifies its relationship to the revived chapter of St Machar's Cathedral: the principal of the college was to be dean of Aberdeen; the subprincipal was to be subchanter, and one of the regents was also to be a member of the chapter.[61] As this affected the constitution of King's College, it may well have been decided that a general confirmation of the college's position was appropriate.

This chapter has been concerned almost entirely with attempts at the national level by state and church to reform King's College. The college has appeared largely as a plaything, pulled in differing directions according to political and religious developments. Repeated attempts were made to improve—or at least change—the college's circumstances. In each case evidence is fragmentary and all turn out in the end to be abortive or enjoy only partial success. The main theme is clear however: the church sponsored the extension of Melvillian reform to Aberdeen, and sometimes the state went along with it. But then, at the last minute, the state—in the person of the king—always drew back from final commitment to such a development, and though it never explicitly and unambiguously rejected such reform, it did, in the end, ignore it. But in the new era which was about to dawn for the university with the appointment of a new and energetic Bishop of Aberdeen, the 1617 act was to be instrumental in tilting the scales decisively in favour of the Old Foundation.

Chapter 3

Miserable Men in Dead Times?
Internal Responses to the New Foundation

. . . miserable men, who in dead times, not being controlled, have
so securely sacked that estate [of King's College], as if neither God
had been in heaven to account with, nor men on earth to examine
their ways.

Bishop Patrick Forbes to James VI, 4 July 1620[1]

In the years 1575 to 1597 talk of further reform at King's College, of a New
Foundation, was almost continuous. They must have been bewildering
years for the staff. Final confirmation of a New Foundation repeatedly
seemed to be imminent, but was always withheld for political reasons.
There were repeated orders to commissioners to visit the college—and
some of these visitations actually took place. It is now time to consider
what was actually going on in the college in these years. Did the college
continue to try to conform to the Old Foundation as far as possible,
though making the changes necessitated by the coming of Protestantism
in 1569? Or did the staff try to implement the New Foundation? Before
this can be discussed, it is necessary to look at the New Foundation and
see what it sought to do and how it differed from its predecessor.

As already indicated, the Melvillian plans for educational reform
enshrined in the new foundations of Scotland's universities do not
represent any dramatic break with developments already taking place:
rather they were attempts to hasten, intensify and systematise the
processes already initiated by the coming of Protestantism to the
colleges. Nonetheless, Melvillian reform undoubtedly did reflect an
impatience with the effects of the initial introduction of Protestantism
into the colleges, a feeling that often only the minimum of change
had been made. Protestantism and other new intellectual ideas had
been introduced into what remained basically mediaeval institutional
frameworks. Further, little consideration had been given to whether the
universities had sufficient resources to flourish as centres of Protestant
learning, suffering as they were from the twin ravages of past financial

41

mismanagement and high inflation. As to what was taught, theology had become satisfactorily Protestant, but apart from this changes in curricula were slow, perhaps hampered by teachers who were sound in religion but conservative and backward-looking in other respects.

Melvillian reform entailed major changes in three distinct but overlapping aspects of the universities—the content of teaching, teaching methods, and establishment or staffing. On the content of teaching, Melville's ideas were based on the educational reforms of Peter Ramus (Pierre de La Ramée), a French Huguenot scholar whose ideas attracted immense interest. Melville advocated the introduction of the anti-scholastic Ramist logic and philosophy, and reform in such basic subjects obviously had implications for the many other subjects which they underlay.[2] In essence this differed little from the sort of change that George Hay had heralded in his oration at the purging of King's College in 1569—perhaps not surprisingly, as the Regent Moray was acquainted with Ramus, who had talked in 1568 of coming to Scotland to visit him.[3] But Melville wanted a more thorough and systematic introduction of such ideas, and the full working out of their consequences in all aspects of teaching. Moreover, he wanted to ensure that Ramist influence on curricula was guaranteed for the future by enshrining it in written new foundations, so that it was clear that all teachers were committed to it.

To those who remained loyal to the older traditions of the schoolmen, the scholastic philosophers, Ramism seemed mainly destructive, doing little more than create confusion by attacking the long-established central authority in philosophy, Aristotle, whose word had frequently been taken as almost infallible. The Ramists would have replied (as, again, George Hay had argued in 1569) that they were not trying to destroy Aristotle's authority, but to reinterpret him critically. This might involve questioning or even rejecting some of his ideas, but far more central than this was trying to rediscover his original ideas, cutting through the mass of later interpretations and glosses which were often wrongly accepted as the thoughts of Aristotle himself. Aristotle, as it has been nicely put, was no longer to be a despot, but a limited, constitutional monarch— or, changing the metaphor somewhat, 'Aristotle, though deposed, was reassessed, not ousted'.[4] Thus, for example, the general assembly which approved the New Foundation for King's in 1583 also condemned twenty points drawn from Aristotle's works: but it did not condemn the works themselves.[5]

Seen in a longer perspective, it is clear that the craze for Ramism was out of all proportion to the insights Ramus had to offer, that his radicalism was often more apparent than real. He has been accused of 'attacking the genuine weaknesses of the scholastic heritage while preserving unwittingly the basic presuppositions responsible for these

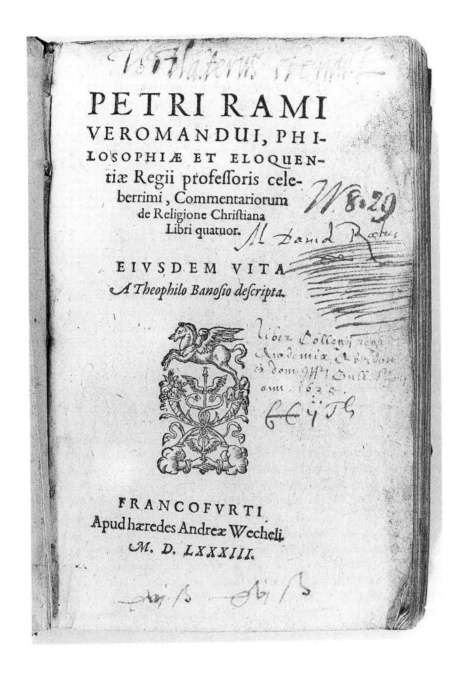

PETRI RAMI
VEROMANDUI, PHI-
LOSOPHIÆ ET ELOQUEN-
tiæ Regii professoris cele-
berrimi, Commentariorum
de Religione Christiana
Libri quatuor.

EIVSDEM VITA
A Theophilo Banosio descripta.

FRANCOFVRTI,
Apud hæredes Andreæ Wecheli,
M. D. LXXXIII.

5   Title page of a copy of Ramus's *Commentaries on the Christian Religion* bearing the signatures of Principal Walter Stuart (1584–92), Principal David Rait (1592–32), and the latter's son, Mr William Rait, who presented the volume to King's College Library in 1635. AUL, π 2304 La R.

weaknesses', of creating an intellectual system of which the 'central element is a logic or dialectic which cannot be taken seriously by any competent logician'. But many sixteenth-century scholars overlooked these basic flaws, excited by his attack on obscurantism and attracted by his claims that his approach could provide a orderly, methodical analysis of any subject, logically breaking it down into its component parts for ease of exposition and learning.[6]

In curricular reform Melville's main interest lay in reorganising the philosophy-based four year arts course leading to the degree of master of arts and then on to the study of theology. In addition to advocating a Ramist approach to all subjects, he favoured more emphasis on classical literature (again foreshadowed in Hay's oration), and the study of Greek, Hebrew and other Near Eastern languages as an aid to close textual study of scripture.[7] Other disciplines, such as law and medicine, held little interest for Melville. They were inessentials, for the central function of the universities was the production of orthodox and well educated ministers for the kirk.

The New Foundation of King's College laid down a typically Melvillian arts course.[8] It has been stated, quite correctly, that no works by Ramus are known to have been prescribed texts at King's until 1641,[9] but it would be wrong to conclude from this that Ramist influence on teaching was limited or absent before then. Almost nothing is known in detail of teaching and the works it was based on in the decades around 1600, and given the general acceptance of Ramus in the Scottish academic world the assumption that his influence was fully reflected in teaching at King's is plausible. There are, moreover, some fragments of evidence supporting such a view. Principal Walter Stuart (1584–92) owned a copy of *Commentaries on the Christian Religion*, Ramus's only theological work—which has been denounced as attempting 'to reduce religion to an art similar to the arts of expression, grammar, rhetoric and logic'[10] through the author's relentless determination to fit every subject into neat, simplified logical schemes. After Stewart's death the volume passed to Principal David Rait (1592–1632). Rait also owned another work, much more central to Ramus's reforms, the *Rhetoric* published under the name of his collaborator Audomarus Talaeus (Omer Talon) but in reality largely Ramus's own work. Both these works were given to King's College in 1635 by David Rait's son, William.[11] Rait's successor as principal, William Leslie (1632–40), had a copy of the 1599 edition of Ramus's *Lectures on Mathematics*, and records in an inscription that he bought it with a gift of money he had received—perhaps at about the time he became grammarian in 1603. In another inscription he testifies in alliterative and punning Latin to the high value he placed on the book:

> Ad Lectorem. Hic Liber est terno ter tersus pumice, lecto, ter lege, ter lectus, ter tibe gratus erit,

which may be translated as:

> To the reader. This book has been polished three times with triple pumice; reader, read it thrice; thrice read, it will be three times as pleasing to you.

Scouring with pumice was part of the process of preparing parchment before writing on it, a process referred to here metaphorically, symbolising Ramus's painstaking scholarship.[12]

The survival of these books hints at the influence of Ramus on the teaching staff at King's. Another fragment of evidence points to enthusiasm for Ramist ideas among students. In about 1584 Robert Howie and John Johnston both graduated at King's and, as was still common, left for the Continent to continue their studies. Once there, each chose to attach himself to a different scholar: but each chose a well-known disciple of Ramus. The obvious (though admittedly not inevitable) conclusion is that the two students were pursuing aspects of scholarship inculcated at King's. That they were not, on the contrary, reacting *against* what they had been taught earlier is indicated by the fact that Johnston, on his death, left Robert Mercer, who had been his regent at King's College ('my old and kind master'), a white cope.[13] Both students went on to distinguished careers. Johnston became professor of theology at St Mary's College, St Andrews, and was one of those commissioned to examine the foundation charter of Marischal College and to visit King's College in 1593, while Howie was to be the first principal of Marischal and subsequently principal of St Mary's.[14] The conclusion that they had probably received at King's in the 1580s an education similar to that which they would have received at St Andrews or Glasgow, known to have been reformed on Melvillian lines, is justified.[15]

The text of the New Foundation (see Appendix II) outlines in general terms the arts curriculum to be followed. In the first year the emphasis was to be on teaching Greek, introducing students to 'the easiest and best authors' in both Latin and Greek, and training them first in Latin and then in Greek composition. In the second year the literary and linguistic emphasis was to be continued, with the teaching of the rules of 'invention, disposition and elocution'—that is, the collection of information and other material on a topic, the arrangement of it logically and effectively, and finally the effective verbal exposition of the topic or argument before an audience. This, with further study of ancient authors and practice of written composition, was intended to fit students to 'grasp the rules of philosophy'. Year three saw the student studying the rudiments of arithmetic, parts of Aristotle's work on logic, and his books on ethics and politics, while to make sure skills in Latin were maintained as well as to inculcate good morals, Cicero's On Duties was prescribed. Study of the various branches of philosophy was extended in the final year, with work on physiology and on some aspects of the nature of animals (both from Greek texts of Aristotle). These were combined with work on geography, astronomy, cosmography and 'the computation of times from the foundation of the world, which subjects bring no small light to bear on other disciplines and the knowledge of history'. As if this was not enough, towards the end of the final year students were introduced to 'the sacred tongue'—Hebrew.

Thus prepared, students could graduate and hasten on to studies 'of greater importance'—the assumption being that most would move on to theology in preparation for entrance to the ministry. Indeed, throughout the four years of the arts class, the New Foundation decreed that religious education should proceed alongside languages, literature and philosophy. One book of the New Testament was prescribed for each year to be expounded by each regent to his class on Sunday mornings, and examined in the afternoons: and students also attended the public worship of the parish, where they would hear the principal preach in his capacity as minister of St Machar's. In addition, the principal was supposed to lecture on weekdays, alternating between expounding difficult passages from the Scriptures and lecturing on Hebrew. Probably these lectures were intended primarily for postgraduate theology students.

In teaching methods the Melvillian reforms were primarily concerned with the question of specialisation among teachers. Traditionally each regent in arts took his class through all four years of the arts course, then moved back to take a new first year class. Melville advocated greater specialisation; each regent should be confined to the subjects of a single year, so a class would be taught by all four specialist regents as it progressed through its course. Along with this specialisation went a tendency for regents to be called professors of the subjects assigned to them. The New Foundation enjoins that regents should stick to the same 'professions'—though without calling them 'professors'. However, it was provided that if there was general agreement in the college, regents might exchange the years of study they specialised in: and indeed this would be essential at times, because it was intended that the final year class should always be taken by the subprincipal, thus forcing a regent promoted to that post to teach new subjects.

The history of teaching at King's is so obscure that it is not known whether in the first flush of enthusiasm for the New Foundation such a 'professorial' system was indeed substituted for the old 'regenting' one. If it was, it must have been quickly abandoned, for when relevant records of classes and their teachers do survive, from 1601, the old system is in force.[16]

On one aspect of the college's experience in these decades, however there is enough evidence for some firm conclusions to be reached as to which foundation was in operation, though the sources are still fragmentary. It is in this area that reform had the most outwardly visible effects. By the Old Foundation of 1529 (which represents Bishop Elphinstone's final plans for reorganising the college, incomplete at the time of his death in 1514) King's College had forty-two members; by the New Foundation it only had twenty-two (see Appendix I). By contemporary standards a staff of this size was by no means ludicrously small, as it might seem to modern eyes: after all Glasgow's *Nova Erectio*, on which King's New Foundation was based, provided for only twelve founded members.

The most significant changes in staffing at King's concerned the academic teaching staff. The Old Foundation had provided for fourteen adult teachers and postgraduate students/teachers: the New only had room for six. Thus while total establishment was intended to fall by about 48%, the cut in teaching staff was to be about 57%. The new slim-line college Melville and his supporters planned concentrated teaching in the hands of the principal (teaching theology), four regents in arts, one of whom was also subprincipal, and the grammarian or humanist—and (as under the Old Foundation) the grammarian divided his time between college teaching and running the grammar school of Old Aberdeen. Academic staff lost comprised the canonist, the civilist, the mediciner, the three postgraduate students in law, and two of the six regents in arts (originally known as students in theology).

There were two arguments in favour of such dramatic retrenchment. One was financial. Fast inflation, combined with incompetent or corrupt management of college property, meant, it was argued, that the college had to be reduced in size if it was to carry out its functions effectively and members of staff were to have adequate salaries. The new salaries proposed were still far from generous. By the end of the sixteenth century the church was working towards the ideal of each parish minister having a minimum stipend of 500 merks (a merk being two-thirds of a pound Scots), plus a manse and glebe. The New Foundation set the salary of the college principal far below this, at the equivalent of about 300 merks—though of course he was also provided with bed and board at the expense of the college. Even setting salaries at such modest levels meant that the salary bill for the twenty-two man New Foundation college would be well over three times (in money terms) that of its forty-two strong predecessor (see Appendix I). Moreover, it was recognised that even the new salaries proposed were inadequate, and provision was therefore made for increasing them if improvements in the college's financial position made this possible.

The second argument justifying the cuts in academic staff in the college was that, independently of the financial situation, there were many posts that could be suppressed with little or no real loss to the college. The chapel staff of eight prebendaries and six choir boys had no place in the reformed worship of the college chapel after 1569, and abolishing their posts was simply giving formal recognition to this. Where teaching staff were concerned, the law and medical faculties were characterised more by suspended animation than by active life in the years before and after 1560. Teaching of these subjects was at best intermittent, so suppressing them so as to strengthen financial provision for the core subjects of arts and theology made sense. The First Book of Discipline's plans for Aberdeen University had involved the abandonment of canon law and medicine,[17] and the New Foundation merely went one step further by abolishing civil law as well. An alternative approach, of course, would have been to try to find extra resources to finance the threatened faculties of medicine, canon law and civil law adequately, but with Melville's attention being concentrated on universities as seminaries for producing ministers this was ignored.

The change in staffing has been seen by some as necessary and realistic, by others as a sad betrayal of the vision of the founder, Bishop Elphinstone. The Old Foundation has been described as 'grand if not grandiose',[18] implying that it may have been overambitious and that this contributed to the problems experienced by the college in later generations. Confirmation that this was indeed the case is supplied by recent calculations which indicate that revenue from the endowments Bishop Elphistone provided for the college can only have met about two-thirds of the recurrent costs envisaged by the Old Foundation. It appears that he planned to make up the shortfall out of the revenues of the bishopric of Aberdeen, but the latter were greatly reduced by the later sixteenth century. The first Protestant bishop of Aberdeen, David Cunningham (appointed 1577), complained that all the revenues of the bishopric had been 'wasted and dilapidated' by his Catholic predecessor, Bishop Gordon.[19] As a former dean of faculty in Glasgow University, Cunningham may have sympathised with the problems of King's College, but he was in no position to provide support to correct the financial weakness inherent in the college since its foundation. Even before 1560 the inadequacy of its endowments had evidently caused strain, and it is likely that the members of the college who were active in teaching were already largely confined to the six defined in the New Foundation. Thus so far as staff establishment is concerned the New Foundation should perhaps not be seen as introducing revolutionary changes, expelling officials and narrowing teaching, but as an attempt to bring the formal constitution of the college into line with existing practice.

In the years immediately after the 1569 purge the intention had evidently been to continue to try to maintain all the five traditional faculties at King's. As noted previously, after the canonist submitted to Protestantism in 1573 he was granted extra revenues so he could teach law (perhaps both canon and civil) in the college—though this would seem to indicate that the nominal civilist, Nicholas Hay, was not at this time active in the college. That the mediciner, Gilbert Skene, was also being encouraged to regard his post as more than a sinecure is suggested by a new grant of his office to him in 1571.[20] But this policy of maintaining five faculties appears to have quickly been abandoned. The surviving fragments of evidence suggest that by the 1580s the college was moving towards New Foundation staffing. Permanent staff now defined as surplus to requirements were accepted as having the right to retain their posts for life, but when they died they were not replaced. Alexander Cheyne, canonist, died in 1587.[21] Nicholas Hay, civilist since at least 1558, died in the 1590s. For many years he had been commissary of Aberdeen (judge in the commissary court which dealt mainly with testamentary matters). By 1591 he had resigned as commissary, but was in no condition to turn his attention to his position as civilist: he appealed for a pension as he was disabled by 'great age and wearied with long travails taken in study and teaching of the civil laws' and acting as commissary.[22] But there is no sign that he had taught in the college for many years—and clearly if he was being paid anything as civilist it was not enought to live on. Yet he retained a connection with the university until his death: he was appointed rector in 1592, and he is said to have provided funds to help support bursars in the college.[23] Gilbert Skene, the mediciner, made a cleaner break with the college. He evidently moved to Edinburgh in 1575, and in 1581 he became James VI's physician.[24] It has been suggested that he used his influence at court against the New Foundation which threatened his post,[25] but there is no evidence for this, and the fact that he and the college agreed to dispose of the the mediciner's manse in Old Aberdeen in 1587 suggests that by that time he accepted that medicine had no future at King's. He died in 1599.[26] Skene could have claimed the melancholy distinction of being the longest surviving member of the college staff appointed in its Catholic days.

It is clear, then, that 'so far as these sinecures were concerned' the New Foundation was in operation by 1600.[27] However, the best and earliest evidence indicating that the New Foundation was being enforced at King's is provided by the fortunes of the office of grammarian or humanist. Under the Old Foundation the grammarian enjoyed a higher salary and status than the students in theology who acted as regents. By the New Foundation, however, the grammarian had a much lower salary than regents, and it was customary for a grammarian only to hold office until a regency fell vacant, to which he would have right of succession. This change in part at least represented a recognition that the grammarian did not work fully within the college, and doubtless had a supplementary income from fees paid by his pupils at Old Aberdeen grammar school. Theophilus Stewart, who had been grammarian since the 1530s, died in 1576.[28] His successor, Walter Stuart, was a regent in the College at the time of his appointment in 1577,[29] which indicates that the Old Foundation was still dictating staffing: becoming grammarian was still promotion for a regent. But by 1580 David Rait was grammarian (Stuart having become subpincipal), though he had not previously been a regent. By 1583 Rait was was no longer grammarian, having been promoted to a regency.[30] Thus in this matter of the grammarian's status the introduction of New Foundation practice can be dated to between 1577 and 1580. But, given that the earliest date at which we can be certain that a new constitution for King's had been drafted on paper is late 1581 (see page 30 above), it may be misleading to attribute the change to the New Foundation: it may have been a change already adopted by the college which was subsequently incorporated in the New Foundation. Historians have been obsessed with the reluctance of King's College to accept the New Foundation, but here again it may have been the case that the staff of the college did not always wait for change to be urged on them from outside, sometimes acting for themselves.

Another instance of the early appearance of a New Foundation office is provided by the appearance of Berold Innes (formerly reader of the parish of Old Machar) as economus or steward in 1586.[31] This office appears in the New Foundation, the ecomomus taking over from the Old Foundation's common procurator the administration of college revenues, and from its provisor the provision of food and other necessities for the college community. The common procurator had been elected from the teaching staff, and had continued to hold his teaching post, whereas the economus was a separate official not holding any other office.[32] Thus Innes held a New Foundation office by 1586, and evidently continued to do so into the seventeenth century. However, though he is also sometimes referred to as common procurator, on other occasions the latter office was separate, being held by a member of the teaching staff—by the principal in 1594 and 1612, for example, and by the subprincipal in 1617.[33] Then in the early seventeenth century the office of economus seems to have faded away. Thus here a New Foundation post has been introduced, and then abandoned: but the important thing is that the new name of 'economus' was in use as early as 1586.

To sum up the situation at King's College by the end of the sixteenth century: so far as staffing was concerned the New Foundation was firmly established. As to the arts curriculum, evidence is fragmentary, but it probably conformed to a large extent to the 'Melvillian' teaching found at the other Scottish universities. But in teaching methods King's retained regenting, the old non-specialist teaching. Of the principals since 1569, Alexander Arbuthnot (1569–83) and David Rait (1592–1632) certainly favoured the New Foundation, and the lack of evidence as to the attitude of Walter Stuart (1584–92) probably indicates that he too favoured change. Beyond this, we know nothing about who opposed and who supported change in what must have been a period of prolonged controversy and uncertainty at King's. The likelihood of opposition from those who held offices which were to be suppressed must have been greatly diminished by the fact that they were allowed to retain office for life. Other motives doubtless fueled opposition: selfish interests; general conservatism; regard for Aristotle and the schoolmen; suspicion of the reforms as they were sponsored by the Melvillian faction which disrupted church-state relations for many years. Central also must have been the 'constitutional' arguments. Firstly, drastic change in the college meant defying the intentions of the revered founder, Bishop Elphinstone. All in the college might accept without question that his intentions should be overturned so far as replacing Catholicism with Protestantism was concerned, but doubtless some argued that beyond this the founder's wishes should be respected. There was also a much wider constitutional argument. As first founded the University of Aberdeen had had faculties of arts, theology, civil law, canon law and medicine. Under the New Foundation only arts and theology remained. Traditional definitions of a university assumed that such institutions possessed at least a range of faculties. It could therefore be argued that the New Foundation reduced King's merely to a college of arts or philosophy, surrendering the proud title of university. In reply it could be pointed out that many continental arts colleges (such as some of the French Huguenot ones) were more impressive centres of learning than Scotland's 'universities', so such a change need not necessarily imply degredation. And if King's under the New Foundation did not fully qualify as a university, the same could be said of Glasgow under its *Nova Erectio*, and of the post-Reformation foundations of Edinburgh College and Marischal College.[34]

★

Though by the beginning of the seventeenth century much of the New Foundation was being adhered to at King's, it cannot be said the institution was in a flourishing state as a result of this. Principal David Rait, though evidently a sound scholar, does not seem to have had sufficient energy or ability to protect the college's interests. Implementation of the retrenchment inherent in the New Foundation, and the acquistion of new grants of church property in the 1570s and 1580s, should have made it possible to put the college on a sound financial footing. But for this to have happened, effective and responsible control over college property and revenues, to conserve them for the future, was also necessary. It was not forthcoming. Some action was taken. In 1607 the college obtained from the court of session a general decreet ordering all its feuars and tenants to pay their dues and rents to the college,[35] but such recourse to the law was time-consuming and often ineffectual. Rait and his colleagues therefore appear to have resorted to long term or permanent alienation of land and other property through feuing or granting of long leases at fixed rents. The college benefited in the short term through the large *grassums* or down-payments received when the grants were made, but in the long term, as inflation continued, they created new financial problems for the college. Such policies cannot be blamed entirely on Rait and his colleagues; they were indeed traditional, and had been pursued under earlier principals like Alexander Anderson and Walter Stuart—though it may be significant that there are no allegations of such alienations under Alexander Arbuthnot. But there may have been an increasing tendency under Rait for members of the staff themselves to deal in college property, a lead being taken by the official who was supposed to have particular responsibility for college finances: Beroald Innes, the economus. His dealings in college property stretch at least from 1585 to 1609.[36] Subprincipal John Chalmers had a feu of college lands.[37] It would of course be wrong to assume automatically that all dealings of members of staff in college property must have been corrupt. But the number of these and other alienations of property do suggest mismanagement.

Though David Rait and his colleagues had supported the Melvillian New Foundation, they probably showed little resistance to the tendency seen early in the new century for Scottish universities to move back towards a Protestant version of Aristotelian scholasticism (seen as necessary to counter the scholastic arguments of Counter-Reformation Catholic theologians),combined with continuing lip-service to Ramism. The first decade of the century saw the final defeat of the Melvillians. Andrew Melville was imprisoned and then banished, and support for his policies collapsed as King James established royal control of the church—and thus of the universities—through bishops.[38] In the new atmosphere advocacy of the more radically anti-scholastic ideas became politically suspect. Rait himself was at one point prepared to take part in a gesture of defiance against royal domination. A test of strength between the king and the Melvillians occured in 1605 when the king ordered the postponment of a general assembly which was due to meet in Aberdeen. A number of Melvillian ministers nonetheless met to assert the freedom of the church, and declared themselves a general assembly. David Rait opened the meeting, and evidently presided until a moderator was elected.[39] Most of those who thus defied the king were subsequently punished, and the episode proved a turning point in James's battle to gain control of the church. But Rait escaped punishment, perhaps an indication that he was not regarded as one of the ring-leaders—he had evidently been chosen to open the meeting as he had been moderator of the previous meeting of the synod of Aberdeen—and perhaps because he submitted quickly. Certainly the fact that he was a member of the assembly of 1610,[40] a body carefully packed by the king's supporters, indicates that he had abandoned support for Melvillian policies by that time.

If Rait and his colleagues on the staff of the college had had some degree of Melvillian sympathies, these were probably largely confined to approval of his educational ideas. In other respects the staff seem to have fitted into the fairly conservative Protestantism which was becoming widespread in the North East as the new religion spread, and which found the king's episcopalianism more acceptable than the radical ideas of his opponents in the church. Rait seems to have been regarded by Peter Blackburn, Bishop of Aberdeen 1600–16, as a senior cleric of the diocese to whom he was happy to delegate certain tasks. Sometimes these were of more than parochial importance: in 1597 Rait (and Peter Udny, the subprincipal) were among ministers appointed to negotiate with the Earl of Huntly and others about ending bloodfeuds in the north and releasing Catholic nobles from excommunication.[41]

Like his predecessors since the deanery of Aberdeen had been annexed to the college in 1574, Rait acted as minister of Old Aberdeen—though the difficulty of combining academic and ministerial duties caused problems for both Rait and his colleagues. In 1600 it was:

> given in before the presbytery as a grief that the youth of the college and grammar school were neglected that week that the regent or master teaches in the kirk, in special the grammar school.[42]

Thus Rait got the grammarian and the regents to take it in turn to teach in the parish church, St Machars Cathedral, with the result that their students were left unsupervised. Neither the staff nor the parishioners were happy with this arrangement. During the presbytery's visitation of the parish in 1601 it was complained that though Rait was diligent in teaching in St Machar's once each Sunday, he should teach twice.

Rait replied that he was only required to teach once. The presbytery concluded that Rait should teach on Sunday mornings, the subprincipal of King's in the afternoon—though as the subprincipalship was vacant, until it was filled Rait and all the other masters of the college should teach in turns.[43] Shortly afterwards John Chalmers became subprincipal, and he acted as minister of the second charge at St Machar's.[44] But the problem of providing an adequate parish minister had not been solved. At the 1602 visitation by the presbytery Chalmers asked for help, and it was agreed that the other masters should continue to alternate with him— something they were evidently not willing to do, as Chalmers protested that if they failed to help the lack of teaching should not be blamed on him. He also resisted orders to take over responsibility for baptisms in the parish when Rait was absent,[45] which suggests that he was a most reluctant recruit to the ministry. Moreover, the preaching of academics was not always suited to the needs of the congregation. In 1604 Rait was ordered 'to apply himself more diligently to his study and to alter his text from Daniel to some other text not so difficult, and to choose a text more plain for the capacity of the vulgar people'.[46] In 1607 he was criticised for not ensuring that elders attended meetings of the kirk session, not enforcing church attendance, and not being active enough in catechising.[47]

The dominance of the college by the church was of course seen as vital—it was primarily a seminary training ministers. But the link was clearly too close for the college's academic health. As the demands made by the presbytery indicate, the parish ministry was itself a full-time occupation, involving taking services, pastoral work with the congregation, administrative and judicial work in the kirk session. The presbytery of Aberdeen met weekly, alternately in Aberdeen and Old Aberdeen (except in spring and summer, when it visited individual parishes in turn), assembling in King's College Chapel when in the latter. As well as attending these meetings, Rait had to take his turn as moderator.[48]

Moreover it was not just ecclesiastical duties which diverted Rait from academic life. The college held civil jurisdiction within 'College Bounds', on occasion choosing its own baillies to act as judges.[49] As a dominant institution within Old Aberdeen the college was closely linked to the burgh and its court. Sometimes the two little jurisdictions became confused, and the college found itself helping run the burgh. Thus on 9 July 1605 proceedings of the college court, held in the college hall in the presence of the principal and his colleagues, were recorded in the minute book of the burgh council. Berowald Innes, the college economus, was also present—as a baillie of the burgh.[50] A month later 'In presence of the baillies of Old Aberdeen. As also the College Court', brewers in the 'city' were forbidden to sell students meat or drink.[51] Thus the courts of the neighbouring jurisdictions were being combined for convenience, as they were seeking to regulate what was in effect a single community. In 1612 Bishop Peter Blackburn (as superior of the burgh) and David Rait (as principal and common procurator of the college) nominated a regent of the college and a burgess as baillies both of the burgh and of the college bounds, but with provision 'that the several jurisdictions be not confounded'.[52] Provost and baillies immediately proceeded to forbid anyone in Old Aberdeen or College Bounds to lend any student or grammar school pupil more than a merk: if more was lent, the student concerned was to be free to reclaim all the goods he had left as security for the loan without making any repayment. Shortly afterwards, a man and his wife were banished for being 'receivers' of stolen goods and for abstracting students from their studies.[53] In a more positive way college and burgh can be seen working together through the former helping to pay part of the stipend of the master of the latter's song school.[54] This merging of jurisdictions was only temporary, but it emphasises how intimately the college was involved in burgh life.

In some respects the fact that the college worked so closely with local civil and church authorities can be regarded as a source of strength, as it indicates that the college was closely intergrated into the wider local community. Yet it is likely that one result was the distraction of time and energy of college staff from the academic functions of the college. David Rait might have been a good principal or a good minister, but it was impossible to be both at once. But shortage of resources, the way in which the new church reluctantly followed the old in seeking to finance university education out of parish revenues, meant that he had to hold both offices.

The decades on either side of 1600 allow for the first time a glimpse of King's College's relations with the church and the burgh, through the survival of presbytery and burgh court minutes. From the same years there survive the first regular records of the names of students: thus at last the size of the college community can be assessed—though still only within fairly broad limits. In 1601–10 an average of 19.1 students are listed as entering the college each year. Had all completed the full four-year arts course, this would indicate an undergraduate population of the order of seventy-five. But in fact many failed to complete the course, and taking account of this would lower the total. Of this 1601–10 cohort of 191 students, only about 104 are known to have graduated.[55] Thus only about 54% of students listed as enrolling ever graduated—and since there is probably significant under-recording of enrolments the percentage of students who graduated may well be considerably lower.[56] The high drop-out rate is not surprising. Some died or fell ill; a considerable number never intended to graduate, as they did not want paper qualifications; others decided that further academic study was not for them. But most of the drop-outs doubtless failed to complete their university careers through poverty. Many of those who aspired to a career in the ministry were drawn from relatively humble backgrounds, and for some the struggle to survive at university was lost. How tough the going was for some is illustrated by he fact that poor university students were recognised as one sub-group in Scotland's mass of beggars.[57] Taking into consideration all these factors, an undergraduate population of between fifty and seventy at King's College in this decade is a reasonable guess, and to this should be added a handful of postgraduate students of theology.

Obviously by modern standards these numbers are tiny, but more to the point is the fact that they indicate that the college was smaller than the other Scottish universities for which figures survive for the same period. Alongside King's average of 19.1 entrants per year can be put the Glasgow average of 27.4 matriculations a year in 1601–10,[58] and Edinburgh's 26.6 graduations a year in the same decade.[59] For Marischal College information on entrants is only available for five years of the decade (1605–6, 1608–10), but this indicates that King's had been overtaken narrowly by its local rival, which enlisted an average of 22 first year students annually.[60] No figures for St Andrews have been published, but it was probably the largest of Scotland's universities. Combining all this information suggests that perhaps 150 students a year were entering Scottish universities, though the margins of possible error are wide. Interestingly, it has been estimated that in England in 1600–9 there were about 700 entrants to university each year.[61] Given that England's population was about five times that of Scotland, this indicates that roughly the same proportion of total population attended university in each country—though in the Inns of Court England had extra institutions of higher education which had no counterpart in Scotland.

Of the life led by the students attracted to King's College in these decades little direct or detailed evidence survives. The text of the New Foundation lays down the official view of what university experience was intended to be—a sober, hard-working, godly and tightly disciplined life for youths who were, by modern standards, of secondary school rather than university student age. Admission to the college depended on the judgement of the principal and his colleagues as to the academic abilities of the candidates, and there was emphasis on only the properly qualified being admitted, and subsequently promoted at the end of each year to the next. However, in view of the college's financial plight and the fact that fees were means-tested, there must have been a considerable temptation to admit students from the right backgrounds without too much investigation. The annual tuition fee or *minerval* (from Minerva, the Roman god of wisdom) was £6 Scots for the higher nobility; £4 for the lower nobility, £2 for farmers, merchants and craftsmen: no fees were payable by 'the poor'—some at least of whom were supported on the college foundation as bursars. Deciding which social category students belonged to was a matter for the regents concerned—who had a financial interest, no doubt, in encouraging social snobbery so sons of landowners and their parents would be willing to accept being classified as higher rather than lower nobility. In addition examination fees were to be collected each year, the amount increasing each year (6s. 8d.; 13s. 4d.; £1; £1. 10s. 0d.), though the poor were again exempt. Finally, each student was to pay annually 4s. to the 'general attendant'. The attendant is not mentioned anywhere else in the New Foundation, but he appears also in the Marischal College foundation charter where, helpfully, it is added that he was known as the beadle.

When it came to eating and sleeping arrangements, the New Foundation implicitly sanctioned three alternative arrangements; sleeping and eating in college; sleeping and eating elsewhere; sleeping in college but eating elsewhere. Whether it was permitted to sleep elsewhere but eat in college in not clear. For those sleeping in college the day began at 5 a.m. when they were woken and (in winter) brought lights by the bursars. Students living outside were to be in the college by 6 a.m., when, presumably teaching began. Breakfast was at 9 a.m., with those eating out required to be back in college by 10 a.m. They were permitted to leave again for dinner at 12 noon, but whereas those living in Old Aberdeen had to be back by 1 p.m., those eating in Aberdeen itself, two miles away, did not need to return until 2 p.m. Clearly dinner was the main meal of the day, so students living in Aberdeen were encouraged to economise by going home, whereas presumably they took their breakfast in Old Aberdeen. After dinner the students worked until 6 p.m., unless permission for play had been given, in which case one of the regents would lead them all out to play and then back afterwards in a body. It may be assumed that the place for this physical recreation was the links, the sandy grassland separating Old Aberdeen from the sea. Play was not to last for more than two hours. It is not specified when the afternoon session of work ended and supper was taken, but the day ended at 9 p.m. when the duty regent for the week who had supervised the students' play made a round of the college bedrooms to check that all his charges were safely settled.

The course of studies pursued within this framework has already been discussed. Much of the teaching was done by regents who were themselves young, and doubtless as in other colleges much of their teaching was based very closely on notes they had taken from their own regents a few years before. The endless routine of note-taking—often, it may be suspected, virtually dictation—and Latin and Greek composition was varied by the emphasis on public speaking and disputation. Such verbal skills were central to university education, with a student's career culminating in the public disputation of theses prepared by the regents. Students in each class were to be divided into groups of ten, and each month the member of the group who had shown himself most learned was singled out for praise: the New Foundation indicates that he was to be chosen by voting, presumably among the students in the group, which suggests the distinction was based mainly on ability at public speaking.

The college disciplinary code was strict—and over-optimistic, no doubt, as to what could be achieved in practice. Students were to live together in the utmost harmony, abstaining from shameful conversation, cursing and blasphemy. They were only to speak in Latin and Greek. Upright in morals and diligent in their studies and religious worship, they were to abstain from carrying a blood-curdling list of weapons: in a society in which the landed social elites still regarded it as acceptable to pursue their quarrels through the violence of the bloodfeud, care of adolescent boys frequently drawn from landed families was a far from easy task. However, the carrying of small knives had to be permitted in an age when knives were not supplied at meals. A first offence against the weapon-code incurred only confiscation of the forbidden item, but a second offence led to a public beating, a third to expulsion from the college. To limit possible occasions for violence, no lavish festivities were to be allowed in college, and postgraduate students were particularly enjoined to set a good example of sober behaviour to their juniors.

Doubtless the easiest students to control were the bursars, since they were financially dependent on the college, and were likely to come from relatively humble social backgrounds and therefore be more amenable to discipline than their higher-born companions. As well as waking other students in the morning the bursars had duties in hall at dinner and supper, helping to serve the meals, and they were to act in turn as janitor or porter at the gate of the college—until the college could afford to employ a janitor.

Subject to strict discipline and constant supervision by superiors both supicious and apprehensive of the potential for disorder inherent in their charges, the status of the undergraduate students in the college appears lowly. Yet they were regarded as members of the college and university, and their role in the life of these institutions was enshrined in their part in election of the rector. Mediaeval tradition divided university students into four distinctly arbitrary 'nations' of origin for this purpose. The

New Foundation for the first time in any surviving source defines the four nations at King's, though it is doubtless merely re-stating an existing division. The diocese of Aberdeen was divided into the nations of Marr and Buchan. All Scotland to the north was to comprise Moray, all that to the south, Angus. Procurators chosen by the students of the four nations joined together to elect the rector, a process symbolic of the principle of student power, whatever the reality.[62]

The general question of how far the New Foundation's ivory-tower ideal of student life accords with the actual experience of students is unanswerable in detail, though it may be said with confidence that that experience must have been more chaotic and confused than the Foundation had hoped, and that in practice the rules laid down must often have been varied or ignored. Yet study of what the Foundation has to say about student life at least provides a general framework in which to envisage students pursuing their educational ambitions—and seeking to subvert the wishes of those set over them. Of the many students who passed through the college in these decades, only one has left us a direct comment about what having studied there meant to him—and it suggests that while he was generally satisfied with his education at King's he came to believe that it had instilled complacency. David Leech mused in Latin verse 'On himself, on finishing his course in philosophy, 1614, in King's College, Aberdeen':

> the muses of Elphinstone instructed me in everything and crowned my head with the laurel. A boy philosopher, I thought I was omniscient. My utter nescience now bothers me. I scarcely know one thing, my own total ignorance.

Still, if the beginning of wisdom is recognition of one's own ignorance, perhaps Leech's masters had taught him well—even if he was rather slow in waking up to his own limitations. Certainly he respected his regent, Robert Dunbar, 'who first taught me philosophy from the learned page of Aristotle' and gave him career advice about the good prospects of the learned professions—the church, medicine and law.[63]

The smallest university in Britain King's College might be, but given its location, the continuing problem of strong Catholic interests in the north, and lack of resources, the state of the college was far from disgraceful, and its graduates were accepted into the ministry on an equal basis with those of other universities. Still, the impression the fragmentary records convey is of an inward-looking and rather complacent institution, providing adequate teaching but perhaps not supplying as much as it might have done in the way of intellectual stimulation. It is symptomatic that neither David Rait nor any of the three subprincipals who served under him in the years 1592 to 1619, nor the grammarians and regents of the period, are known to have left any significant published works behind from which their scholarship might be judged. Repeated attempts by national authorities from the 1570s to the 1590s to intervene and bring new life to the institution all ended in failure. The staff, left to their own devices by such failures, introduced many of the features of the Melvillian New Foundation, but were hamstrung by financial and other constraints. Once the initiative of the New Foundation had been accepted, the (admittedly fragmentary) evidence suggests that Principal Rait and his colleagues settled back, accepting the position of their college as worthy perhaps, but certainly not outstanding even in a Scottish context. In the long term such complacency was all but certain to lead to decline.

Small in size, limited in cash and scholarship though King's College was, there is little evidence of positive efforts in the early seventeenth century to improve the situation. Perhaps, after all the indecisive activity over the New Foundation in previous decades, Rait and the rest of the staff had given up, accepting that nothing much could be done to deal with deep-seated problems. The same seems true of the early Protestant bishops of Aberdeen—whose influence as chancellors of the university is notable by its absence. But the situation was not to be acceptable to Patrick Forbes of Corse, who in May 1618 was consecrated bishop of Aberdeen. To him the college was a corrupt and decayed institution, blatantly ignoring its responsibilities, staffed by men for whom he had little or no respect. They had betrayed the ideals of his great (if Catholic) predecessor, Bishop Elphinstone, and must be brought to account for this treachery.

Chapter 4

A Second Founder? Bishop Patrick Forbes

Your worthy and famous university, founded by Bishop Elphinstone, and hospital [nurtured?] by Bishop Dunbar, may vaunt [boast] of him as of a second founder

John Guthrie, Bishop of Moray, 1635[1]

Patrick Forbes was born in 1564 into the old and moderately prosperous Aberdeenshire family of the lairds of Corse. His education was dominated by his second cousin, Andrew Melville. He was sent to study under him in Glasgow, and moved with him to St Andrews in 1580. When Melville had to flee to England for safety in 1584, after the escape of James VI from the Ruthven Raiders, Forbes accompanied him, and this and other evidence suggests that he was very much a supporter of the Melvillian or presbyterian faction in both church and state. He returned to St Andrews with Melville in 1586 and studied theology. It is said he was offered a post as regent in arts there but declined it to please his father, who saw an academic career as unsuitable for the heir to the estate of Corse and wanted him to settle down and raise a family. This Forbes did, living in Montrose until he inherited the estate in 1598.[2]

Throughout the years in which he lived the life of a laird, Forbes retained a close interest in the affairs of the kirk, and his involvement in the religious life of the area, his character and his ability evidently led to him being urged to enter the ministry. This he at first refused to do, perhaps feeling that he should not do so until his family had grown up. Of his links with King's College before he became bishop of Aberdeen in 1618 very little is known, though he witnessed a document signed by Principal Rait in 1600, indicating some acquaintance with college staff.[3] But his attitude to the college may be deduced from his wider interests. His early Melvillianism was modified in time, partly it seems by his worries about the religious situation in his native region. Catholicism was better organised and more strongly supported there than in any other part of Lowland Scotland, and Forbes considered the Catholic threat so serious that he concluded that the first priority for Protestants must be unity if

61

this menace was to be overcome. No doubt Forbes interpreted the local situation in terms of the broader European context, in which crusading Counter-Reformation Catholicism was triumphantly pushing back the frontiers of Protestantism in many places. In these circumstances quarrels between Protestant factions were a luxury which might well prove fatal, weakening and discrediting Protestantism and thus playing into the hands of its enemies. This became the central point in Forbes's teaching. Protestants must unite and love one another, concentrating on the essentials they held in common instead of becoming obsessed with the relatively minor matters on which they differed. Thus in Forbes's thought there was a willingness to compromise in some aspects of religion, but this was combined with—and indeed inspired by—obsessive fear and hatred of Catholicism.

This preoccupation with the Catholic menace must have influenced his attitude to King's College, for he held the common view that the chief purpose of the college was the production of well-qualified ministers. The church was still short of parish ministers in the north, and some of those it had left much to be desired. Yet ministers were supposed to be the spearhead of resistance to popery. University reform aimed at increasing both the quantity and the quality of candidates for the ministry therefore became as high a priority for Forbes as it had been for Andrew Melville. Aberdeen's two colleges, lying in the region where the threat was greatest, were obviously of particular importance. Perhaps this was why Forbes chose to send his second son, John, to King's College in 1606 rather than to his own university, St Andrews.[4] It is also interesting that he chose King's College for his son, and not Marischal. Certainly it must indicate that at this time, one of the most obscure in the history of the college, Patrick Forbes was satisfied that his son would receive a sound education there. A man with so strong an interest in religion and education would surely have established that much before sending there a boy who may already have been showing signs of his later academic brilliance. Yet it is possible that subsequently his son's reports on King's College from a student's point of view were among the influences which led Patrick Forbes to impose reform on the college as soon as he had a chance. John Forbes may well have expressed discontent at the rather uninspiring character of King's under Principal Rait.

It was a former teacher at King's College who persuaded Patrick Forbes to enter the ministry in middle life. In 1610 John Chalmers, subprincipal and second minister of St Machar's since 1601, resigned to become minister of Keith. The following year he committed suicide by cutting his throat. But though the wounds eventually proved fatal, the unfortunate Chalmers lingered on for a week before dying. Patrick Forbes was summoned to his deathbed, and this visit to the dying man proved a turning point in his life, for, in response to Chalmers's pleading, he agreed to enter the ministry, and indeed became minister of Keith in 1612. In taking this step Forbes was much influenced by the way that Chalmers's suicide was exploited for propaganda purposes: the Marquis of Huntly, the great patron and protector of local Catholics, was alleged to have hastened to cross-examine the dying man, trying to get him to admit that he had been driven to despair by doubts about the validity of Protestant beliefs.[5] By succeeding Chalmers at Keith, Forbes could strive to undo the harm caused by his suicide. Thus the episode which brought Forbes into the ministry intensified his obsession with countering Catholicism—and tragically illustrated the importance of making sure that those who entered the ministry were suitable in character and training. As seen in the previous chapter, Chalmers had been reluctant to act as second minister at St Machar's, and once he had left King's for a full-time ministry he had fallen into despair within a year. Chalmers's obvious unsuitability for the profession for which King's was supposed to have trained him may well have contributed to Forbes's belief that radical reform of the college was necessary.

Patrick Forbes had by now sufficiently modified his earlier presbyterian inclinations to accept episcopal ordination as a minister. At Keith his energy, ability and anti-Catholic publications[6] soon made him an outstanding figure, and in 1618 he was appointed Bishop of Aberdeen by James VI. He accepted office with, it seems, genuine reluctance, both through personal disinclination for high office and because he knew that in such an office he could not escape involvement in the bitter controversies in the church over innovations in worship and other changes imposed by the king. Perhaps also his presbyterian past had left him with a lingering distaste for bishops. But his appointment had widespread support locally and from the other Scottish bishops. In March 1618 the recently re-established Dean and Chapter of Aberdeen formally elected him bishop—and the dean was, *ex officio*, Principal Rait of King's College.[7]

Reluctant to accept office or not, Forbes was resolved to be an energetic and effective bishop, as David Rait soon discovered. At the new bishop's instigation, in March 1619 James VI ordered the issue of a commission under the great seal for a visitation of the colleges and hospitals of Aberdeen because of the 'sloth, negligence and connivance' of those in charge of them. The commission went on to speak of the 'dilapidation and the unnecessary and idle spending and wasting of the proper rent and patrimony' of both Marischal and King's College, together with:

> the ruin and decay of the buildings and edifices within the same, and the neglect of the ordinary teaching . . . and [of] the constitutions established within the said colleges . . . the professors are become careless and negligent. The number of professors and founded persons is not fully complete, and all good order and government within the said colleges is become in contempt.[8]

Clearly Bishop Forbes's report, on which the commission was based, had been strongly worded and sweeping in its denunciation of the state of the Aberdeen colleges. Later (1620) Forbes recalled that he had obtained the royal commission for visitation of King's College because its condition was so bad that he did not think his powers as chancellor of the university were sufficient to reform it, and he gave a highly-coloured picture of the college. This may owe something to what he had discovered during the 1619 visitation, but basically it reflects his opinion of the state of the college when he had asked for issue of the commission. King's was in a distressed state through:

> the abominable dilapidation of the means mortified thereto by miserable men, who in dead times, not being controlled, have so securely sacked all that estate, as if neither God had been in heaven to count with, nor men on earth to examine their ways.[9]

Support for Forbes's strictures is provided by the son of one of the 1619 commissioners for visitation, who recalled a generation later that at that time the revenues of the professors 'by the avarice of such as had been members of the university, were feued or let out for payment of so little as could not maintain them, and their very dwelling houses impropriated'. There was not 'so much left undilapidated . . . as to maintain all the professors according to their institution'.[10]

This interpretation of the state of the college in 1619 was to be the justification for all Forbes sought to do to reform it in the following fifteen years. But one central feature of the interpretation was highly controversial. It was based on the assumption that the college and its staff should be judged according to the pre-Reformation Old Foundation. The conduct of the visitation confirmed this. On 14, 15 and 16 September 1619 Bishop Forbes and the twelve other commissioners assembled in the college, and Principal David Rait, Subprincipal Patrick Guthrie and the three other regents appeared before them. The text of the Old Foundation was read, and the staff were told to produce written evidence of their elections to their offices in conformity with it. This they could not do, so the visitors declared that none of them had been correctly elected or admitted. Thus Forbes immediately seized the initiative, announcing that none of the college staff had any legal right to their offices. It followed from this that all their actions must have been illegal, no defence of them valid. For good measure in this preliminary 'softening up' of those who might oppose change, the principal was denounced for having illegally acted as common procurator, a post he had no right to hold.

Next, the visitors declared that 'the greatest part of the founded members were quite abolished and out of use, especially such as had special voice in nomination and presentation of members, wherethrough formal and canonical election had fallen away'. The principal was denounced for not teaching according to the foundation; in the past year he had only taught 'some few precepts of the Hebrew grammar'. In his dealings with college property while procurator he 'had not only been negligent but also harmful' by granting leases and feus unfavourable to the college, whereby its annual income 'was reduced to small importance, and as he alledged was presently three thousand pounds in his debt'. Breaches of college statutes had led to revenues of bursars being misused and promotion silver (a fee paid by students) diverted to private use. Each bursar was supposed to present the college with a silver spoon, but the college only had six.[11] Members did not live in college as they should. A paid porter was employed, whereas one of the bursars should have performed his duties. There was even a shortage of plates and table cloths in the college hall. All the buildings were ruinous, through funds set aside for maintenance being diverted to other uses. Finally, in spite of grants of extra revenues to the college since the Reformation, it had been so corruptly administered that it 'is not the less in miserable estate; and withall, no ministry of the gospel in the kirks of the deanery, but lamentable heathenism and such looseness as is horrible to record, albeit even about the cathedral kirk of the diocese'.[12]

This adds up to a comprehensive and damning indictment of the college under Principal Rait—though it is noticeable that it is on the administration of the college that the attack is concentrated. No criticism is made of the teaching apart from the reference to the principal's idleness. Having defined what was wrong with the college, the 1619 visitors moved on to remedies. Prime responsibility for the existing state of affairs was laid on David Rait, but he was to be given a chance to redeem himself, though under stringent conditions. After negotiations, agreement was reached with him as to what he would promise to do to improve the state of the college, to avoid having the visitors sentence him to any punishment. Rait was to give up the ministry of St Machar, which since the annexation of the deanery of Aberdeen to the college in 1579 had come to be held by the principal. Out of the deanery revenues he would provide 500 merks a year as stipend for the new minister, and more when the college's financial position made this possible. By Michaelmas 1621 Rait would provide another 500 merks a year to support

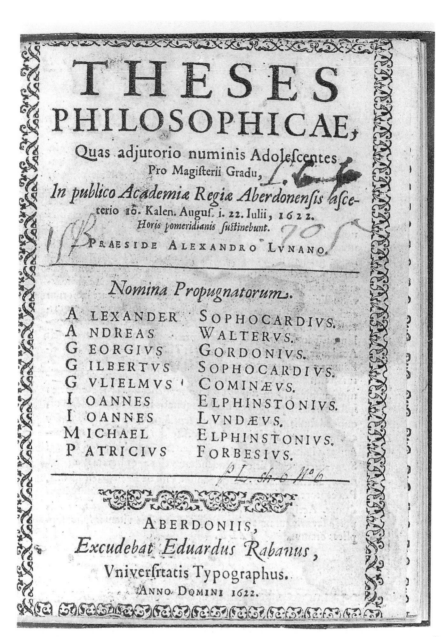

THESES
PHILOSOPHICAE,

Quas adjutorio numinis Adolescentes
Pro Magisterii Gradu,

In publico Academiæ Regiæ Aberdonensis asce-
terio 16. Kalen. Augus. i. 22. Iulii, 1622.
Horis pomeridianis sustinebunt.

PRAESIDE ALEXANDRO LVNANO.

Nomina Propugnatorum.

ALEXANDER	SOPHOCARDIVS.
ANDREAS	WALTERVS.
GEORGIVS	GORDONIVS.
GILBERTVS	SOPHOCARDIVS.
GVLIELMVS	COMINÆVS.
IOANNES	ELPHINSTONIVS.
IOANNES	LVNDÆVS.
MICHAEL	ELPHINSTONIVS.
PATRICIVS	FORBESIVS.

ABERDONIIS,
Excudebat Eduardus Rabanus,
Vniversitatis Typographus.
ANNO DOMINI 1622.

6 Title page of the earliest (or earliest surviving) King's College graduation
theses to be printed, 1622. Alexander Lunan, the regent whose students
were graduating, prepared the theses, which were then defended in debate
by his students, whose names are listed. The printer, Edward Raban, had
only recently arrived in Aberdeen, and describes himself as printer to the
university. AUL, SBL 1622 R 2.

a minister at Monykebuck (New Machar), and by the same date he was to have repaired all the college buildings, using the same materials (lead, slates, oak and fir) as in the original work, and provided adequate table cloths and other necessities for the dining room. A number of overseers were appointed to supervise Rait's performance of this work. Finally, by Michaelmas 1623 Rait was to free the college from all debts. If he failed to fulfil any of these promises he was to pay the college 2,000 merks and loose all right to debts owed to him by the college. To enable him to carry out these reforms the visitors appointed Rait common procurator for four years, though he was to grant no leases or other alienations of rights without the consent of Bishop Forbes (as chancellor) and other members of the university.[13]

On 15 November 1619 the humiliation of Principal Rait was completed: he signed a formal obligation, for registration in the register of deeds, binding himself to carry out the obligations imposed on him. By an additional clause he was bound only to grant leases 'for augumentatioun of rentals and not for grassums', to ensure that Rait did not try to get out of his financial difficulties by granting leases which brought in large 'grassums' or down payments with low rents thereafter which would decrease college revenues in the long term. However, it was evidently decided that entrusting Rait with sole responsibility for restoring administrative and financial efficiency was unwise in view of his past record, so it was agreed that he need not serve as procurator— though he would have to be cautioner (guarantor) for whoever was appointed.[14]

Having dealt with the principal, the 1619 visitors proceeded to the restoration of many of the old offices which had been abolished under the New Foundation. Thomas Nicolson was elected civilist, William Anderson canonist, and Patrick Dun mediciner. In addition David Wedderburne was appointed grammarian in an effort to restore the status of the office as superior to that of regent—he was already master of Aberdeen grammar school and a well known Latin poet. Well qualified Latinists were evidently thin on the ground, because in 1620 Wedderburne agreed to give weekly lessons in Marischal College as well.[15] Two university (as opposed to college) posts which had come to be of very limited importance in previous decades were revived. John Leith was elected rector, William Forbes (one of the regents) dean of the faculty of arts.[16]

The 1619 visitation initiated the most radical upheaval in King's College since the purge of 1569, exactly half a century before. The coming of the New Foundation in the generation after 1569 had been gradual and piecemeal: 1619 saw the abrupt return of the Old Foundation— or at least of as much of it as was compatible with Protestantism. In the same post-1569 years, and even before them, the supervisory role of the university over the college had virtually vanished. Now it was back with a vengeance, for the new Bishop of Aberdeen clearly had a very different concept of his duties as chancellor from that held by his immediate predecessors.

The reforms demanded of David Rait himself were justified, and indeed long overdue. He had clearly neglected many of his duties, though it is true he had inherited financial problems from his predecessors. But the insistence of Forbes and the other visitors on judging Rait and his colleagues according to the Old Foundation was harsh and unjust. The legal situation was admittedly confused, but for many years the college had been run in the sincere belief that the New Foundation had replaced the Old. If the Old was to be re-introduced, the integrity of those who had conformed to the New should surely have been accepted. Moreover, even if Bishop Forbes's determination to rebuild the college on Old Foundation lines is accepted as a worthy ambition, the way he went about it is highly questionable, and gave rise to a very real sense of grievance among the existing staff that made Forbes's task harder than it need have been. The 1619 visitation's immediate restoration of a number of Old Foundation offices might look good on paper. Overnight the university grew from two faculties (arts and theology) to five. But in reality this meant no growth in the college community, no increase in teaching. Appointments had been made of canonist, civilist, mediciner and grammarian. But none of these men received salaries from the college, so though they had gained grandiose new titles they continued to make their living in their old professions. The new canonist, William Anderson, can probably be identified with the man of the same name who was sheriff clerk of Aberdeen. If this is the case, it provides an explanation of why Anderson soon disappeared from the college records: in the 1620s the canonist/sheriff clerk was denounced as a Catholic—a highly embarrassing presence in a college Patrick Forbes was seeking to rebuild as a bastion of Protestant resistance to the threat of popery.[17] The other new appointees at least were not controversial in this sense. The civilist, Thomas Nicolson, was commissary of Aberdeen. The mediciner, Patrick Dun, was a regent a Marischal College, and became principal there in 1621. The grammarian, David Wedderburn, was master of Aberdeen grammar school and also a regent at Marischal. At the most these men can have made occasional visits to King's for formal occasions, perhaps giving occasional lectures, but they added virtually nothing to the real academic strength of the institution.[18] It might be argued that the appointments were nonetheless justified as a sort of declaration of intent on the part of Forbes: undoubtedly he did plan to appoint proper salaried men to these posts once resources were found to pay them. But in the eyes of the existing staff at King's the appointments had a far more sinister effect. They gave office in the college to four supporters of Forbes who could then be trusted to help him to supervise and reform it as he wished. Nicolson and Dun were indeed themselves members of the 1619 visitation commission, and thus henchmen of the bishop from the start.[19] As there were only five other academic staff in the college (principal, subprincipal and three regents), Forbes's four placemen put him in a strong position.

The nominal appointments were thus bound to lead to bitterness and tensions within the college. Five staff did the work, but these four outsiders had in college affairs power without responsibility (normally held to be the attribute of a rather older profession). In the event Forbes was never able to do more than make the first moves towards providing salaries for these four offices, but even after his death the 'real' members of staff constantly feared that these interlopers would conspire to demand salaries out of existing revenues—at the expense of existing salaries.[20] Forbes may have been so convinced that the college staff would oppose what he was trying to do that he saw no point in wasting time trying to gain their willing co-operation. But the way he tackled the major problems the college undoubtedly had created a bitterness that lasted long after his death, though while he lived his authority was such that it remained largely below the surface.

News of what the zealous new bishop and the other visitors had done at King's caused panic at Marischal College. When the visitors attempted to move there on 16 September the gates were locked against them,[21] this being justified by a constitutional argument backed by the Earl Marischal claiming that neither the bishop or nor a royal commission could authorise interference in his college. Eventually the earl was forced to give way and the visitation took place, its most dramatic feature being the forced resignation of the principal, Andrew Aidy or Adie.[22] The contrast in the treatment of the two principals by the visitors is interesting. It suggests that the bishop saw some good in Rait, for all his faults, which justified giving him another chance.[23] Other evidence points to the same conclusion The pre-Reformation degree of doctor of divinity was revived by James VI as an encouragement to learning among ministers, being first granted in 1616 at St Andrews. The first award of the degree in Aberdeen, in 1620, was to David Rait.[24] This may have been partly because the Old Foundation stipulated that the principal should hold such a degree,[25] but Forbes would hardly have bestowed it on Rait unless he respected his learning. Further, in describing his actions at King's to James VI Forbes implied that Rait was no worse than his predecessors or colleagues: Rait was singled out for punishment as an example to others and because the office he held meant the prime responsibility for the financial mess at King's was his. Promises had been forced from him 'for a just punishment of his own bygone prevarication, that both he and others might hereafter walk more circumspectly'.[26]

In November 1623 Forbes carried out another visitation, this time merely as chancellor, without a royal commission, to see if Rait had fulfilled his promises. The visitation records[27] are incomplete, but Rait evidently gave satisfaction as there is no evidence of any penalty being imposed on him—though a new contract in 1624 between the bishop and college staff on the one hand, Rait and his sons on the other, dealt with some of his remaining financial obligations to the college.[28] Progress in providing parish ministers out of deanery revenues was however slower than planned: Rait was not replaced as minister of St Machar until 1621, and Monykebuck did not get its own minister until 1626.[29] In the interim Forbes had continued to be active in the work of college regeneration. A long series of legal actions had begun to try to recover alienated college property, and where the law provided no remedy attempts were made to buy back property.[30] In 1620 Forbes appealed to the king for benefit of the 'laws of recovery' to help the college, and asked him to intercede for return to it of the right to some teinds (tithes): no other part of college property had been 'more corruptly put away' than the teinds.[31]. What effect the appeal to the king had is not known, but in the years between 1620 and the outbreak of the 'troubles' in 1637 much alienated property was returned to the college. In 1622 the chaplains' chambers were bought back for use by the new professor of divinity.[32] The year 1624 saw the return of the civilist's croft,[33] followed by the canonist's manse[34] and the humanist's manse.[35] In March 1637 the Court of Session set aside a tack of the teinds of St Machar dated 1579 as it had been granted without the consent of the bishop and chapter of Aberdeen, and it was noted that this was the third such decision in favour of the college on such grounds. In the same month a tack of some of the deanery lands was set aside for the same reason.[36] The fact that the first Protestant bishops of Aberdeen had neglected their duties as chancellor of the university thus provided convenient legal arguments for helping regain college rights. Many other cases were also pursued before the session and the sheriff court.[37] The 1606 decreet summoning all holding property from the college to pay their dues to it was revived, letters of horning being issued on it in 1626.[38]

All this legal and financial activity was combined with attention to the reform of teaching within the college. Little of this is known in detail, but two major innovations took place: a new chair was established and funded, and the regenting system was reformed. In April 1619, before the visitation of King's later in the year, the synod of Aberdeen met for the first time with Forbes as bishop, and proposals for endowing two new chairs of divinity were discussed, presumably on his initiative. By December the plans for such a chair at King's were complete, and shortly thereafter the bishop's son, John Forbes, was appointed to it and granted the revived degree of doctor of divinity. Endowment of the chair was completed in 1629 when money collected by the presbyteries within the synod and by the bishop himself were used to purchase land for 10,000 merks from the bishop's brother, William Forbes of Craigievar, to provide an income for the professor.[39] The revival of theology at King's required students as well as a professor, and Forbes was evidently instrumental in diverting money raised to support bursars in theology in St Andrews to the two Aberdeen colleges, while as a further encouragement it was declared that Aberdeen graduates would be preferred (other things being equal) in appointments to the parish ministry in the diocese.[40] The appointment of the bishop's son to the chair, and purchase of land from his brother, must have led to mutterings about nepotism, but the choice of professor quickly justified itself. Since graduating at King's in 1610 John Forbes had studied at Heidelberg, Sedan (under his exiled kinsman, Andrew Melville) and elsewhere, and in the years following his taking up the new chair at King's he emerged as one of the leading Scottish theologians and scholars of the age.[41]

In setting up the new chair Bishop Forbes demonstrated that he was not a rigid supporter of the Old Foundation in every detail, nothing more and nothing less. Teaching of theology needed to be strengthened at King's (not least because the principal, who was supposed to teach theology, was the neglectful David Rait), so innovation was justified. In substituting a 'professorial' for a regenting system for arts teaching Forbes again showed himself flexible. Here he did not add to the Old Foundation but defied it and introduced an element from the New Foundation. The attribution of the change to the bishop himself rests only on circumstantial evidence. All that is known is that from the academic year 1628–9 onwards the subprincipal and the other three regents each ceased to take a class through the entire four year course and instead took each class for a single year, thus specialising in that year's subjects. Simultaneously the regents begin to be referred to sporadically as professors of the subjects in which they specialised.[42] As Forbes took such a close interest in the college, supervising its reform in detail, it is highly likely that he was responsible for the change, and it is tempting to link it with a visitation of the college he undertook in May 1628, though the only change that is known to have resulted from it was the abolition of the custom of students paying for a banquet for their teachers before graduation. In future they were to donate books to the college library instead.[43]

The change in teaching methods might be interpreted as raising the status of the regents by making them specialists. But another of Forbes's reforms worked in the opposite direction. The pre-Reformation regents, chosen from among the students of theology, had only served as regents until their theological studies were completed,[44] and after the Reformation this tradition continued, with most regents eventually entering the parish ministry. Bishop Forbes tightened up this custom by stipulating that after serving for six years a regent had to make himself available for the ministry if any parish wanted him. Moreover, as he saw the regents as still being essentially the old students of theology under another name, he insisted that they were subordinate to the new professor of theology—his own son—even though they might themselves be called professors. According to a later writer Forbes saw these changes in the position of regents as 'a great advantage to the church, a preventive of the regents' negligence in their study, and a spur to their diligence', while also providing regular vacancies of regencies to be filled by youths 'of pregnancy and parts'.[45] Thus regencies would be used to supply the diocese with mature, scholarly and experienced candidates for the ministry. Given Forbes' over-riding concern to have the best possible ministers, making the regents temporary members of staff made sense, but from the point of view of the development of scholarship within the college his decision was questionable. Moreover, those involved could hardly fail to notice that the change strengthened his hold over the regents. To his four cronies in revived offices he had added his son as a professor, and he had now given him authority over the four regents, including the subprincipal. The control of the university chancellor over college staff was now overwhelming. To David Rait his proud title of principal must have seemed to mean little any more.

The fears of existing salaried staff that in time attempts would be made to give salaries to the newly intruded officials were realised when William Gordon was assigned a stipend on his appointment as mediciner in 1632.[46] When James Sandilands younger took over the post of canonist from his father James, commissary of Aberdeen, it was agreed (1 January 1634) that though the masters and members of the university were willing to grant him a full stipend, because of financial difficulties he would be content with whatever was assigned to him, which would be whatever could be afforded without diminishing the stipends of the existing masters and servants of the university.[47] Further, in February 1634, Gilbert Ross, already reader and chorister of St Machar's Cathedral, was appointed cantor and master of the music school of King's College—the first cantor since the Reformation. He agreed to serve without any stipend 'in respect of the many and great both ordinary and extraordinary burdens presently incumbent upon the said university and college' and that he would not seek any more for his duties at St Machar's than the £60 Scots a year already assigned to him. But Ross was promised something when 'the said rents may conveniently permit and bear it', rising eventually to 'a reasonable competent stipend'.[48] Thus by the end of 1634 of the Old Foundation college officials restored by Bishop Forbes only the absentee civilist, Roger Mowat (an Edinburgh lawyer), was without a stipend or the prospect of one. The stipulation that the canonist would only be paid if this did not entail reducing the stipends of others was clearly an attempt to reassure those who felt their interests were threatened. But it was soon to become clear that the attempt had failed.

The return to essentially Old Foundation staffing at King's was given official approval in 1633 when Charles I visited Scotland. The king:

> moved with fervent zeal of the propagation and advancement of religion, and with a special regard to the education and upbringing of the youth within this kingdom in piety and learning, and specially within the north parts of the realm,

ratified the Old Foundation of the college and university, which, it was now declared, had also been ratified by the 1617 act of parliament. 'All and sundry the forsaids old foundations' were confirmed in perpetuity.[49] This expression of deep interest in the college was of course simply a matter of form—ratifications of the foundations of Glasgow and St Andrews were also granted[50]—and it is typical of Charles I that the only matter concerning the Scottish universities that he took a personal interest in as a result of his 1633 visit was a trifle of ceremony. In May 1634 he wrote to Bishop Forbes that while in Scotland he had seen some things which should be put in better order. Nothing, he stated, 'appeareth unto us more necessary than the well settling of our universities, both for the service, of God and good education of youth there'. But he had heard that in the universities of both Old and New Aberdeen staff and students when attending their parish churches sat intermingled with the rest of the congregation, 'which looseth much of the honour and dignity of the universities, being quite contrary to the course held in other well governed places of the like nature, and in diverse respects very inconvenient'. He had therefore instructed the authorities in the two burghs to provide special places for the members of the universities, and in future staff and students were to go to the churches in orderly processions wearing their gowns. So important a matter did the king consider this to be that he ordered that he be informed when this practice started, and that he be assured at least once a year that it was being continued.[51] As a top educational priority this left something to be desired. Bishop Forbes doubtless believed that ceremonial had its place in the life of an institution, but he can hardly have failed to reflect that there were matters more central to the revival of the Aberdeen colleges on which royal support would have been welcome.

By 1634, indeed, Forbes's reforms at King's were entering a new phase, though his personal circumstances may have led to alterations in his plans, and certainly forced him to play a less direct part in the college than previously. In 1632 the aging bishop suffered a severe stroke which left his right side paralysed. Though not impaired in speech or thought he was unable to walk and had to be carried about in a chair. Realisation that no recovery could be expected led him increasingly to work through his son John, already professor of divinity, in reforming King's College. It is probable that from 1619 Bishop Forbes had been working to tighten up and regularise 'management' of the college and university after a long period of neglect, and by 1630 rector and college staff are found meeting in a 'quarter session of the King's College of the University' with a college clerk, Mr Alexander Reid, recording decisions taken in 'the book of acts and registrations of the said university'.[52] This 'book' has not survived, but in 1634 regular recording of the proceedings of visitations of the college in a minute book began, and over the next few years many aspects of college and university life were regulated. The timing may be coincidental, but it looks very much as though Bishop Forbes was preparing the college for the time when his guiding hand would be removed. In the first of these visitations, in June 1634, it was ruled that rectors and deans of faculties should be elected in June each year, and John Forbes was elected rector for the coming year.[53] Present at the meeting were the four 'procurators of the nations' who had votes in electing rectors. On this occasion three of the procurators were regents, the other a theology student.[54] Was Patrick Forbes making sure that the election was carried out in full conformity with the Old Foundation, and all the details recorded, so that no challenge could be made to his son's authority when, as rector, he continued his father's reforms?

John Forbes's career was to change in other directions as well in 1634. Later in the year he resigned the chair of divinity to become a parish minister in Aberdeen.[55] It seems likely that this development was unwelcome to him, for when his successor died after a few months he returned to his chair with alacrity. Behind the move probably lay, yet again, the hand of his father: a plausible scenario is that Bishop Forbes had persuaded his son to resign to demonstrate that senior academics had a duty to enter the ministry, and perhaps also in the hope that his son, no longer a teacher in the college, would have greater authority as rector of the university. If this was indeed the bishop's plan, it was thwarted by the coincidental deaths of himself and of his son's successor as professor of divinity early in 1635, allowing John to sneak back into academic life.[56]

Rector John Forbes held his first visitation of the university on 7 July 1634, accompanied by Principal Leslie, Robert Baron (dean of divinity), Patrick Dun (mediciner and dean of medicine), James Sandilands (canonist and dean of law), David Leech (subprincipal and dean of philosophy), John Lundie (grammarian), Gilbert Ross (cantor), the three regents, and Dr James Sibbald. This list raises some problems. There is no evidence that any elections had been yet held for the newly revived posts of deans (except for that of philosophy or arts), and Sibbald, minister of Aberdeen, held no office in the university. What seems to have happened is that those stated to have held this visitation included those elected to office during the visitation. Certainly all the deans named as if already in office were voted into office for the coming year, and Sibbald (along with Baron and Dun) were among the four rector's assessors elected. Rules were then laid down for the conduct of such elections in future. Each faculty was to elect its own dean, the rector having a casting vote in case of equal voting. It was also agreed that in future rectorial visitations should be held twice a year.[57]

As with the appointments made at the time of Patrick Forbes's visitation in 1619, those made in 1634 are open to the charge that they amount to little more than window-dressing, an impressive array of titles that did not denote any real change in the university or its activities. The canonist at King's College became dean of the university faculty of law—a faculty whose staff consisted of himself and the absentee civilist, Roger Mowat. The new dean of medicine was principal of Marischal College, and similarly the dean of divinity was professor of divinity at Marischal. The only staff member of the medical faculty was the mediciner, Dr William Gordon, an active and able doctor but without, so far as is known, students. In 1619 two lawyers and a Marischal regent had been called in to give nominal existence to three professorships at King's. In 1634 two Marischal professors were similarily used as deans at Old Aberdeen, and this must have increased the feeling, dating back to 1619, of the principal and regents at King's that they, the men who formed the real core of the college and its teaching, were being swamped by holders of fancy titles who had power to vote in visitations and elections.

Having supervised university elections, the July 1634 rectorial visitation proceeded to other matters. Charles I's letter about church attendance was read, and it was agreed that all staff and students of both Aberdeen colleges should wear their gowns in college, in the parish churches and in the streets.[58] Regulations, applying to both colleges, were approved for admission of students into classes other than the first year class: such cases were to be considered by a committee of at least two masters of each college, decisions being approved by the 'rector' of the 'university'.[59] These rules have a significance beyond matters of academic dress and admissions, for they demonstrates that the rectorial visitation regarded itself as qualified to legislate for both colleges. The king's letter had specifically referred to the two universities of Old and New Aberdeen, and had been addressed to the bishop as chancellor of both. But the rector and deans of faculty now elected at King's were acting as if there was only one university, of which they (along with the bishop/chancellor) were the officials, with two colleges within it. They had met to carry out a visitation of King's College, but as university officials they appear to have assumed that they could legislate for Marischal. Marischal College was in a sense represented at the visitation in that two of the deans who had been elected were officials of that college: but it appears that only King's College staff had taken part in the election of rector and deans. Was there one university of Aberdeen or two? It is probable that this confused state of affairs reflects the attitude of Bishop Forbes, and that he tended to think in terms of there being a single Aberdeen University. The foundation charter of Marischal College had not made its status clear, but this had not been of any real practical significance at first; rectors and deans of faculty had probably been appointed in both institutions only intermittently, and the bishops/chancellors of the day had taken so little interest in either college that the question of whether he was chancellor of one university or two had not arisen. The university had been little more than an abstract concept: the colleges were what mattered, and they developed as if there was no link between them.

The coming of Patrick Forbes had changed the situation. With him as chancellor the university, as opposed to the colleges, came to life. Having to accept the bishop's jurisdiction over it in 1619 had clearly been a major shock for Marischal College. Nothing had been said at that time as to whether there was one university or two, but it is likely that from the start Bishop Forbes intended that in time the separate 'universities' within which the two colleges regarded themselves as existing should become one, and that his policy of giving members of Marischal's staff posts in Old Aberdeen's university—and King's staff posts in New Aberdeen's— was intended to facilitate this merger by bringing what had been two distinct academic communities into frequent contact.[60]

Other acts of the July 1634 visitation concern the academic and administrative reform of King's College alone. William Gordon, mediciner, was common procurator, and provision was made for examining his accounts annually—and for auditing his accounts of a special fund established to raise money to rebuild the crown on the tower of the college chapel, which had blown down the previous year. Compilation of an inventory of the charters of the college was to be undertaken. The academic year was defined: students were to assemble on 29 September, and teaching would last from 15 October to 15 July.[61]

The July 1634 visitation had evidently worked on the assumption that though it was visiting King's College and primarily concerned with its affairs, it was a visitation by university officials whose jurisdiction included Marischal College. Yet at the end of the same month the rector sanctioned a major initiative which was based on the assumption that King's was the only college in a university limited to Old Aberdeen. John Forbes, with consent of the chancellor his father, signed instructions to William Gordon listing representations to be made to the king from the university of Old Aberdeen. It is as if how many universities there were was regarded as a matter of expediency.

The detailed instructions to Gordon may be taken as the old bishop's attempt to crown his fifteen years of work at King's. The instructions fall into three parts, the first being intended to show why it is necessary that the traditional jurisdiction of the university should be confirmed and extended. Former corruptions and present problems were listed. Men had unjustly maintained possession of university houses, lands and revenues, and teinds and annuities due to it were not being paid. Those who made payments in kind did so with bad grain—or did not pay at all when prices were high and they wanted to sell on the open market. As the university's jurisdiction had not been fully exercised its members were open to contempt and injury from others—to 'tumults with neighbours' and 'amongst themselves in defect of due order and justice'. As a result of all this members 'are often forced to plead before the lords [of session] in Edinburgh, and so are pitifully withdrawn from their studies and functions'. Those who remained were frequently diverted from study by the need 'for advising and labouring to get in some small means for their necessary maintenance'; often they had almost to beg for what they should have received by right, being treated with scorn and disdain.

The second section of the instructions detailed grants of jurisdiction formerly made to the university, and the third, running to thirteen clauses, details powers and rights the king was to be asked to grant to college; full powers of 'barony, sheriffship, chancellery and regality' in temporal causes (civil and criminal) within the university precincts and all lands held by the university, without right of appeal to anyone but the king, the council, or the court of high commission. The university also wanted power to withdraw its degrees from graduates who proved unworthy or ungrateful, jurisdiction over all schools, colleges, printers and stationers in the diocese, and that the precedence of university staff in relation to burgh magistrates and country gentlemen be settled. Finally, it was asked that the Bishop of Aberdeen be excused payment of taxes so the money could be devoted to repairing the crown tower.[62] The chancellor and rector also wrote to the Archbishop of Canterbury, the Bishop of Ross (who was at court) and Dr Alexander Reid (who on his death in 1639 was to leave his medical books and £100 Scots a year to the college) asking them to assist William Gordon in his mission at court.[63]

Gordon was prompt in setting off on his journey, for in October William Laud, Archbishop of Canterbury, wrote to tell Patrick Forbes that Gordon had shown him his instructions and that he, Laud, had spoken to the king and would continue to show all the favour he could to the university on the matter. But he warned that the king was being asked for many things, some relating to matters he was not well acquainted with, and that he would need to take expert advice before replying.[64] The prediction was accurate. On 30 September the king commissioned five Scottish archbishops and bishops (including Patrick Forbes) to examine the charters of King's College to ascertain its privileges, to recommend which should be renewed, and to decide on what new privileges and immunities enjoyed by other 'famous universities' should be granted. A report was to be submitted to the king so a new charter under the great seal could be issued to the university. Meanwhile, with the advice of Patrick Forbes as chancellor, the bishops were to visit the university 'and repress such abuses and settle such good order therein as you can lawfully and conveniently do'. To give immediate help, the Court of Session was instructed to hear cases in which the university was involved as soon as possible, and Sir Thomas Hope (the king's advocate) was to help the university in such cases.[65]

To back up Gordon's endeavours, Rector John Forbes also wrote to Dr William Davidson, an Aberdonian who was a professor of chemistry in Paris, for a copy of the rights and privileges of that university, as the Old Foundation had been based on Paris and Bologna. In September 1634 Davidson sent a printed copy of the Paris privileges, and announced he had got permission to copy that university's manuscript registers— though he warned that they were 'bigger than any great Bible'.[66]

Meanwhile the more routine work of reforming and tightening up discipline and procedures at King's continued. Meetings of college staff in October 1634 arranged a visitation of the library: all the books in the catalogue were found to be present, and books recently bought by Robert Ogilvie, regent and 'last bibliothecar' were added to the catalogue: this is the first surviving reference to a college librarian.[67] Several scientific instruments were also listed, including two globes, a quadrant and an astrolobe.[68] The next rectorial visitation (November and December 1634) examined and approved the conduct of the regents. Penalties were specified for failure to wear gowns and for absence from college. One session of the visitation was held in Bishop Forbes's presence in his palace, and Principal William Leslie (David Rait had died in 1632) was admonished for not dining regularly in hall, not going to church in procession with the students, and not reading the laws of the college to the students. Leslie had previously been common procurator, and he was now ordered to present satisfactory accounts or be fined—or even be deprived of office. For these offences he was eventually fined 500 merks. Thus, as in 1619, Bishop Forbes indicated that principals would be closely supervised, their conduct being one of the keys to the college's morale and efficiency. Later Leslie was also instructed to give two lectures on divinity and four on Hebrew each week, and the grammarian, John Lundie, was instructed to employ a second doctor of grammar—though he was only to be paid forty merks a year. Regular visitations of the library were ordered. On the complaints of the minister of St Machar about his stipend (paid by the college) provision was made for increasing it, and payment of £40 a year to the university's clerk was authorised—provided he was a public notary. The rector's action in sending William Gordon to court was approved, and he was asked to write again to Dr Davidson in Paris for a copy to be made of 'the evidents and registers of the university of Paris concerning their conservatory, jurisdiction, privileges and immunities'.[69]

This confusing mass of developments in 1634 make that year almost as important a date in the history of King's College as 1619. Regular biennial visitations began, the status of the rector was enhanced, regular elections of rector and deans were introduced, regulations on many disciplinary, administrative and academic matters were passed. And, potentially most important of all, a major initiative had begun to get the powers of the university extended. This, and the attempt to get hold of the Paris documents on which to base developments at King's, surely indicate that Patrick Forbes was hoping to complete his work with a 'new foundation' of his own, updating the Old Foundation in the light of Reformation and other changed circumstances, and finally extinguishing the despised late sixteenth-century New Foundation. But reform under his supervision was to proceed no further. The already crippled bishop died on 28 March 1635.

The bishop's death was genuinely regretted in King's College, even by those who were soon to be striving to undo much of his work in the college—men like Principal Leslie, Subprincipal David Leech and John Lundie, the grammarian. They joined with the bishop's supporters in contributing to the massive memorial volume of tributes that was prepared.[70] Such men might think some of what he had done in the college was misguided and unjust, but they nonetheless had respected him for his personal life, ability and energy. Adam Bellenden, who succeeded him as bishop, wrote that succeeding ages would be in his debt 'for the restitution of the college, wholly ruinated, till it pleased God to stir him up', and John Guthrie, bishop of Moray, was evidently responsible for coining the phrase which was often to be applied to Patrick Forbes: he wrote that the college 'may vaunt of him as of a second founder'.[71]

His achievements at King's College were undoubtedly impressive. He had improved its financial position, enlarged the staff, restored internal discipline, introduced the professorial system of teaching, ensured teaching was done conscientiously, and encouraged scholarship. One indication of the improved reputation of the college is that it began to received donations from well-wishers—though modest in scale. Dr Alexander Reid (a London physician and King's graduate) gave £1,200 to help maintain bursars, a 'good number' of books, two globes and some mathematical instruments—probably those listed in the 1634 library visitation. Andrew Strachan (professor of divinity 1634–5) left his books to the library and most or all of Principal Rait's books also ended up there, given by his son. Thomas Merser, notary public, gave £100 worth of books: he had been clerk to the 1619 visitation, and in 1635 (when his books were being catalogued) was acting as the college's agent in a legal case in Edinburgh.[72]

Higher degrees had been revived—the doctorate of medicine (first known to have been awarded in 1630) certainly;[73] that of both laws perhaps (see page 83 below); and, above all, the doctorate of divinity. Most of the small group of holders of the degree of doctor of divinity[74] shared not just that honour but a common approach to theology. The inspiration was Bishop Patrick Forbes, and his *Commentarie upon the Revelation of Saint John* published in 1613 gave the Aberdeen theologians their hatred of the Roman Catholic Church and their identification of it with Antichrist. This of course was commonplace among Protestants of the age, but what was distinctive in Forbes and his disciples was a determination to combine the fight to the death with Rome with a willingness to agree to differ with fellow-Protestants on matters seen as inessential. All Protestants must unite in the great conflict with evil if it was to be overcome. However, this willingness to accept differences of opinion on things not central to true religion was not merely a policy adopted out of expediency, but a matter of principle. John Forbes was fully in agreement with his father's attitude, and his *Irenicum Amatoribus Veritatis et Pacis in Ecclesia Scoticana* (Aberdeen, 1629) applied his father's outlook to a particular problem, the controversy over the Five Articles of Perth. John Forbes sought to prove that these reforms of details of worship, which had caused much controversy in Scotland, should be accepted as they concerned matters indifferent. But John Forbes did not just copy his father, and he probably has prime responsibility for another distinctive feature of the Aberdeen theologians: emphasis on the importance of the works of the Early Christian Fathers, and determination to claim them for Protestantism. His *Instructiones Historico-Theologicae* (Amsterdam, 1645) was a massive theological compendium displaying his great patristic scholarship—while at the same time providing an example of the revival of Protestant scholasticism.[75]

Robert Baron (professor of divinity at Marischal) was a theologian in very much the same mould, again deeply learned in the Early Fathers, strongly anti-Catholic, scholastic in approach in both theology and philosophy.[76] Judging by the number of reprints of his books[77] his work was more highly regarded in the mid-seventeenth century than that of John Forbes—indeed his textbook on scholastic philosophy was to be still in use in Oxford and Dublin late in the century.[78] The theses compiled by King's College regents such as Alexander Lunan, William Leslie, and David Leech in the 1620s and 1630s for disputation by their students reveal them to be men learned in commentaries on Aristotle and other neo-scholastic literature, frequently citing the works of the great Catholic philosophers of the Counter-Reformation, accepting their scholastic philosophy but adapting it to support Protestant conclusions.[79] Andrew Strachan's books show him as teacher in very much the same mould.[80] Both Strachan and Alexander Lunan reveal knowledge of Copernicus's heliocentric concepts, but nonetheless remained basically Ptolemaic in their astronomy, accepting an earth-centred universe.[81] From a modern viewpoint the college certainly might seem to be backing the wrong horses in the long-term intellectual stakes, remaining stubbornly Aristotelian; but in the general intellectual context of its age it was backing the favourites, remaining in the mainstream of European thought. More specifically, the college had a role in the development of Protestant neo-scholasticism, and if it is true that the Aberdeen colleges under Patrick Forbes became 'the most Aristotelian' of all Scotland's colleges[82] as Ramism waned, this was something in which their masters took a positive pride rather than seeing it as a sign of embarrassing backwardness. The school of theologians which emerged in Aberdeen came to be regarded by some as the most distinguished in Scotland,[83] with John Forbes as an outstanding figure.

However, it has been said that the praise given to John Forbes's theology is 'somewhat exaggerated',[84] and if indeed he deserves to be called the greatest of Scottish theologians[85] this is perhaps partly a reflection on the competition rather than proof of outstanding intellectual distinction. The courageous stand that some of the Aberdeen divines were soon to make against the overwhelming strength of their enemies merits admiration for their characters and the strength and consistency of their principles, but it has perhaps tended to lead to uncritical exaggeration of their academic achievements.

The work of Patrick Forbes at King's has been criticised for being 'perhaps too exclusively devoted to rendering [the university] a school of sound theology',[86] but the same could be said of all the regimes which had dominated King's since its foundation, and at least his emphasis on theology had brought results. Moreover, King's could boast of some progress in other disciplines as well. David Wedderburn's association with the college after his appointment as grammarian in 1619 was short lived, and the post fell back into obscurity for a decade. But with the appointment of John Lundie the office's status was revived. Lundie had been a regent in 1625–8, probably became a bachelor of divinity in 1631, and was admitted as grammarian in 1634 to teach grammar, poetry and rhetoric.[87] In medicine as in grammar the 1619 reforms did not have any significant practical effect at first. Patrick Dun had become mediciner, but as he was unpaid he not surprisingly devoted his energies to other activities, becoming principal of Marischal College in 1621. Eventually he resigned, opening the way for the appointment of William Gordon in 1632.[88] He quickly became, as already seen, highly active in college administration, and was evidently active in teaching as well. In 1636 in a petition to the Privy Council he explained that he had exercised his students in the dissection of animals for two years and now needed human bodies for the same purpose. He therefore requested that the relevant authorites in the shires and burghs of Aberdeen and Banff be ordered:

> to deliver to the said supplicant two bodies of men, being notable malefactors, executed in their bounds, especially being rebels or outlaws, and, failing of them, the bodies of the poorer sort, dying in hospitals, or abortive bairns, foundlings, or those of no quality, who have died of their diseases, and have few friends and acquaintances that can take exception.[89]

If he got approval for this, he promised that he would exercise his rights with such moderation and discretion that the university would offend 'no man of quality'. It is notable that though the supplication states that it was common for bodies of both men and women to be delivered to universities teaching medicine, permission was only sought to seek male corpses. Perhaps this reflected some compromise with those who viewed with distaste such human butchery being carried out under university auspices. Unfortunately, though William Gordon's name was to be prominent in the controversies which were shortly to wrack the college, this is the only hard evidence of his teaching. But in introducing dissection at King's Gordon was copying a widespread continental practice which was relatively new to Britain: if King's was late in adopting it, Oxford had only done so twelve years before.[90] Of all the university's faculties under Bishop Forbes's management law is the most obscure. Roger Mowat, who became civilist in the 1620s, was an Edinburgh advocate, thus continuing the unhappy late sixteenth-century tradition of absentee officials. The canonist, James Sandilands (succeeded by his son, another James, in 1634) was at least resident in Old Aberdeen, but was mainly concerned with his work as commissary of Aberdeen. He is not known to have done any teaching, but his acquisition of the degree of doctor of both laws (canon and civil) sometime in the later 1620s may indicate some activity on the part of the law faculties.[91]

The revival in King's College in the 1620s and 1630s was one aspect of a wider cultural and intellectual revival in the North East of Scotland, which made Patrick Forbes's task in the college easier than it would otherwise have been. He clearly wanted the college to benefit from close contact with this thriving cultural hinterland, and wanted it to contribute to the region's intellectual development—primarily though not solely through its graduates entering the parish ministry. The impression of inward-looking self-absorption the college had given in the past was to be replaced by a much greater degree of interaction with the community. As already seen, he probably planned to link the college formally with Marischal College within a single university, and he sought to bring them closer together by college and, above all, university appointments of rectors and their assessors and deans of faculties. The emphasis in this study has been on Marischal staff becoming involved with the administration of King's, but appointments the other way round were also made—Professor John Forbes was dean of faculty at Marischal in 1632.[92] University appointments also served to bring some of the more intellectually-inclined parish ministers into active contact with the college—as did the granting of doctorates of divinity.

Whatever Forbes's vision of King's College was, it was not of an ivory tower, but an institution in close touch with the church, professions and general culture of the region. A key development here was the settlement of Edward Raban in Aberdeen as printer to the town and university. Raban, an Englishman, had printed in Edinburgh in 1620 but moved to St Andrews to become printer to the university there. It is uncertain what persuaded him to come to Aberdeen in 1622: perhaps realisation of how small the local market in St Andrews was influenced him, but it is likely that Bishop Forbes had a hand in the move, seeing easy access to a printing press as central to the thriving of Aberdeen's colleges. Andrew Strachan firmly claims the credit for Forbes, he having 'perceived the printing-press to be a nursery of the Library'.[93] The output of the press in the years that followed amply justified such an assumption.

7   Patrick Forbes, Bishop of Aberdeen and chancellor of the university, 1618–35.
Engraved portrait which appeared as the frontispiece in some copies of the
memorial volume issued after his death. AUL, SBL 1635 R 3⁴.

The custom was emerging in Scotland of printing graduation theses, both individual theses defended by candidates for higher degrees, and those drafted by regents to be defended by members of the final-year undergraduate class at the time of their graduation. The earliest of the printed class theses to survive is an Edinburgh one of 1599, and such a Marischal College thesis was printed in Edinburgh in 1616. Resort was had to Edinburgh printers again in 1620, when David Rait's doctoral thesis and John Forbes's inaugural thesis on appointment to the chair of divinity appeared. As soon as Raban was established in Aberdeen in 1622 King's undergraduate class theses and individual higher degree theses began to roll from his press,[94] providing a rich source of information about the teaching of individual regents. In Aberdeen as elsewhere the theses confirm the continuing domination of Aristotle, with the earliest of the King's College class theses indicating that 'Here too Aristotle rules— and rules, indeed, with even greater stringency' than elsewhere.[95]

The printed theses tell us much of what went on at college graduation ceremonies. Alexander Strachan, through Raban, gives us another glimpse of academic ceremony through his *Panegyricus Inauguralis*, delivered during the graduation ceremony of 1630 to mark Alexander Reid's gift of money, books and instruments to the university. The speech, 'somewhat exaggerated in its eulogisms and full of pagan rehetoric',[96] praises Reid by setting him in the context of previous benefactors of the college.[97] It may have been reaction to Strachan's solemn and high-flown excesses that led a 1632 graduate, William Lauder, to produce a rival panegyric, a burlesque 'abounding in puns, comic compounds and ironical compliments to the Principal and Regents', evidently delivered before the assembled arts students (and perhaps staff) in the college hall.[98] This was not thought worthy of being immortalised in print.

Theses obviously were printed for the use of those concerned in the colleges, but Raban's press also offered opportunities for publication of less specialised works, and theological, philosophical and other works by Patrick Forbes, John Forbes, Robert Baron and other Aberdeen academics were soon appearing for general sale.[99] It also made possible the publication of the eulogistic memorial volume, unrivalled (in Scotland at least) in its scale and literary quality, produced after the death of Patrick Forbes. The volume is largely the work of men from the North East, most of them linked in some way with King's or Marischal. Virtually all senior academic staff contributed, along with a few undergraduates and postgraduate students of theology (the latter including William Lauder), lairds, lawyers and others. Largely composed of Latin prose and verse, the volume arouses little interest today, but in an age in which Latin literature was still central to literary culture, it is an impressive tribute both to the

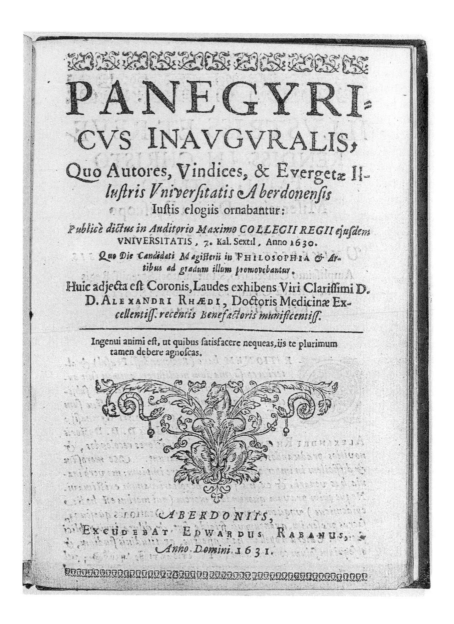

8 Title page of Andrew Strachan's *Panegyricus Inauguralis* of 1630, delivered at the graduation ceremonies and, while praising Dr Alexander Reid for a recent bequest to the college, taking the opportunity to extol the virtues of the college's teachers, past and present. AUL, in SBL 1623 R 4.

wide circle of Patrick Forbes's friends, and to their cultural abilities.[100] Nearly all of the figures who were responsible for the modest cultural and intellectual renaissance that the North East was experiencing were linked to Forbes and 'his' Aberdeen colleges in one way or another.[101]

Even a man as strongly opposed to bishops as the presbyterian historian Robert Wodrow could write of Patrick Forbes that at King's College he:

> Found all out of order, and with the greatest vigilance and diligence restored that University to its ancient glory, revived the liberal sciences, recovered and bettered the college revenues, repaired the buildings, restored the professions that were disused, and brought their excellent old statutes into practice again; quicked the masters to their work, and reformed the manners of masters and students by his own excellent example.[102]

Yet though Patrick Forbes deserves much credit for his work at King's, the praise heaped on him has tended to be exaggerated, creating a saintly figure without blemish rather than a warts and all human being. There are several reasons for this. First, the reformed church in Scotland in the late sixteenth and early seventeenth centuries was distinctly lacking in bishops pious in their personal lives, able and energetic, with real intellectual and administrative achievements to their credit. It is thus not surprising that episcopalians, in the increasingly bitter controversies which marked the seventeenth century and the struggle for survival in later generations, should turn to Patrick Forbes as a shining example of a good and effective bishop, demonstrating the potential virtues of episcopacy. Secondly, twentieth century church historians have sometimes had their historical judgments swayed by the fashion for ecumenicism, and they tend to hail Patrick Forbes as a kindred spirit for his wish to reconcile the different branches of Protestantism (though the fact that his reason for this was hatred and fear of Catholicism is something of an embarrassment). Certainly historians favourably disposed towards Patrick Forbes can cite plenty of contemporary statements which stress his outstanding qualities, but most of them are drawn from the memorial volume of tributes produced just after his death. No man is on oath when composing epitaphs, and too much reliance on them as evidence does not make for entirely satisfactory history—though of course the very fact that so elaborate a memorial volume was thought appropriate can itself be taken as evidence of Patrick Forbes's stature.

Nonetheless, a cool look at the man and his achievements indicates that some modifications are needed to the conventional picture of his work in King's College. His attack on the incompetence and corruption of the college in 1619 and thereafter was entirely justified. But, as already suggested, it was grossly unfair to insist on judging college staff according to the Old Foundation when they had for decades acted on the reasonable assumption that it had been legally superseded by the New Foundation. Instead of arguing that the staff had been mistaken to accept the New Foundation, he ignored its existence and denounced the college staff as corrupt not only for their many real failings but as perverters of the Old Foundation purely through greed and laziness. He even burnt the text of the New Foundation when it came into his hands, so that his opponents would not have evidence with which to try to justify themselves. Moreover, though Forbes was continually throwing up his hands in horror at the wickedness of perverting the Old Foundation when it suited him, he himself contravened it when expedient. Such flexibility was of course sensible. The Old Foundation in every detail was obviously not appropriate after the Reformation and other developments, and his evident ultimate aim of introducing a new foundation of his own was logical. But his attitude that his own perverting of the Old Foundation was justified, while for others to do the same was a great evil, was hypocritical. Forbes might be pious, but he could also be ruthless and even unscrupulous, no doubt justifying this as necessary if the very deep-rooted problems of the college were to be solved.

Again, while it was a worthy ambition to seek to restore the faculties of medicine and law, was his insistence in 1619 on the immediate appointment of purely nominal mediciner, canonist and civilist the best way to go about it? Would it not have made more sense to have restored the offices gradually as funds became available? This would have avoided the charge of packing the college with his own nominees to outvote those who actually did the teaching. In the event, not just what he did but the way that he did it left a lasting legacy of bitterness in the college which was to surface after his death.

How successful Forbes was in dealing with the college's financial problems is hard to assess. A rental dated 1637-8 shows income due to the college from land and teinds as totalling about £5,300,[103] and this constituted the great majority of college income: revenue from various fees collected from students (exam silver, chamber mails and spoon silver) totalled only £89 in 1623-4.[104] It is hard to know how adequate these college revenues were, with New and Old Foundatation supporters making conflicting partisan claims. Considering that under the New Foundation the total salary bill had been about £1,150[105] an income of well over £5,000 looks impressive, but fast inflation in intervening years had rendered salaries proposed half a century before totally inadequate, and there is no evidence of what was actually being paid to staff in the 1630s. Much of the college revenue was collected in grain and consumed in the college—which had its own facilities for baking bread and brewing[106]—

9 'Logo' or device adopted by the Library of King's College. This first appears
on the back of the title page of some copies of the memorial volume for
Bishop Forbes, published in 1635. AUL, SBL 1635 R 3².

so the figure calculated above for 'revenue' does not represent cash at the college's disposal, and reflects rising grain prices. Further, out of the revenues of the deanery of Aberdeen the college had to pay the ministers of St Machar and New Machar. It is probable that Bishop Forbes very considerably increased the revenues from land through more efficient collection, enforcement of the college's rights and higher rents, but with the major exception of the endowment of the chair of divinity he had not managed to gain for the college any significant new sources of income. All the indications are that at the time of his death the college was better off than it had previously been, but that financial stringency remained the order of the day.

Certainly growth of income derived from fees paid by students can only have been slow. In spite of the much improved intellectual reputation of the college under Forbes's guidance, the increase in student numbers seem to have been disappointingly slow. If the surviving records are accurate, under Principal Rait's unreformed management an average of 19.1 undergraduate students per year had entered the college in 1601–10. In 1620–34, after Forbes's reforms, this rose to 22.4 entrants per year.[107] This represents a rise in average undergraduate enrollment of 17%, and this was welcome. But it is not very impressive when set alongside Edinburgh University's increase in graduations of 33% and Glasgow University's rise in matriculations of 41% between the same two periods. That Marischal College only increased its first year numbers by 7.3% was little consolation to King's.[108] The sluggishness of growth in undergraduate numbers in Aberdeen suggests that the existence of two separate colleges represented academic over-provision. However, there was almost certainly also a more significant rise in the number of graduate students in the college—students of theology, and perhaps also one or two students studying law or medicine in some years.[109]

In conclusion, Patrick Forbes achieved a major revival of the fortunes of King's College, but there were considerable limitations to his achievements, and perhaps the term 'second founder' exaggerates them.

Of reactions within King's College to Forbes's reforms during his own lifetime we know almost nothing. But the changes he made were so sweeping, and the language he used about the staff so strong, that there must have been opposition and resentment. That this was indeed the case is confirmed by one remarkable incident. In a supplication about the New Foundation in 1638 it was alleged that 'of late' the New Foundation 'was secretly destroyed and burnt by private persons without any warrant of superior powers'.[110] This is very vague as to both when the burning took place and who did it. But a more detailed account comes from James Gordon, who himself graduated at King's in 1636 and whose father, Robert Gordon of Straloch, had taken part in the visitations of 1619 and 1623.[111] According to James Gordon, the New Foundation (which he believed had been drafted by David Rait), having failed to receive parliamentary ratification in 1597:

> that paper coming afterwards into the hands of Bishop Patrick Forbes, with a solicitation for him to set it anew on foot, he threw it into the fire, where it ended; and instantly, being chancellor of the university, caused set the old institution on foot, as far as it could subsist with the Protestant religion.[112]

Thus responsibility for the burning is placed on the bishop (though in general Gordon shows great respect for him), and though the incident is not dated the impression given is that it was at the beginning of his work in the college—perhaps actually during the 1619 visitation. A third surviving account of the incident, however, suggests a later date. In 1638 Principal William Leslie claimed that:

> about the year 1627 some crafty and corrupt men . . . By their subtle suggestions and persuasions so far prevailed with the late Bishop of Aberdeen of happy memory, that he was induced to be a means of destroying of the said Royal Foundation, and that in secret, without the privity of the members of the college, except only some few that happened to be mere spectators, and without either public authority, or lawful cognition of the cause before any judicatory.

But:

> here behold the work of God . . . in God's secret providence the destroyer thereof gave express order to one of the masters of the college, who yet survives, to cause draw a just double or copy of the said foundation, word for word, subscriptions and all exactly collated and concordant with the original *in omnibus*. Which double, after perusal and collating thereof, he delivered in first to the said master, willing him to keep it *in omnen eventum*, and this was done immediately before the burning of the royal deed.[113]

The more detail we have, the more confusing the incident becomes. The New Foundation, which Leslie presents as an undoubted act of James VI, was destroyed by Bishop Forbes—though he is careful not to blame him personally for this (he was led astray by evil advisers), as to attack Forbes's revered memory at a time when Scotland was in revolt against the king and his bishops would have offended the king. It was destroyed secretly—

SPLENDENTE VIVO
SECEDENTE PEREO

10 James Sandilands elder, canonist at King's College from the early 1620s until 1633, when he resigned office in favour of his son. Portrait by George Jamesone dated 1624. The inscription 'Splendente vivo; Secedente pereo' expounds part of the meaning of the symbols above it—the sun 'in splendour' and a pink: 'When [the sun] shines bright, I [the flower] live; when it withdraws into darkness I perish'. The life-giving properties of the sun could symbolise the truths of religion or the inspiration of learning— or indeed both. Aberdeen University Picture Store

but spectators were present. It was destroyed presumably because Forbes thought it had no legal force and to put an end to controversy—but he had a copy of it made. The impression given is of Forbes, at some particularly bitter point in the confrontation between supporters of the New Foundation and the Old, making the grand symbolic gesture of flinging the document into the fire, to demonstrate once and for all that it was invalid.

The master who copied the text before the burning is not identified; it it is an intriguing possibility that it could have been Principal Leslie himself. He had been at King's since at least 1617, when he was promoted from grammarian to regent, and his promotions to subprincipal in 1623 and principal in 1632 suggest that he had not then been an open opponent of the bishop's reforms, whatever his real feelings. The burning of the New Foundation was not, as Patrick Forbes hoped, the last that was heard of it. While he lived he managed to keep the bitterness and frustration that lingered on in the college under the surface through the mixture of fear and genuine respect with which he was regarded. But once he was dead and this constraint was removed pent-up grievances erupted into open conflict.

Chapter 5

The Eclipse. The Coming of the Covenanters

Through the absence of this shining light, we see
Th' eclipses of this university.
Her sun's gone down, and darkened is her day
John Lundie, grammarian, on the
death of Patrick Forbes, 1635[1]

The legacy of Bishop Patrick Forbes at King's College was two-fold, and both aspects of it were to have disastrous consequences. The first was the tensions within the college between those who felt they had been done an injustice by the more arbitrary aspects of his reforms on the one hand, and those who had benefited from these changes on the other. The second aspect of his legacy was much more positive than this internecine strife: the emergence of the college as a centre of what has been called the Aberdeen school of thought, but which it would be more accurate to describe as a shared cast of mind, a religious and intellectual outlook, since it lacked the coherence of a 'school of thought'. These intellectual developments in Aberdeen make her colleges the most interesting in Scotland in the 1630s, but they were to bring down on Aberdeen the wrath of those who were soon to seize control of Scotland from Charles I, the covenanters. It is ironic that the first episode in which Aberdeen could boast of real intellectual distinction since the Reformation led directly to disaster for its colleges.

The development of the feud within the college after Forbes's death is at first hard to trace in detail. Probably all those concerned were happy to see the continuation of many of the reforms which Forbes has begun and which aimed at creating more efficient administration and higher academic and teaching standards, but tension mounted when attention turned to plans for expansion and reorganisation which raised the old issues of establishment and finance. Moreover, while Bishop Forbes's guiding hand had often been painfully strong, the hands of those who succeeded him in running the college appear to have been weak. Adam Bellenden was appointed to succeed Forbes as bishop of Aberdeen, and

94

the importance of his role as chancellor of the university was stressed when he was informed that the king expected him to reside in Aberdeen as it had a university and was a place of consequence: he 'relies much upon you for the well ordering of that place'.[2] But though Bellenden was often present as chancellor at rectorial visitations at which major disagreements clearly emerged, there is no sign of him taking any initiative or seeking to influence the outcome of such arguments. The conclusion that 'the short time that he sat there he touched nor did innovate nothing' seems justified.[3] Principal William Leslie seems to have sat on the fence at first, and though he eventually became leader of the New Foundation faction he appears to have lacked the strength of character necessary to control the situation. Contemporaries paid glowing tribute to his great learning,[4] but scholarship alone was not enough to provide effective leadership for the college in the difficult years that lay ahead.

Controversy probably began at the first rectorial visitation of the college after Forbes's death, in June 1635. Agreement was reached that the stipend the college paid to the minister of Monykebuck (New Machar) should be increased. Strain on college finances was further increased by the provision of a salary for James Sandilands, the canonist. That deciding on a salary for the cantor, Gilbert Ross, was delayed until the next visitation indicates that there was opposition to these new financial commitments.[5] This was confirmed when the visitation held in May and June 1636 again delayed assigning a salary to the cantor— though the crafts of Old Aberdeen had just agreed to contribute to his support as master of the music school[6]—and ruled that no new salaries should be allocated until the college buildings were inspected and properly repaired.[7] Clearly there was disagreement as to where the college's financial priorities should lie.

At this point internal disagreements over salaries suddenly broadened in scope, both in that they led to the revival of the question of Old Foundation or New, and in that the dispute was now to be fought in Edinburgh and London as well as Aberdeen. Who brought the college's problems to the king's attention is unknown, but it may well have been the work of William Gordon, mediciner and common procurator, whose position in the college was threatened by the attack on the offices which had been abolished by the New Foundation. A letter from the king in September to his Scottish Privy Council stated that he was informed of abuses in the college and infringements of his foundation. Recalling that he had (at the college's request) ordered a commission to carry out a visitation of the college to investigate its privileges and draw up a new charter for it, he pointed out that it had failed to take action. It was now to do so.[8] A few weeks later the king decided to commission an investigation into the financial plight of all Scotland's colleges: their health was central to the health of the church, yet they were so poor that teachers were abandoning their posts for lack of proper maintenance.[9] As a result, the council wrote to the various colleges asking them to send commissioners to Edinburgh to give information about abuses and financial problems so that action could be taken.[10]

King's College chose to send William Gordon as its commissioner.[11] As he had been the common procurator for some years and had been active in court cases concerning college revenues he was a natural choice— but as he was a supporter of the Old Foundation his appointment represented a victory for one faction in the college over the other. The New Foundation party fought back. At the June 1637 rectorial visitation the regents (presumably including the subprincipal, David Leech) demanded increases in their stipends, thus arguing that any funds available for increases should go to them, the core teachers of the college, and not the revived Old Foundation officials.[12] The unsettled matter of a salary for the cantor was also raised,[13] but the visitation was dominated by an obscure row centring on the principal. He evidently refused to attend the visitation, and summonses were issued against him for 'rectification of his carriage'. At the end of the last session a message was sent to him ordering him to deliver the newly revised college laws to the rector under threat of punishment for contumacy.[14] Work on revising the college laws (relating to internal government, discipline and teaching) had been in progress for the past year,[15] but what was it in them that William Leslie objected to? It might be that he opposed the definitions of his own duties and responsibilities: but equally it could be that he objected to them as they made the assumption that the Old Foundation was in force. The laws do not survive, but as they included details of courses to be taught in medicine and law[16] accepting them would seem an admission that the New Foundation was without authority.

Just six days after the end of this disastrously divisive visitation the Privy Council in Edinburgh found itself faced by two rival petitions from the college. In the first Subprincipal Leech and the three other regents put their New Foundation case. After the Reformation many of the Old Foundation college posts were unnecessary, so they had been abolished and 'in regard of the meanness of the provision allowed in the first foundation' their salaries had been used to provide for the remaining members of the college. This arrangement had been ratified by parliament. But lately certain persons had 'usurped upon them places in the said university' and were trying to get salaries 'by defrauding the supplicants'. They therefore craved the council, and the commissioners appointed by the king, to rectify the matter.[17] Mediciner William Gordon then put forward his party's very different version of events. His was the voice the council should listen to, as he had been appointed as the commissioner to represent the state and grievances of both Aberdeen colleges. David Leech was holding his post as a regent illegally, as he had married two years before. Further, he lived outside the college, and took more from the college revenues than his lawful stipend. Seeking to avoid punishment, he was conspiring against the college, combining with its enemies 'by devising and divulging a new foundation of their own' which was not authentic, seeking to appropriate for himself and the regents the salaries of the other professors. Leech's appearance in Edinburgh was the second time that year he had deserted his post to prosecute his 'sinistrous designs', and he should be sent home to attend his class and be punished. The council, no doubt with relief, referred the matter to the commissioners appointed to reform abuses in Scotland's colleges.[18]

It soon had second thoughts, however, perhaps recalling that the king had been issuing commissions to visit King's College for three years without effect, and itself named commissioners, three bishops and three nobles, headed by the Marquis of Huntly, to investigate.[19] Not only was Huntly the leading magnate in the region, he had contact with the college through having sent two of his sons there in 1630,[20] thus earning the praise of the king for providing them with a Protestant education at the price of offending his mainly Catholic friends and kinsmen.[21]

The response of David Leech to the appointment of the new commission was a Latin poem, 'Philosophy in tears', bemoaning the troubles of the university and emphasising the high hopes placed on its 'patron', the Marquis of Huntly. Only he could 'bring us aid and restore Philosophy. Marquis, bring a time of joy to brother Scots, bring back happy days to sinking Philosophy'.[22] But before this poetic propaganda had time to have any effect a further attempt was made to reach a decision on some of the matters at issue by the rector, the physician and noted Latin poet Arthur Johnston. If his interests as a poet might have inclined him to sympathy with Leech, his profession as a doctor (he was one of the king's physicians) would counter-balance this by giving him interests in common with William Gordon. At a meeting on 22 July 1637 Johnston enacted a compromise. The stipends of regents were to be in accordance with the Old Foundation (once the college's debts were paid): but they were all to have the stipends that that foundation had assigned to subprincipals. This was hardly logical, but was doubtless seen as expedient. In effect it was a ruling in favour of the Old Foundation, but with an element of compromise aimed at making it acceptable to all: regents would be entitled to rather more in stipends than they had feared (especially as the new stipends were defined largely in terms of bolls of grain, and this was inflation-proof), and it was established that though the Old Foundation was in force, it was legitimate to tinker with it.

11 William Gordon, mediciner at King's College 1632–8 and champion of the Old Foundation. Aberdeen University Picture Store.

Whether this was acceptable to the regents is unknown, but it was not to William Gordon. As common procurator he immediately protested that no rector had power to alter stipends except with the unanimous consent of all members of the college.[23]

Gordon's hard-line stance seems to have lost him credibility: by October he only had the support of James Sandilands, and was forced to resign as procurator, protesting vigorously and declining to recognise the jurisdiction of the rector.[24] Months of further argument followed as attempts were made to get Gordon to return to the college charter chest various documents he had taken to produce as evidence in court cases. As late as March 1638 he was refusing to return 'the Old Foundation'—Bishop Dunbar's 1529 Foundation—saying he would only produce it before the royal commissioners who were to visit the university.[25] The supporters of the Old Foundation having burnt the New Foundation, Gordon perhaps feared a similar fate for the Old if he let in fall into his opponents' hands.

That the initiative had now passed to the supporters of the New Foundation for the first time since Patrick Forbes had become Bishop of Aberdeen was confirmed by a letter from Charles I to the council. This indignantly related that the college's foundation, a good and pious work of his royal father, had been deliberately destroyed. Investigations were to be made to reveal the delinquents, and that foundation—clearly the New Foundation—was to be re-established.[26] Charles sent a similar letter to the college, which promptly dispatched David Leech to Edinburgh to distribute copies to all members of the commissions for visiting Scotland's colleges.[27] Leech, only months before denounced for visiting Edinburgh as a sinister conspirator, was now the college's official representative there; but early in 1638 he resigned to become parish minister of Ellon, appointed by the king himself.[28] Leech choose his moment to leave well, for the triumph of the New Foundation party was short lived, as Charles I's understanding of the situation in the college had changed yet again in a way which typified the problems of absentee monarchy: the distant king was at the mercy of whatever interested party gained his or an influential courtier's ear, and tended to believe what he had been told most recently. Perhaps through the machinations of William Gordon, he had now been told that:

> the principal and four regents of philosophy, having these many years been liable to the censure of deprivation through manifest contempt and violation of their original foundation, are now of late come to that height of presumption as to abolish, as much as in them lies, the ancient and true foundation . . . and to bring in a new one of their own forging, both to palliate their past malversations and appropriate to themselves only the whole revenues.

Law and medicine were being extinguished, the college being reduced to 'a bare school of philosophy'. Therefore in February 1638 Charles ordered his commissioners for visiting the college—from whom he had expected to hear long before—to punish and remove the transgressors, and to restore the Old Foundation.[29]

In the light of this the dominant party in the college must have awaited the long-heralded visitation with trepidation. Acting in real or (more likely) pretended ignorance of the king's latest letter, the New Foundation party—rector, principal, subprincipal and the three other regents—nailed their colours to the mast, and claimed to be doing this out of their zeal to obey the king's earlier letter. The king had lately instructed that the New Foundation be observed, so they all swore 'under pain of perjury and infamy to maintain according to the uttermost of our power the said New Foundation'—unless the king declared it null.[30] There is great irony in the date—28 February 1638—on which the staff of the college signed this bond to stand together for their cause. On the same day in Edinburgh the National Covenant was being signed for the first time, binding men to fight together for the cause of what they saw as true religion. Thus while the college staff were obsessed with their petty, inward-looking squabbles the great movement was being forged which was to sweep across the nation and bring a far greater revolution to King's College than any threatened by the king's commissioners.

The proceedings of the royal commissioners of visitation opened on 12 April with the reading of the king's letter, and William Gordon's production of Bishop Dunbar's Foundation which he had been guarding carefully for months.[31] The rector, Arthur Johnston, countered by casting doubt on the authority of the visitors: of the confusion of commissions ordered by the king in the past few years, which were still valid, and under which were the commissioners acting? The four commissioners (led by Huntly and including Bishop Bellenden) were confident enough of their own authority to dismiss this as merely a delaying tactic. Johnston then produced a copy of 'the new alleged foundation', the original having been destroyed some years before 'as they alleged', protesting that if the visitors did not act in accordance with it the college staff would ask the courts to nullify their proceedings. Only the mediciner and canonist opposed this, and they were given until the next day to produce their response to it. Thus it seemed that the commissioners were willing to leave the question of the foundations open for the moment, but when they proceeded to examine Principal Leslie's conduct the fact that they were committed to the Old Foundation became clear. They found him defective, negligent and worthy of censure, though as he was a man of 'good literature, life and conversation' they were unwilling to be rigorous. But in future he was to teach two lessons weekly, one in Hebrew and one in theology (which

12 Arthur Johnston, distinguished physician and poet, rector of the university 1637–8 and champion of the New Foundation. Aberdeen University, Elphinstone Hall.

hardly sounds very arduous), and perform all other duties incumbent on him 'by virtue of the Old Foundation'.[32]

However, the visitors recognised the very real ambiguities of the college's legal position and the lack of resources which had led to the dispute between the foundations, and therefore though they ruled the next day that the king's intention was to restore the Old Foundation, they accepted that college revenues were insufficient for this to be done immediately. Lack of money was why 'the whole present controversy, which is amongst the members of the college, arises and results upon a posterior foundation alleged'. Therefore all college staff were to keep their present offices until the king's wishes were known. Meanwhile, college funds were not to be used by the rival parties in pursuing court cases against each other.[33] It was a lot fairer an assessment than Bishop Forbes had made in 1619 when he had condemned the New Foundation outright. Nonetheless, the judgement was not acceptable to the New Foundation party. They protested, drawing attention to the fact that the king had previously written in favour of the New Foundation, and claiming that it had long been in force until secretly destroyed 'of late'—thus skating over the awkward fact that Bishop Forbes had suppressed it nearly twenty years before. As the king had written two letters, it was wrong to ignore the one which had been based on true information. And summonses had already been issued against Gordon (mediciner), Sandilands (canonist) Roger Mowat (the nominal civilist) and Gilbert Ross (cantor) seeking judgement that they were not members of the college. The burners of the New Foundation and those abusing the king with lies should be punished. The visitors should try 'what fruit and benefit the country has received of the public lectures in medicine and canon law these sundry years bygone, and what scholars the professors have had, either private or public, that the country be not gulled any longer by mere ciphers and shadows'.[34]

facing page

13 Title page of David Leech's 'Philosophy in tears'. Leech was subprincipal of King's College 1632-8 and a strong supporter of the New Foundation. In 1637 the second Marquis of Huntly had just been appointed to lead a visitation of the college, and Leech took the opportunity of the university's graduation ceremonies in July to deliver this poem, no doubt hoping that flattery might help influence the visitation's result: he laments the decay of philosophy in King's College and claims that only Huntly can save it! Leech delivered his poem just three days after the riots in Edinburgh which sparked off the Scottish revolt against Charles I, which was to prove far more destructive to Aberdeen philosophy than the internal squabbles Leech was concerned with. BL, 8403. ddd. 3.

PHILOSOPHIA ILLACHRYMANS,

Hoc eſt,

QUERELA PHILOSOPHIÆ,

Et *PHILOSOPHORVM SCOTORVM*, (præſertim verò *Borealium*) *oratoriè expreſſa:*

Publicè habita in Auditorio Maximo Collegii *Regii Aberdonenſis* 26 *die Iulii*, 1637;

Quo die Adoleſcentes nonnulli, Magiſterii Candidati, curriculum Philoſophicum emenſi, & cum Laureâ emittendi, *Philoſophici examinis rigorem ſuſtinebant,*

In ſolenni Clariſſimorum Virorum conſeſſu.

Perorante *DAVIDE LEOCHÆO*, Philoſophiæ Profeſſore, & συζητήσεως Philoſophicæ Moderatore ordinario, *dicti Collegii Subprimario.*

Frugalitatem Philoſophia deſiderat, non inopiam, præmium Philoſophus non pœnam. *Senec. in Epiſt.*

ABERDONIÆ,
IMPRIMEBAT EDWARDUS RABANUS,
Almæ Academiæ Typographus. 1637.

Gordon and Sandilands (who were brothers-in-law) replied with equal bitterness on behalf of the Old Foundation, giving their version of the college's history and showing an equally cavalier attitude to the truth when it suited them—as in claiming that there had been unbroken successions of canonists, civilists and mediciners since pre-Reformation times. If James VI had wanted the New Foundation to be enforced, why had the 1617 act of parliament ignored it and ratified the Old? As for the supposed act of 1597 ratifying the New Foundation, it had been rejected by the Court of Session in a case in 1636 since it had not been revised as parliament had ordered in 1597. As for financial problems, increases in college revenues over the past few years (presumably resulting from better administration and the many court cases the college had pursued to exact payment of rents and other dues) were more than adequate to pay the extra salaries in dispute. The regents complained of their poverty, but they were better paid than their counterparts at Marischal College, Edinburgh or St Andrews, 'and yet have the fewest scholars of any of them'. Significantly, the suggestion of their enemies that there were no students in medicine and civil law were ignored by Gordon and Sandilands, which must surely be an indication that they could not deny it.[35]

The two parties in the college had now stated their cases, but the visitors had already made their decision: the Old Foundation was valid, but the college was too poor to implement it. When their report reached the king is unknown, but the most influential voices to gain his ear in the following months favoured the New Foundation, and this led in May to yet another royal reversal, contradicting the decision of his own visitors. Charles announced that he had formerly ordered his father's foundation to be enforced, but since then another letter by him, issued on new (and evidently now discredited) information, had hindered this. He wanted to see the university flourish and his father's work preserved. Bishop Bellenden should therefore investigate the situation anew, and recommend what should be done.[36]

It was presumably this royal letter that led to the rout of the Old Foundation supporters at the rectorial visitation of June 1638. Gordon and Sandilands did not appear, and were denounced for contumacy and for having neglected all their duties and teaching since the April visitation, and indeed long before it.[37] To back up its case, the triumphant New Foundation party commissioned Principal William Leslie to write to one of the courtiers whose favour had brought them success, Patrick Maule of Panmure. He had previously had financial dealings with the college, holding a lease of some teinds from it, and had procured the king's recent letter to Bishop Bellenden. Now Leslie thanked Maule for his help and provided him with a skilfully constructed exposition of the case for the New Foundation, to give him ammunition to counter the continuing plots of the Old Foundation party, which was trying to get a charter issued under the great seal confirming it.[38] At this point King Charles came to the conclusion that he would have been better to reach months or even years before: that it was impossible for him to sort out the truth of the situation in the college from London, listening alternately to contradictory cases and issuing contradictory orders. He therefore washed his hands of the matter—though evidently leaning again towards the Old Foundation. Its supporters had taken their case to the Court of Session, and Charles informed the court that he might, through being misinformed, have issued orders prejudicing their rights. Now, notwithstanding any previous orders and letters from the king, the court was to administer justice to either party according to equity and the laws of Scotland.[39]

Principal Leslie took a leading part in 1637–8 in attempting to destroy one aspect of Bishop Patrick Forbes's legacy, the restoration of the Old Foundation. Simultaneously he played a lesser role in a much greater and more significant controversy in which he fought to uphold the bishop's intellectual legacy. The cause he supported was to be lost, but the fight he and his colleagues put up deserves respect, especially as they were to be vanquished by force and threats while remaining undefeated in debate. The conflict was that between the 'Aberdeen Doctors' and the covenanters. Defiance of Charles I's religious innovations in Scotland, especially in worship, had begun in mid 1637, and soon snowballed into a great national revolt whose supporters were bound together by swearing the National Covenant. Enthusiasm for the covenant was widespread throughout most of the Lowlands, but support in the North East was patchy, and largely lacking in Aberdeen itself. As in 1559–60, Aberdeen was to be forced into conformity with a religious revolution made in the south, and just as some of the staff of King's College at the Reformation had been among the few with the courage to stand up for their beliefs, so in 1638–9 the Aberdeen Doctors, all holding the degree of doctor of divinity granted by the college (or more strictly, by the university), were prepared to resist the narrow-minded fanaticism of the covenanters.

To the covenanters the king's attempts to reform the worship of the church to introduce more in the way of ritual and ceremony were not only displeasing to God and Scotland's Protestant traditions, but raised fears of a secret move towards Catholicism. This was certainly not Charles's intention, but in an age when the revived Counter-Reformation Catholic Church was continuing to regain lost territory in many parts of Europe the covenanters' fears are understandable. Moreover, the king favoured the spread in Scotland of Arminian theology, derived from a Dutch theologian's ideas and seeming to threaten belief in predestination, the core of Calvinst theology in Scotland since the Reformation—and, again, it seemed to threaten established religion in a way which could be seen as tending towards Catholicism. The church must be purged of these corruptions if God's wrath was not to fall on Scotland. The outlook of the covenanters obviously had many similarities to that of Andrew Melville in a previous generation, and many of their leaders were committed presbyterians. But at first there was no direct attack on episcopacy as such, though there were demands for reductions in royal power in ecclesiastical affairs. Instead, to help win moderate support, it was simply argued that the existing bishops must be punished for cooperating in introducing corruptions into the church.

In the controversy that followed the covenanters denounced the Aberdeen Doctors as believers in 'popish' ceremonies and suspect theological ideas, but what really distinguished the two sides was not so much specific beliefs as wider attitudes to religion. The covenanters tended to work on the maxim that he who is not for us is against us, and must be attacked as ungodly. Under the influence of Patrick Forbes and his son Professor John Forbes, the Aberdeen Doctors saw room for more flexibility in religion. Insistence on complete agreement on every detail of religious belief and practice simply led to division and weakness among Protestants. Certainly there were some fundamental beliefs on which agreement was essential, but in other matters diversity could be accepted. Thus Charles I believed that episcopalianism was the only lawful form of church government; the covenanters were soon to be claiming that on the contrary only presbyterianism was acceptable to God. The Aberdeen Doctors would not accept either argument. Within limits, forms of church government were a matter of expediency. They supported episcopacy in Scotland because that was what the king had ordained, because it had historical arguments in its favour going back to the New Testament, and because it had strengths in maintaining order and discipline in the church. But this did not mean that presbyterian government was unlawful or displeasing to God. Similarly, the ceremonies the king was introducing in worship were to be accepted because the king had the authority to impose them, because they did not conflict with the will of God, and because historical precedents could be cited in their favour. But, in other circumstances, other forms of worship could be valid.

Thus intellectually and theologically the Aberdeen Doctors' response to the narrow and exclusive claims of king and covenanters was not that either was inherently right or wrong: the differences between them were minor, and the overwhelming priority was not fighting over them but concentrating on the far more important elements they had in common as Protestants so they could stand together against Rome. But, if forced to choose between the contending parties, they would support the king. In principle their position was one which was not fully acceptable to the king, but in the circumstances this was overlooked and in practice they came to be regarded as the king's champions. In the eyes of the covenanters, this meant they were in effect in league with the sinister Catholic forces which were believed to lie behind the king's policies. Thus the intellectual trend established by Patrick Forbes in the hope of uniting Protestants against Catholics came to be seen as itself pro-Catholic.

The clash between the Aberdeen cast of thought and the rising tide of opposition to royal policy was clear long before the troubles began. It was illustrated dramatically in 1636 when one of the leaders of the opposition, Samuel Rutherford, was banished from his parish in the south west to Aberdeen. There, in the conservative North East, his seditious ideas would not find a receptive audience—and who knows, he might even be tamed by the prevailing intellectual climate. The experiment failed. Rutherford addressed an immense stream of apocalyptic letters to sympathisers predicting the wrath of God to come before Scotland was cleansed. These were dispatched from what he called 'Christ's Palace in Aberdeen'—his own lodgings in which he was marooned in a sea of corruption. The inhabitants of the town consisted of 'papists or men of Gallio's naughty faith'. Junius Gallio, a Roman official in Greece, had dismissed a case brought by the Jews against St Paul as being a matter of trifling differences,[40] and Rutherford was indicating that Aberdonians showed a similar shocking tendency to regard as unimportant differences that were crucial to a stickler like himself. Typically, when the ministers of the town greeted him, Rutherford sneered at their 'pretended great love' for him, unable to accept that they could differ from him in some beliefs but still feel friendship. He debated controversial matters with some of the doctors—especially Robert Baron (professor of theology at Marischal College). They probably regarded the debates as sincere attempts to discuss their differences, to try to understand each other. Rutherford by contrast saw the debates as life and death struggles against the powers of darkness. 'I am here assaulted with the Doctors' guns; but I bless the Father of lights, that they draw not blood of truth'. He debated ceremonies and Arminian controversies with Baron three times, and claimed to have won. He concluded that 'all are corrupt here': 'I never knew so well what sin was as since I came to Aberdeen'. Further, he reported that he had learnt that the university professors were working on a confession of faith which would be acceptable to Lutherans as well as Calvinists, a move towards Protestant unity which he inevitably saw as treachery—and equally inevitably concluded was a first step towards the ultimate evil, reconciliation with popery.[41]

When the troubles first broke out in 1637 the Aberdeen Doctors showed no inclination to become publicly involved on either side, though no doubt their sermons and lectures reflected their deep disquiet at the likely consequences of opposing the king. While their principles might incline them to the king, his doctrinaire and blundering innovations in religion doubtless led them to feel that he was himself partly responsible for provoking conflict. They were peaceable, conservative and relatively tolerant men who must have been saddened by the narrow-minded rigidity of both sides. Further, for those directly involved in King's College's affairs the renewed and bitter controversy between the two foundations must have consumed much time and energy, distracting them from national issues. The intellectual leader of the doctors, Professor John Forbes, is notable for abstaining completely from these internal college conflicts, doubtless distressing to his sensitive soul: or, to be more cynical, it may be pointed out that he was the only member of the college staff whose salary was secure whatever the outcome of the dispute, as the establishment of his chair postdated both foundations. But he also abstained at first from the growing national controversy, instead agonising over such matters as whether his guests at a dinner party had been 'more overcome with wine than was seemly'. Had he been over zealous in pressing drink on them until they 'exceeded the bounds of lawful hilarity' and on leaving presented a scandalous example to citizens and students?[42]

Yet it was to be Forbes who was the first of the Aberdeen Doctors to extend opposition to the covenanters from the pulpit and classroom to a wider audience. Already by April 1638 the king had thanked King's College for its support,[43] and at about this time Forbes wrote and circulated manuscript copies of his 'Peaceable Warning' to the king's Scottish subjects about the dangers of supporting the covenanters. It was a step he soon regretted, for though he had no intentions of causing offence his tract could be read as casting aspersions on the noblemen leading the covenanting movement. This gave them a chance to attack Forbes on this personal issue, thus distracting attention from the general principles he propounded. The unfortunate author was soon threatened with criminal charges against him. Desperately he offered grovelling apologies that some 'rash and foolish speeches did escape me in the sudden inadvisedness of my first writing'. Nonetheless, even while fearfully craving pardon, Forbes stuck to his principles, rewriting the 'Warning' to remove the causes of offence and moderating his language. This he proceeded to have printed by Edward Raban.[44] But his arguments would probably have had more impact if he had not had to withdraw and apologise for the earlier botched manuscript version.

Aberdeen's continuing hostility to the covenant led the covenanters to send a delegation of nobles, lairds and ministers north in July 1638 to try to persuade it to submit. In spite of his unhappy experience with

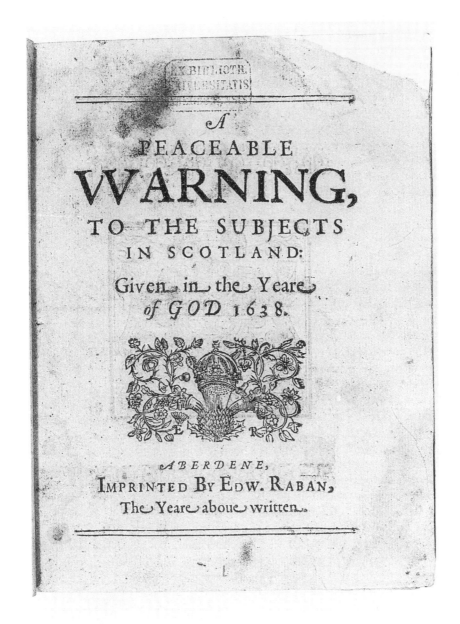

A
PEACEABLE
WARNING,
TO THE SUBJECTS
IN SCOTLAND:

Given in the Yeare
of *GOD* 1638.

ABERDENE,
IMPRINTED BY EDW. RABAN,
The Yeare aboue written.

14 Title page of Professor John Forbes's *Peaceable Warning* of 1638, urging Scots of the dangers of opposing King Charles I. AUL, in π MN. 4. 3.

his 'Warning', Forbes again led resistance, probably playing the major role in organising the 'Demands', a series of questions concerning the covenant and the actions of the covenanters to be put to the covenanting ministers. Signing this document was to define the 'Aberdeen Doctors' in the sense of those prepared to make a public stand for their beliefs. At first they numbered seven, but one of their number (William Guild, minister in Aberdeen) soon fell by the wayside and signed the covenant. The other six were John Forbes, Robert Baron, Principal William Leslie, Alexander Scroggie (minister of St Machar's and rector of King's College 1636–7), Alexander Ross (minister in Aberdeen and rector of King's 1638–9) and James Sibbald (minister in Aberdeen).[45] In spite of all the theological mud to be thrown at them by the covenanters, most of them were orthodox Calvinists in their basic beliefs. Leslie, Scroggie and Ross (and Guild, for that matter) were never specifically accused of Arminianism. Forbes was accused but cleared. Baron and Sibbald undoubtedly were influenced by Arminian ideas,[46] however, and this enabled the covenanters to tarnish the whole group—after all, in their eyes the willingness of the the majority of the doctors to tolerate and cooperate with their Arminian-infected colleagues was tantamount to adopting the heresy themselves: guilt by association.

By the time the covenanters' delegation reached Aberdeen the Doctors had their 'Demands' ready, and indeed had them printed. This roused the fury of the covenanters: the resistance of Aberdeen was an embarrassment to them, and they had hoped to persuade their opponents to submit in private debate. Instead the Doctors insisted on making it a public one— though a minor success was achieved by the covenanters when the grammarian of King's College, John Lundie, and the sacrist, Patrick Innes, agreed to sign the covenant.[47] A vigorous paper war followed, in which the parties concerned never met face to face and which continued even after the covenanters' delegation had returned to Edinburgh. The Doctors' 'Demands' were countered by the covenanters' 'Answers', which in turn provoked the Doctors' 'Replies'. The covenanters responded with their 'Second Answers', but the succeeding 'Duplies' of the Doctors proved the last salvo in the exchange of fire. The covenanters broke off the engagement as they were getting nowhere, and the publicity given to the debate was benefiting their opponents—all the papers were quickly reprinted in both Edinburgh and London.[48] The fame of the 'Aberdeen Doctors' and their bold stand against overwhelming odds now spread throughout Britain: at last the king could claim that there was a coherent group of intellectuals in Scotland offering sustained and reasoned opposition to the covenanters. John Forbes's signature appeared first on all three of the papers the doctors issued, and he, Robert Baron and James Sibbald were probably mainly responsible for their contents.

GENERALL
DEMANDS
CONCERNING
THE LATE
COVENANT :

Propounded by the Ministers and Professors of Divinitie in Aberdene, to some Reverend Brethren, who came thither to recommend the late Covenant to them, and to those who are committed to their charge.

TOGETHER WITH
The ANSWERS of those Reverend Brethren to the said DEMANDS.

AS ALSO
The REPLYES of the foresaid Ministers and Professors to their ANSWERS.

1 PET.3.15.16.
Sanctifie the Lord God in your hearts, and be ready alwaies to give an answer to every man that asketh you a reason of the hope that is in you, with meeknesse and fear: Having a good conscience, that whereas they speak evil of you, as of evildoers, they may be ashamed that falsly accuse your good conversation in Christ.

EDINBURGH,
Printed by ROBERT YOUNG. *Anno* 1638.
CVM PRIVILEGIO.

15 Title page of one of the editions of the first three rounds of the paper conflict between the Aberdeen Doctors and the covenanters, 1638. Here, as in the next illustration, the publication gives the Doctors the last word in this propaganda war. AUL, in π 2852(41) Sco.

Forbes knew well the dangers of putting himself at the head of opposition to a movement which had by this time established what amounted to a provisional government in Scotland, and the courage shown by this mild academic is all the more creditable in view of the terror he admitted to in private, in letters and his diary.[49]

The next challenge, however, was too much for Forbes and his colleagues. The king had agreed that a general assembly should meet in Glasgow in November 1638 to consider the religious controversies which had dominated the country for the previous year, but it soon became clear that the covenanters had so rigged the elections that in much of the country it was virtually impossible for any of the king's supporters to be elected—and threatening noises were made to deter any royalists who were elected from attending. The Aberdeen Doctors were encouraged in their stand by praise, thanks and promises of favour from the king,[50] and it was decided that some of them should represent Aberdeen in the assembly. But their nerve failed. Their presence could do no good, they argued, and their past activities would single them out for victimisation.[51] Later it was decided specifically that Forbes, Baron and Sibbald should attend. They agreed to do so if possible, but regretfully reported that their great infirmities, well known in Aberdeen, would probably mean they would not be able to travel. Further declarations of good intentions coupled with references to ill health and the difficulties of travelling in winter combined with arguments that going would probably do more harm than good anyway. Finally they were driven to admit that they did not want to go, fearing for their lives if they did, such was the hatred of them whipped up by the covenanters.[52]

It was an ignominious end to the spirited resistance Forbes and his colleagues had put up, but understandable. They had only been able to get away with publicising their opposition to the covenanters because they were cocooned from their enemies by the widespread support they had in Aberdeen. In Glasgow they would have been isolated: they would never have been given a fair hearing and would have been simply targets for abuse and possible violence. Considering that none of Scotland's bishops dared attend the assembly, it was unreasonable and unrealistic to expect the Aberdeen Doctors to do so. When the assembly met a commission for Baron and Sibbald to sit for Aberdeen was in fact presented, but was immediately rejected in favour of a rival one commissioning William Guild and another local minister who had signed the covenant to sit[53]— confirming the correctness of the Doctors' belief that there was no point in their going to Glasgow.

King's College did, however, have a representative sitting as a member of the assembly—though this was unintentional, the result of the interaction of the internal feud in the college between the foundations and

THE
ANSWERS
O F

Some Brethren of the Minifterie to
the Replies of the Minifters and Profef-
fours of Divinitie in Aberdene,

CONCERNING
THE LATE COVENANT.

ALSO,
DUPLIES
O F

The Minifters and Profeffors of Aberdene, to the fecond Answers of
fome reverend Brethren,

CONCERNING
THE LATE COVENANT.

If thou take forth the precious from the vile, thou fhalt be as my mouth : Let them
returne unto thee, but returne not thou unto them, Jer.15.19.
Honour all men : Love the Brotherhood: Feare God : Honour the King, 1 Pet.2.17.

Printed by *R.Y.* His Majefties Printer for Scotland,
Anno Dom. 1638.

16 Title page of one of the editions of the last two rounds of the paper
conflict between the Aberdeen Doctors and the covenanters, 1638. After
this the covenanters broke off the controversy, realising it was being
successfully exploited for propaganda purposes by the royalists. AUL, π
285(41) Chu an.

the external controversy over religion. As one of the Aberdeen Doctors Principal William Leslie had won royal favour. But the situation looked unpromising for the New Foundation faction in the college which he headed. Both the royal visitation in April 1638 and the most recent indication of the king's views (his July letter to the Court of Session) indicated that the Old Foundation was likely to be confirmed. But with the rise of the covenanters an alternative authority had appeared that might be persuaded to take a different view—especially if they could be persuaded that the Old Foundation was 'papist'. Conveniently one of the academic staff, John Lundie, had signed the covenant and would thus be acceptable to the assembly; and as he had been common procurator since William Gordon had been ousted from the post he was well versed in the college's business. Principal Leslie and the regents therefore commissioned Lundie to appear before the assembly and supplicate it in favour of the New Foundation. The attempt to use the assembly for their own ends backfired: instead the assembly used Lundie's commission for its own purposes. Lundie's commission merely authorised him to give in a supplication to the assembly. But the assembly chose to read it as a commission to sit as member of the assembly for Aberdeen University, thus demonstrating that even that institution, so closely identified with the king's cause, now accepted the legality of the covenanters' proceedings. Lundie duly took his seat, and he continued to attend even after the assembly refused to obey the king's orders to dissolve.[54] His submission to the assembly was truly extraordinary considering that he had been commissioned by a college headed by one of the Aberdeen Doctors. William Leslie had defended episcopacy, but now, in opportunistically seeking to exploit a national controversy for factional ends, he had created a situation in which the college's agent, encouraged by the covenanters, appeared to join in the attack on episcopacy—in the hope of winning the assembly's support for the New Foundation.

Lundie related to the assembly how the college had been miserably oppressed by the bishops, who had taken revenues from the regents and the grammarian (who were diligently teaching their students) and given them to the professor of the superstitious canon law and others, according to the old popish foundation. In the past the New Foundation faction had been reluctant to name Bishop Forbes as the unscrupulous destroyer of the document on which their claim rested, as attacking so revered a figure could be counter-productive. But now, in an assembly which had just abolished episcopacy and established presbyterianism, all bishops were fair game and Forbes could be denounced. Immediate opposition to Lundie's attack on the Old Foundation came from an unexpected quarter. Lord Balmerino might be one of the foremost of the covenanting nobles, but he was after all an Elphinstone, and family honour would not let him remain silent when the achievements of the great Bishop Elphinstone were being questioned—even if he had been not only a bishop but a Catholic one. Balmerino therefore demanded that his kinsman's foundation be maintained. Lundie hastily moderated his tone: he sought no more than abolition of 'the popish offices opposed to the reformed religion which their bishop [Patrick Forbes] of new had [im]posed on them'. On this basis Balmerino agreed with the rest of the assembly that Lundie's request for a visitation of the college be granted. With luck, as plotted by Lundie in another nice example of guilt by association, it would agree to abolish mediciner, civilist and cantor through lumping them together with the popish-sounding canonist.[55]

The covenanters must have been delighted that King's College had actually asked the assembly to interfere in its affairs, and visitors were to meet there in April 1639 to remove surplus, unqualified and corrupt members.[56] Lundie returned home to find—surely not entirely to his surprise—that his actions had horrified all his colleagues. The Old Foundation supporters smugly pointed out that they had had nothing to do with his presence at the assembly, while the chastened New Foundation party admitted commissioning him, but denounced him for going beyond his instructions. He should not have sat as a member of the assembly, and certainly not attended after the king had ordered its dissolution. Lundie protested (not very convincingly) that he had not heard of the ordered dissolution at first, that in any case many of the king's own councillors had continued to attend, and that he had stayed on because the assembly had not at that point considered the college's supplication. Nonetheless, all united in condemning his activities, in order to avert 'the king's majesty's wrath'. But Lundie was not deprived of office lest that brought down on the college the rival wrath of the covenanters.[57]

After the Glasgow Assembly both king and covenanters prepared for war. The covenanters' grip on the rest of the Lowlands was strong, but in the North East royalists were ready to resist—though their leader, the Marquis of Huntly, was to prove both incompetent and uninspiring. He occupied Aberdeen (whereupon John Lundie hastily signed the King's Covenant—the royalists' rival to the National Covenant).[58] But when the Earl of Montrose approached at the head of a covenanting army, Huntly withdrew. Montrose announced that the purpose of his advance was to see that the assembly's visitation of King's College could take place: one royalist remarked wonderingly that cannon were 'strange ingredient for the visitation of a university'[59] As the covenanters approached all the staff and students of the college scattered in panic (for the second time: they had only just re-assembled after an earlier alarm). Principal Leslie was among three of the Aberdeen Doctors who fled by ship to Berwick, having decided that it was not wise to await the visitation which his plottings in favour of the New Foundation had helped to bring about.[60] However, by 11 April most of the staff had returned and the visitation took place. All those present signed the National Covenant, and were ordered to do public penance for receiving communion from Bishop Bellenden after the Glasgow Assembly had excommunicated him—though in the end this public humiliation was not insisted on. The visitation ordered the suppression of the offices of canonist as papist and of cantor as unprofitable, which would have gladdened Principal Leslie's New Foundation heart. But the visitation also deposed him and the absent regent (Alexander Scroggie younger, son of the Aberdeen Doctor of the same name) because they had failed to appear, Leslie also being convicted of consorting with the bishop, refusing to acknowledge the Glasgow Assembly, and fleeing the country.[61] A further session of the visitation to impose further reform was planned for May, but this proved abortive: only one of the visitors turned up and the college staff refused to let him in.[62] The covenanters' hold on the North East was still weak, Aberdeen changing hands several times in the months that followed, and they did not feel it expedient to impose a harsh purge of the college: 'things were not ripe enough: it was therefore laid by for that time'.[63] Even the depositions of the principal and regent were not immediately enforced, though the former cautiously delayed his return to his post until August 1639. He still refused to sign the covenant, but kept a low profile and lived quietly in the college at his own expense[64]—presumably so that if his deposition was upheld he could not be charged with illegal use of college funds.

The April 1639 visitation indicated that the covenanters were not interested in the full imposition of either the Old or the New Foundation. The fact that canonist and cantor were removed involved no judgement about foundations and thus it was not seen as implying that the posts of mediciner and civilist should be abolished as well. Even the canonist managed to win a reprieve: James Sandilands appealed to the general assembly in August 1639, arguing that though canon law was indeed pre-Reformation Catholic law, teaching of it should not be abolished entirely, for in Scotland matters relating to marriages, testaments (wills) and teinds were still judged by canon law—though other aspects of that law should indeed be suppressed as they 'smelled of popery'.[65] Thus the faculty of canon law should be limited, not abolished—or perhaps it should be merged with that of civil law.[66] The assembly accepted Sandilands' arguments, tendentiously interpreting the judgement of the visitors to mean not that the canonist should be deprived, but that he be limited to teaching aspects of canon law consistent with true religion.[67]

Less lucky was William Leslie, who also presented a supplication begging to be restored to office, offering to accept the legitimacy of the church's recent reforms and obey it in future. The supplication was simply referred to new visitors appointed to investigate the state of the college.[68] This visitation was delayed by the continuing political confusion, and though a start was made with further reform in October, when William Guild was elected rector and the deposition of Alexander Scroggie younger was confirmed, the further intention of making Guild principal was delayed.[69] The choice by the covenanters of William Guild to take over the college indicated moderation on their part, for though he now supported their cause he had (albeit briefly) been one of the Aberdeen Doctors, and retained much in common with their outlook. During his first rectorial visitation in October his conciliatory approach was startlingly demonstrated: James Sibbald, perhaps the most Arminian of the Aberdeen Doctors, was elected dean of the faculty of theology, and William Gordon was restored to the office of common procurator to replace Lundie, who had not been forgiven by his colleagues for his behaviour in the Glasgow Assembly. If the subprincipal and the other three regents were worried by seeing Gordon, tenaciously opposed to raising their salaries, return to office, they must have been mollified by the announcement that in future 'exam silver' collected from students would be divided equally among them.[70] But tensions remained. When Sandilands returned and began teaching canon law the regents muttered that the revenues that supported him were in effect lost to the college, as he taught so little and had such small audiences: the money should have gone to the regents 'who endured pains, day and night, for upbringing the youth'. Sandilands' qualifications were also called in doubt: 'strange to see such a man admitted to teach laws who was never out of the country studying and learning the laws'.[71] Then, early in 1640, Sandilands pulled off a coup that must have intensified jealousy of him. Though restored to office he must have felt insecure: the name of canon law still smacked of popery to many, and the fact that he was now forbidden to teach most of such law obviously strengthened arguments that he was not worth his salary. Sandilands was therefore probably responsible for persuading the absentee civilist, Roger Mowat, to resign office. Sandilands then offered to resign as canonist—provided he was promised appointment as civilist, and his salary as canonist was transferred to that office. The idea was obviously beneficial to Sandilands, but it was also sensible. One law teacher was obviously quite enough (if not more than enough) to meet demand for his services; the embarrassment of having a canonist in a Protestant university was removed; and at last one of Bishop Patrick Forbes's disastrous (from the point of view of college morale) absentee and largely nominal teachers disappeared. And again William Guild as rector showed a desire both to conciliate former rival interests in the college and to reconcile all to the new covenanting regime, for the stipends of the regents were increased at the same time as Sandilands became civilist—

though they still grudged him his salary, especially as he continued also to collect fees as commissary clerk of Aberdeen.[72] Conveniently, the mediciner, William Gordon, had just died,[73] removing an opponent of generosity to regents and also perhaps providing the wherewithall for such generosity—he was not replaced, and it may have been his salary as mediciner which was divided to pay more to the regents.[74]

Others benefited less from Guild's conciliatory policies as rector. There was no repreive for William Leslie, and the covenanters were determined to examine the orthodoxy of John Forbes as professor of theology. He spent whole days late in 1639 agonising about whether to sign the covenant if it was pressed on him, but his examination was repeatedly delayed by the confusion of the times (for which he praised the Lord) and he was allowed to continue to teach.[75] Not until July 1640 did he appear before the visitors, terrified about what was going to happen to him, but nonetheless determined not to take the covenant—and remembering to pray that his persecutors would avoid sinning against God by acting against him. In the event, since the next general assembly was due to meet in Aberdeen at the end of the month, the visitors simply referred the further reform of King's College back to them: Forbes escaped with being forbidden to teach until then, which he happily pointed out was hardly a burden as it was now the university vacation.[76]

When the assembly did meet it confirmed Leslie's deprivation and chose William Guild to succeed him as principal. Sandilands' change of professorial horses was ratified, and his father and predecessor as canonist acted as chancellor of the university in place of the bishop when Guild's position as principal was legitimised by his formal election, the traditional 'procurators of the Four Nations' being recorded for the first time as taking part in such an event: a case perhaps of the more arbitrary the proceedings, the more elaborate the formalities required to give them a show of legitimacy. The covenanters' control of the college was now complete, and the assembly had chosen to meet in Aberdeen to demonstrate their domination of the region. But there was still restraint, a wish to avoid vindictiveness. Leslie was quietly allowed to keep his room in the college he had served for over twenty years, and he was probably relieved to be out of the limelight.[77] James Gordon, who knew him, explained away the charges of laziness and drunkenness made against him:

> his retired, monastic way of living, being naturally melancholian, and a man of great reading, a painful student who delighted in nothing else but to sit in his study, and spend days and nights at his books, which kind of life is opposite to a practical way of living. He never married in his lifetime, but lived solitary; and if sometimes to refresh himself, his friends took him from his books to converse with them, it ought not to have been objected to him as drunkenness, he being known to have been

sober and abstemious above his accusers. He was a man grave and austere, and exemplary. The university was happy in having such a light as he, who was eminent in all the sciences above the most of his age . . . Pity it was that he left not more behind him of his learned works; but the reason was his natural bashfulness, who had so small opinion of his own knowledge, that he could scarce ever be gotten drawn for[th] to speak in public.[78]

The portrait is a sympathetic one, but it does not delineate a man suited to governing a college riven with bitter faction or to guiding it through a great national upheaval such as Scotland had experienced since 1637.

John Forbes too was shown some clemency: he was again questioned but no further action was taken against for the moment. If Leslie was left alone as being harmless, Forbes was treated relatively gently because of his theological eminence. If his fears could be played on sufficiently to persuade him to sign the covenant this would be a great propaganda coup: it was accepted that he was pious, learned and orthodox, and it was only on church government and the covenant that his views were unacceptable, so there did seem some hope of winning him over. Moreover, persecuting him harshy would be likely to offend many, not least Calvinists abroad.[79] But eventually, early in 1641, Forbes reached a final decision that he would not submit, sadly asking that if he were not to be allowed to remain as professor a successor should be appointed 'that the church be not defrauded'.[80] He was duly deposed, his reaction to the news being to pray God to bring further afflictions on him for his sins.[81]

William Guild, who continued to be rector as well as principal, must have lamented the departure of John Forbes, the college's greatest scholar, but he could do nothing to avert it. In 1641 he presided over two major changes at King's, but though he obviously supported them it is impossible to know whether the initiative was his. The first change was retrogressive. In June it was decreed that 'the subprincipal and regents shall follow their scholars and continue with them from their entry'.[82] In other words, the concentration of each regent on the teaching of one year of the four year arts course, advocated by the New Foundation and introduced by Bishop Patrick Forbes, was to be abandoned. No explanation was given, and it is impossible to know whether it reflects the innate conservatism of the staff—or that of the covenanters. In academic matters the covenanters made much noise in denouncing the neo-scholastic teaching of their episcopalian opponents, but they were themselves thoroughly Aristotelian in philosophy, and though they revered the name of Ramus they never sought to impose his ideas systematically: they themselves were indeed much closer to neo-scholasticism than Ramism.[83] Given their general tendency to look to the past and reject recent 'innovations', they may well have mistrusted the specialist regents or professors at King's College as an episcopalian novelty.

The second major change introduced to the college in 1641 is perhaps more likely to have originated at the national level than in Aberdeen itself. In August Guild represented the university in the general assembly,[84] and doubtless he had a part in drafting overtures concerning the universities of Scotland which were to be sent to the king and parliament. These declared that:

> the good estate both of the kirk and commonwealth dependeth mainly on the flourishing of universities and colleges, as the seminaries of both, which cannot be expected unless the poor means which they have, be helped, and sufficient revenues be provided for them and the same well employed.

Therefore, it was urged, the revenues of the now abolished bishops should be devoted to upholding:

> a competent number of professors, teachers and bursars in all faculties, and especially in divinity, and for upholding, repairing and enlarging the fabric of the colleges, furnishing libraries, as suchlike good uses in every university and college.

Moreover, to prevent abuses and promote piety and learning, continuing contacts between the colleges should be encouraged, with yearly meetings of representatives of them all consulting on matters of common concern and making relevant recommendations to the general assembly and parliament. Finally, special care should be taken in appointing professors (especially of divinity) from among the ablest men—and the most loyal to reformed religion and presbyterianism.[85]

The response was prompt. Charles I had come to Scotland in the vain hope that, by making all the concessions that the covenanters demanded, he would win their support against his enemies in the increasingly defiant English parliament. One of the concessions he made was to agree to the

facing page

17 James Gordon's view of King's College from the south west in about 1660. The only significant change from the buildings depicted in plate 1 (p. 3 above) is the appearance in the north east corner of the quadrangle of the unfinished 'New Work', now known (inappropriately) as the Cromwell Tower. Key to numbers:

1	The Chapel	8	The 'Capitols' or round towers
2	The New Work	9	The Grammar School
3	The Great Hall	10	The churchyard
4	The Second School	11	Part of the College Garden
5	The Jewel House	14	The Grammar School close
6	The Bibliotheck (Library)	15	The Crown Tower
7	Chambers	16	Window of the Great School under the College Hall

diversion of the revenues of some of the bishoprics to the universities. A charter in favour of the Aberdeen colleges related that he had commissioned an investigation into them, and it had reported that to provide 'a competent maintenance in a reasonable way to the professors and founded persons' additional revenues of £500 sterling were needed. Therefore the two colleges were to be united 'in one university, to be called in all time coming, King Charles's University of Aberdeen'. To this university the revenues of the bishopric of Aberdeen would be assigned, two thirds for King's College and one third for Marischal. In assigning the revenues the king was responding to the plea from the general assembly, but where the idea of uniting the colleges came from is obscure, though it seems to have had the whole-hearted support of William Guild. The move was a sensible one. It cleared up the confusion of previous years in which the two colleges had usually acted as if entirely separate from each other, but in which at times Bishop Forbes and others had acted as if they were part of the same university. Moreover to link two small and struggling colleges situated just a couple of miles apart was an obvious thing to do. But it is significant that the proposal to devote bishops' revenues to universities had first emerged in the First Book of Discipline in 1560 and that the book had also planned that there should be a two-college university in Aberdeen.[86] The covenanters liked to see themselves as restoring the early purity of the reformed church in Scotland, later swamped by royal and episcopal corruptions, and the First Book was frequently consulted as a guide to that early purity. Aberdeen conveniently had two colleges; combining them in one university at last fulfilled an eighty-year old pious ambition.

King Charles's charter gave special attention to the needs of King's, saying nothing of specific problems at Marischal, which suggests that the problems of the former were seen as the greater. King's College was in debt: its buildings needed major repairs; and it 'has not a sufficient library'. Therefore half the new revenues due to the college were to be devoted each year to paying off debts, making repairs, and providing a 'competent' library. On 17 November 1641 the Scottish parliament ratified the king's action.[87] Again there was no clear announcement in favour of the Old Foundation or the New, but the indications were that the former was favoured. Thus when the Privy Council recommended a new visitation the old university (meaning college) of Aberdeen it was described as founded by Bishop Gavin Dunbar: and the king ordered the new revenues to be used according to the original and authentic foundations of the colleges.[88]

The staff of King's College must have looked to the future with very mixed feelings. They had accepted the authority of the covenanters, but they had done so reluctantly and must have worried about further interference in the college's affairs by the country's new masters. On the other hand, the promise of extra revenues held out hopes of a more stable future, in which controversy over money would be less central in college affairs. Reactions to incorporation into a single university with Marischal College were doubtless mixed. Some may have seen welcome opportunities for academic co-operation, and the practice begun by Patrick Forbes of having staff from Marischal serve as rectors and deans of faculties meant that the idea was not entirely novel. But it was an arranged marriage, and most in both colleges probably hoped that the link should be a merely nominal one. Fears about the merger on the part of the King's staff must have been lessened by the fact that their principal, William Guild, became rector of the combined university (and retained the post until 1645)—but in Marischal College his appointment must have intensified suspicion about the merger. Rather oddly, when the Caroline University was founded no consideration was given to who should be chancellor now there was no longer a bishop of Aberdeen: perhaps it was implicit in King Charles granting the university his name that he would act as its protector. But in 1643 the staff elected a chancellor for themselves—the Marquis of Huntly.[89] That the royalist champion (however ineffectual) of the North East should be elected to the post when there were clear signs of a new civil war approaching indicates the continuing conservative leanings of the staff in spite of purging by the covenanters.

In the event, King's College was ushered not into a new era of stability and achievement, but into one of increased instability and even chaos. One crude measure of this is that while between 1569 and 1717 five of the ten successive principals of King's College were deposed on ideological grounds, three of the depositions fall in the years 1639 to 1661, with three principals in a row being forcibly ejected from office.[90] Looking back, the days of Patrick Forbes seemed a golden age, its intellectual and cultural achievements remembered, the disputes within the college which had seemed so important at the time dwarfed by the disasters which followed in the 1640s and 1650s.

Abbreviations

Anderson, *FAM*	P J Anderson, ed., *Fasti Academiae Mariscallanae, 1593–1860*, NSC, 3 vols (Aberdeen, 1889–98)
Anderson, *Officers*	P J Anderson, *Officers and Graduates of the University and King's College of Aberdeen*, NSC (Aberdeen, 1893)
APS	*The Acts of the Parliaments of Scotland*, ed. T Thomson and C Innes, 12 vols (Edinburgh, 1814–75)
AUL	Aberdeen University Library
AUR	*Aberdeen University Review*
AUS	Aberdeen University Studies
Bibliographia Aberdonensis	J F K Johnstone and A W Robertson, eds, *Bibliographia Aberdonensis. Being an Account of Books relating to or published in the shires of Aberdeen, Banff, Kincardine, or written by Natives or Residents or by Officers, Graduates or Alumni of the Universities of Aberdeen*, Third SC, 2 vols (Aberdeen, 1929–30)
BL	British Library
BUK	T Thomson, ed., *Acts and Proceedings of the General Assemblies of the Church of Scotland, from the year MDLX*, Bannatyne and Maitland Clubs, 3 vols (Edinburgh, 1839–45) (usually referred to as 'The Booke of the Universall Kirk of Scotland')
CSPS	*Calendar of State Papers relating to Scotland and Mary, Queen of Scots, 1547–1603*, 13 vols (London, 1898–1969)
Gordon, *History*	J Gordon, *History of Scots Affairs, from MDCXXXVII to MDCXLI*, ed. J Robertson and G Grub, SC, 3 vols (Aberdeen, 1841)
Innes, *Fasti*	C Innes, ed., *Fasti Aberdonensis. Selections from the Records of the University and King's College of Aberdeen*, SC (Aberdeen, 1854)
NLS	National Library of Scotland
NSC	New Spalding Club
RMS	*Register of the Great Seal of Scotland. Registrum Magni Sigilli Regum Scotorum*, 11 vols (Edinburgh, 1882–1914)

RPCS	*Register of the Privy Council of Scotland*, 38 vols (Edinburgh, 1877–1970)
RSS	*Register of the Privy Seal of Scotland. Registrum Secreti Sigilli Regum Scotorum*, 8 vols (Edinburgh, 1908–83)
SC	Spalding Club
Scott, *Fasti*	H Scott, ed., *Fasti Ecclesiae Scoticanae. The Succession of Ministers in the Church of Scotland from the Reformation*, 8 vols (Edinburgh, 1915–50)
SHS	Scottish History Society
SRO	Scottish Record Office
STS	Scottish Text Society

Notes

PROLOGUE AND EPILOGUE, pp. 1 to 6

1 Sir Thomas Craig, *De Unione Regnorum Britanniae Tractatus*, ed. C S Terry, SHS (Edinburgh, 1909), 381.

2 J Fraser, *Chronicles of the Frasers. The Wardlaw Manuscript*, ed. W Mackay, SHS (Edinburgh, 1905), 257–8, 260. The list of sports and technical terms has been left in the original spelling. This is the earliest evidence surviving for a 'silver arrow' archery contest at King's.

CHAPTER 1, pp. 7 to 19

1 J Cranstoun, ed., *Satirical Poems of the Time of the Reformation*, STS, 2 vols (Edinburgh, 1891–3), 1, 56.

2 For the progress of Reformation in both King's College and the North East in general, see B McLennan, 'The Reformation and the burgh of Aberdeen', *Northern Scotland*, 2 (1974–7), 119–44 (hereafter McLennan, 'Reformation'); G Donaldson, 'Aberdeen University and the Reformation', *Northern Scotland*, 1 (1972–3), 129–42 (hereafter Donaldson, 'Aberdeen University'); A White, 'Religion, Politics and Society in Aberdeen, 1543–1593' (Unpublished PhD thesis, University of Edinburgh, 1985) (hereafter White, 'Religion'); A White, 'The Reformation in Aberdeen', in *New Light on Medieval Aberdeen*, ed. J S Smith (Aberdeen, 1985); C H Haws, 'The diocese of Aberdeen and the Reformation', *Innes Review*, 22 (1971), 72–84 (hereafter Haws, 'Aberdeen'); and J Durkan, 'Early Humanism and King's College', *AUR*, 48 (1979–80), 259–79 (hereafter Durkan, 'Humanism').

3 White, 'Religion', e.g., 149, interprets the evidence for pre-1560 protestantism in the North East as indicating no real support for new ideas, except briefly in 1543–5. McLennan, 'Reformation', 124–7 and Donaldson, 'Aberdeen University', 132–4 tend to regard the evidence as more significant.

4 McLennan, 'Reformation', 122–3.

5   Ibid., 135–6; Donaldson, 'Aberdeen University', 135–6; R S Rait, *The Universities of Aberdeen. A History* (Aberdeen, 1895), 99 (hereafter Rait, *Universities*).

6   T Middleton, *An Appendix to the History of the Church of Scotland* (London, 1677), [39] (hereafter Middleton, *Appendix*). J Ker, *Donaides*, (Edinburgh, 1725: facsimile reprint, ed. I S Lustig, Augustan Reprint Society, Los Angeles, 1978), [4], [10] n. 12, and W Orem, *A Description of the Chanonry, Cathedral, and King's College of Old Aberdeen, in the Years 1724 and 1725* (Aberdeen, 1791), 155 (hereafter Orem, *Old Aberdeen*), also state that Anderson saved the lead. They may be simply copying Middleton, but Ker (1725) is the first to make it clear that two incidents are being confused: he blames the mob from the Mearns for stripping Aberdeen Cathedral of its lead (1569).

7   J Knox, *History of the Reformation in Scotland*, ed. W C Dickinson, 2 vols (London, 1949), 1, 353.

8   J Leslie or Lesley, *The History of Scotland*, ed. T Thomson, Bannatyne Club (Edinburgh, 1830), 293.

9   J Leslie or Lesley, *The History of Scotland Wrytten first in Latin . . . and translated into Scottish by Father James Dalrymple . . . 1596*, ed. E G Cody and W Murison, STS, 2 vols (Edinburgh, 1888–95), 2, 450. Donaldson, 'Aberdeen University', 136, assumes the debate to have taken place at the December 1560 meeting that later came to be regarded as the first meeting of the general assembly, perhaps being influenced by Knox's use of the word 'assembly'. But the meeting that Knox refers to is much more likely to have been the convention of estates of January 1561. Leslie specifically says the debate was held before the lords in the tolbooth—though the Latin version of his history mysteriously transforms this into a burgess's house.

10 White, 'Religion', 150–1, 172–3.

11 Leslie, *History of the Church of Scotland Wrytten first in Latin*, 294.

12 SRO, CS 7/20, ff. 291r-v; M H B Sanderson, *Scottish Rural Society in the 16th Century* (Edinburgh, 1982), 136; Donaldson, 'Aberdeen University', 136.

13 G Donaldson, ed., *Accounts of the Collectors of Thirds of Benefices, 1561–1572*, SHS (Edinburgh, 1949), 89, 221, 230; Innes, *Fasti*, 126–7; Donaldson, 'Aberdeen University', 137.

14 Gilbert Gardyne was a regent in the 1550s, and is recorded as borrowing books from the college library in 1557, Anderson, *Officers*, 51, and W S Mitchell, *Catalogue of the Incunabula in King's College Library*, AUS 150 (Aberdeen, 1968), 21. By 1561 he owned two works by Calvin, which he signed and dated—Calvin, *Opuscula* (Geneva, 1552) and *Praelectiones . . . Danielis* (Geneva, 1561)—AUL, π f. 2081 Cal 1 and π f. 2245 Cal). See H J H Drummond, *A Short Title Catalogue of Books, Printed on the Continent of Europe, 1501–1600, in Aberdeen University Library*, AUS 156 (Aberdeen, 1979), nos. 866, 871, 880. In the same year he became a parish minister in the new church, Scott, *Fasti*, 8, 495.

However, it is not certain that he was still a regent when he converted to Protestantism.

15 Innes, *Fasti*, xxiii; McLennan, 'Reformation', 119.

16 Durkan, 'Humanism', 259–79; McLennan, 'Reformation', 119–20; White, 'Religion', 90–133.

17 J Durkan and J Kirk, *The University of Glasgow, 1451–1577* (Glasgow, 1977), 239–40; McLennan, 'Reformation', 137–8.

18 Innes, *Fasti*, 259–72; Donaldson, 'Aberdeen University', 134–5.

19 White, 'Religion', 90–9.

20 *CSPS, 1547–63*, 649.

21 A 1567 charter mentions the principal, subprincipal, civilist, canonist, mediciner and grammarian (as well as the non-teaching sacrist) as among the college staff, and the presence of three regents in arts may be assumed (*RMS, 1546–80*, no. 2896)—certainly three were in office in 1569.

22 'Statuta et Leges Ludi Grammaticorum Aberdonensium. 1553', in *The Miscellany of the Spalding Club*, 5, ed. J Stuart, SC (Aberdeen, 1852), 399–402; G P Edwards, 'Aberdeen and its classical tradition', *AUR*, 51 (1986), 412.

23 W P D Wrightman, 'James Cheyne of Arnage', *AUR*, 35 (1953–4), 379–80; J R Pickard, 'A History of King's College Library, Aberdeen, until 1860', 4 pts (Typescript in AUL, 1979–84), pt. 2, 7; *Bibliographia Aberdonensis*, 1, 58–9; R French, 'Medical teaching in Aberdeen: from the foundation of the university to the middle of the seventeenth century', *History of Universities*, 3 (1983), 137 (hereafter French, 'Medical teaching').

24 J Knox, *History of the Reformation in Scotland*, 2, 141; Haws, 'Aberdeen', 76.

25 Donaldson, 'Aberdeen University', 137.

26 Quoted in Durkan, 'Humanism', 271.

27 Anderson, *Officers*, 29–30.

28 Innes, *Fasti*, 127–8.

29 D E R Watt, ed., *Fasti Ecclesiae Scoticanae Medii Aevi ad Annum 1638*, Scottish Record Society (Edinburgh, 1969), 375; Anderson, *Officers*, 24–5; White, 'Religion', 104–6.

30 Innes, *Fasti*, xxviii n; G F Shand, ed., *Funerals of a Right Reverend Father-in-God, Patrick Forbes of Corse, with a Biographical Memoir*, Spottiswoode Society (Edinburgh, 1845), 386 and n.

31 Middleton, *Appendix*, [39]. See also Orem, *Old Aberdeen*, 155.

32 Rait, *Universities*, 99; Innes, *Fasti*, xxviii; White, 'Religion', 4; G D Henderson, *The Founding of Marischal College, Aberdeen*, AUS 123 (Aberdeen, 1948), 52.

33 McLennan, 'Reformation', 127, 135–6.

34 W Kennedy, *Annals of Aberdeen*, 2 vols (London, 1818), 2, 314; *RSS, 1556–67*, nos. 2985, 3522; *RSS, 1567–74*, nos. 672, 1878–80, 2625; *RSS, 1575–80*, nos. 2317, 2467.

35 D Chalmers, *Davidis Camerarii Scoti. De Scotorum Fortitudine, Doctrina, et*

Pietate, ac de Ortu et Progressu haeresis in Regnis Scotiae et Angliae (Paris, 1631), 57, translated in AUL, MS M 116, p. 3507; J Robertson, ed., *Collections for a History of the Shires of Aberdeen and Banff*, SC (Aberdeen, 1843), 211–14.

36 J K Cameron, ed., *The First Book of Discipline* (Edinburgh, 1972), 58–62, 137–55.

37 *BUK*, 1, 33–4, 60; D Shaw, *The General Assemblies of the Church of Scotland, 1560–1600. Their Origins and Development* (Edinburgh, 1964), 281.

38 For an earlier, 1564, attack, see Durkan, 'Humanism', 272.

39 D Calderwood, *The History of the Kirk of Scotland*, ed D Laing, Wodrow Society, 8 vols (Edinburgh, 1842–9), 2, 380 (hereafter Calderwood, *History*); *RPCS, 1545–69*, 535; *BUK*, 1, 108. The act was ratified by parliament a few months later, *APS*, 3, 38.

40 *CSPS, 1563–9*, 455.

41 R Wodrow, *Collections upon the Lives of the Reformers and Most Eminent Ministers of the Church of Scotland*, ed. W J Duncan, Maitland Club, 2 vols (Glasgow, 1834–45), 1, 22–3.

42 *Accounts of the Lord High Treasurer of Scotland, 1566–74* (Edinburgh, 1970), 111–12, 114.

43 *BUK*, 1, 127–8, 129; Calderwood, *History*, 2, 425, 427.

44 *RPCS, 1545–69*, 608–10.

45 See note 6 above.

46 Aberdeen City Archives, Aberdeen Register of Sasines, vol 12, 5 & 6 February 1567/8. It is not certain whether the canonist at this point was Andrew Leslie or Alexander Cheyne (Anderson, *Officers*, 29–30), but both men sign one of the protestations.

47 *RPCS, 1545–69*, 675–6; Calderwood, *History*, 2, 491–2; *BUK*, 1, 141–4; R. Wodrow, *Collections upon the Lives of the Reformers*, 23–5.

48 Anderson, *Officers*, 30, 31, 35, 45, 92.

49 Haws, 'Aberdeen', 76–7; *BUK*, 1, 254; McLennan, 'Reformation', 138.

50 W J Anderson, 'Narratives of the Scottish Reformation, II, Thomas Innes on Catholicism in Scotland, 1560–1653', *Innes Review*, 7 (1956), 117; J Durkan, 'George Hay's Oration at the purging of King's College, Aberdeen, in 1569: Commentary', *Northern Scotland*, 6 (1984–5), 103 (hereafter Durkan, 'Oration').

51 Durkan, 'Oration', 103.

52 Haws, 'Aberdeen', 77.

53 Donaldson, 'Aberdeen University', 129; *RSS, 1567–74*, nos. 2030, 2125, 2198, 2205.

54 *RPCS, 1569–78*, 238; *RSS, 1567–74*, no. 1999.

55 W Cullen, 'The Chronicle of Aberdeen', in *The Miscellany of the Spalding Club*, vol 2, ed. J Stuart, SC (Aberdeen, 1842), 44.

56 *RSS, 1567–74*, no. 2032.

57   Donaldson, 'Aberdeen University', 129–32.

CHAPTER 2, pp. 20 to 40

1   The sole surviving copy of the printed oration is in the National Library
    of Scotland, *M G Hayi Oratio habita in Gymnasio Aberdonensi 2 Iulij. 1569*,
    described in *Bibliographia Aberdonensis*, 1, 304. The translation quoted is
    that of W S Watt, 'George Hay's Oration at the Purging of King's College,
    Aberdeen, in 1569: a Translation', *Northern Scotland*, 6 (1984–5), 91–6.
    For a commentary on it see Durkan, 'Oration', 97–112.
2   Durkan, 'Oration', 98.
3   Durkan, 'Humanism', 259–79.
4   *BUK*, 2, 693–4; Shaw, *The General Assemblies of the Church of Scotland*,
    152.
5   *RSS, 1567–74*, nos. 662, 663.
6   Anderson, *Officers*, 52.
7   Durkan, 'Oration', 103–8.
8   Anderson, *Officers*, 8 lists no rector until 1592, but W S Mitchell, 'The
    Common Library of New Aberdeen, 1587', *Libri. International Library
    Review*, 4 (1954), 334 states that Robert Lumsden of Clova was rector in
    1585–92. H J H Drummond, *A Short Title Catalogue of Books, Printed
    on the Continent of Europe, 1501–1600, in Aberdeen University Library*,
    AUS, 156 (Aberdeen, 1979), 304 states that he was rector 1588–92.
    Neither cites any source, but several of the books which Drummond
    lists as formerly belonging to Lumsden bear inscriptions dated 1585 which
    refer to him as rector of the university. Lumsden, an advocate, was sheriff
    depute of Aberdeenshire, D Littlejohn, ed., *Records of the Sheriff Court of
    Aberdeenshire*, NSC, 3 vols (Aberdeen, 1904–7), 1, 456–7; AUL, MS
    K 281/2/7.
9   Scott, *Fasti*, 5, 452; 6, 18, 196, 200; 8, 575. The church of Arbuthnot
    had been annexed to the university in 1497, Innes, *Fasti*, 18–25.
10 Scott, *Fasti*, 7, 364. See also J Kirk, ed., *The Second Book of Discipline*
    (Edinburgh, 1980), 43–4, 125 (hereafter Kirk, *Second Book*).
11 *BUK*, 1, 186, 190; M H B Sanderson, 'Catholic recusancy in Scotland
    in the sixteenth century', *Innes Review*, 20 (1970), 95.
12 J Spottiswood, *History of the Church of Scotland* (London, 1655), 335.
13 Durkan, 'Oration', 106; McLennan, 'Reformation', 142–3; Durkan,
    'Humanism', 273.
14 Innes, *Fasti*, 129–31.
15 Anderson, *Officers*, 25, 39; Innes, *Fasti*, 133–4.
16 *RSS, 1567–74*, no. 2032.
17 Durkan, 'Oration', 107.
18 Ibid., 103.
19 Durkan, 'Humanism', 273; 'An early Aberdeen graduation formula', *St
    Andrews University Library Bulletin*, 7 (1917), 353–6.

20   Durkan, 'Oration', 108.

21   Kirk, *Second Book*, 231n; *BUK*, 1, 305.

22   Donaldson, 'Aberdeen University', 140; Kirk, *Second Book*, 188–9.

23   Kirk, *Second Book*, 231.

24   Donaldson, 'Aberdeen University', 142; *APS*, 3, 98.

25   J. Melville, *The Autobiography and Diary of Mr James Melville*, ed. R. Pitcairn, Wodrow Society (Edinburgh, 1842), 53.

26   Anderson, *Officers*, 324–5; *APS*, 3, 98–9; Donaldson, 'Aberdeen University', 142.

27   *BUK*, 2, 434–5; Calderwood, *History*, 3, 446.

28   *RPCS, 1578–85*, 199–200.

29   R G Cant, *The University of St Andrews. A Short History* (Edinburgh, 1970), 50.

30   Anderson, *Officers*, 325; *APS*, 3, 214.

31   Anderson, *Officers*, 325–6; *BUK*, 2, 593–4; Calderwood, *History*, 3, 682.

32   *RSS, 1581–4*, no. 2254.

33   Anderson, *Officers*, 326; *BUK*, 2, 614, 624–5; Calderwood, *History*, 3, 705, 707.

34   The document is confused in its form of address: the chancellor and rector were, of course, university rather than college officials.

35   Anderson, *Officers*, 327; R Wodrow, *Selections from Wodrow's Biographical Collections. Divines of the North-East of Scotland*, ed. R. Lippe, NSC (Aberdeen, 1890), 188–9 (hereafter Wodrow, *Selections*). In 1581 there had been an earlier attempt to remove Arbuthnot from the principalship, and make him a parish minister (of Aberdeen), *BUK*, 2, 475; Wodrow, *Selections*, 187. The motivation for the two attempts is not known directly, but there were differing opinions in the church on whether to employ its best talents in the universities or in important urban parishes.

36   *BUK*, 2, 634; Calderwood, *History*, 3, 738, 742.

37   *BUK*, 2, 627, 629; Calderwood, *History*, 3, 732.

38   Anderson, *Officers*, 326; *BUK*, 2, 638; Calderwood, *History*, 3, 732.

39   Wodrow, *Selections*, 68.

40   *RSS, 1581–4*, no. 1857.

41   Ibid., no. 2254.

42   Anderson, *Officers*, 327; APS, 3, 355.

43   Anderson, *Officers*, 333.

44   An early eighteenth-century writer, Professor John Ker, dates the New Foundation to 1592 and attributes it to David Rait, but he cites no evidence for this, Anderson, *Officers*, 324; G D Henderson, *The Founding of Marischal College, Aberdeen*, AUS, 123 (Aberdeen, 1948), 23 (hereafter Henderson, *Marischal*); J Ker, *Donaides* (Los Angeles, 1978), 5, 18 [4].

45   *BUK*, 2, 811.

46   Henderson, *Marischal*, 17–18, demonstrates that the Marischal charter borrows from the Glasgow *Nova Erectio* not directly, but through the King's College New Foundation.

47 E.g., Rait, *Universities*, 249; J M Bulloch, *A History of the University of Aberdeen, 1495–1895* (London, 1895), 91; H Kearney, *Scholars and Gentlemen. Universities and Society in Pre-Industrial Britain, 1500–1700* (London, 1970), 54, 58 (hereafter Kearney, *Scholars*).

48 Henderson, *Marischal*, 17, 20.

49 Ibid., 24.

50 Ibid., 34. R G Cant, 'The Scottish universities in the seventeenth century', *AUR*, 43 (1969–70), 227 concluded that it was 'most unlikely' that the Earl Marischal intended his college to be the nucleus of a university entirely separate from that already existing in Old Aberdeen.

51 Anderson, *FAM*, 1, 64. For a recent, and extreme, re-statement of the old, discredited legend see French, 'Medical teaching', 141: 'the founder of Marischal College had sought to implement ideas that were quite opposed to those held by King's College and its patrons'.

52 AUL, James Fraser, Triennial Travels, part 1, MS 2538/1, f. 5r. Fraser undermines the credibility of his anecdote by garbling Principal David Rait's name into 'John Bate'. But the rhyme Rait/Blate works just as well as Bate/Blate, which helps to restore confidence.

53 Anderson, *FAM*, 1, 77n. The 1590s also, incidentally, saw an attempt by Sir Alexander Fraser to establish a university and college at Fraserburgh, ibid., 1, 78–9.

54 White, 'Religion', 348.

55 Anderson, *Officers*, 327–8; *APS*, 4, 153.

56 Gordon, *History*, 2, 156; Anderson, *Officers*, 328n.

57 Cant, *The University of St Andrews*, 55–6.

58 *CSPS, 1597–1603*, 57.

59 Anderson, *Officers*, 328; *APS*, 4, 576–7; Innes, *Fasti*, 140–2.

60 *RPCS, 1616–19*, xxxvi, 198n.

61 Rait, *Universities*, 124, misunderstands the act, taking it to stipulate that the principal should be dean of the faculty of arts, rather than dean of the diocese. The general assembly of 1616 had ordered a visitation of King's College (Innes, *Fasti*, 297). Nothing is known of the proceedings of the visitors, but their activities might have drawn to official attention the confusion over foundations, and thus helped inspire the 1617 act.

CHAPTER 3, pp. 41 to 60

1 D Laing, ed., *Original Letters relating to the Ecclesiastical Affairs of Scotland*, Bannatyne Club, 2 vols (Edinburgh, 1851), 2, 633 (hereafter Laing, *Original Letters*).

2 J Kirk, 'The New Foundation', in J Durkan and J Kirk, *The University of Glasgow, 1451–1577*, 276–9, 290–1 (hereafter Kirk, 'New Foundation'). Kirk's work contains the best available discussion of the impact of Melvillian reform on Scotland's universities.

3 *CSPS, 1563–9*, 455.

4   J M Bulloch, *A History of the University of Aberdeen, 1495–1895* (London, 1895), 78; Kirk, 'New Foundation', 280.

5   *BUK*, 2, 638–9; Calderwood, *History*, 3, 732, 743–5.

6   W J Ong, *Ramus, Method, and the Decay of Dialogue. From the Art of Discourse to the Art of Reason* (Cambridge, Mass., 1958), ix, 7, 29–30 (hereafter Ong, *Ramus*).

7   Donaldson, 'Aberdeen University', 141.

8   For a note on the texts of the New Foundation and an English translation see Appendix II.

9   Kirk, 'New Foundation', 289. Kirk erroneously cites Anderson, *FAM*, 2, 231 in support of this statement: the correct reference is Innes, *Fasti*, 231.

10 Ong, *Ramus*, 5.

11 *Petri Rami . . . Commentariorum* (Frankfurt, 1583), at AUL, π 2304 LaR; *Audomari Talaei Rhetorica, e P. Rami Praelectionibus Observata . . .* (Frankfurt, 1579), at AUL π 8085 Tal 1; Ong, *Ramus*, 271; W J Ong, *Ramus and Talon Inventory* (Cambridge, Mass., 1958), 82–5; H J H Drummond, *A Short Title Catalogue of Books, Printed on the Continent of Europe, 1501–1600, in Aberdeen University Library*, AUS, 156 (Aberdeen, 1979), nos. 2377, 3836 (hereafter Drummond, *STC*). Drummond fails to note the signatures of the Raits on the *Rhetoric*. Drummond, p.305 identifies the Mr William Rait who gifted these books (and forty-one others, ten of which had previously been owned by David Rait) with the William who was a regent at King's in 1641–3 and principal briefly in 1661, and was the son of James Rait who had been a regent in 1611–17. But as David's eldest son was a Mr William it seems most likely that it was he who donated his father's books to the college.

12 *Petri Rami Scholarum Mathematicorum* (Frankfurt, 1599), at AUL π 5102 LaR S2; Drummond, *STC*, no. 2387. My thanks to Patrick Edwards for the translation of Leslie's inscription.

13 J K Cameron, ed., *Letters of John Johnston . . . and Robert Howie* (Edinburgh, 1963), xiv, xvi. Cameron, 216, states that Johnston left Mercer a diamond ring, but he is confusing the two Robert Mercers to whom Johnston made bequests, *Miscellany of the Maitland Club*, vol 1, pt 2 (Edinburgh, 1834), 343. Johnston also left ten merks to Alexander Davidson, a poor scholar at King's.

14 Cameron, *Letters*, xiv, li.

15 Cameron, *Letters*, xvii. Kirk, 'New Foundation', 289; Henderson, *Marischal*, 16–17 concluded rather more cautiously that 'the evidence does afford a slight balance of probability in favour of the view that the teaching at King's College in 1593 was not markedly pre-Melville'. Kirk surprisingly concluded that not until after 1597 did the New Foundation begin to 'take effect' at King's.

16 Rait, *Universities*, 118–19; Anderson, *Officers*, 313–14.

17 Durkan, 'Humanism', 271.

18 Donaldson, 'Aberdeen University', 134–5.

19   L J Macfarlane, *William Elphinstone and the Kingdom of Scotland,*
     1431–1514. The Struggle for Order (Aberdeen, 1985), 341–2; J
     Kirk, 'Royal and lay patronage in the Jacobean kirk, 1572–1600',
     in *Church, Politics and Society. Scotland, 1408–1929,* ed. N Macdougall
     (Edinburgh, 1983), 136.

20   French, 'Medical teaching', 136; W F Skene, ed., *Tracts by Dr Gilbert*
     Skeyne, Mediciner to His Majesty, Bannatyne Club (Edinburgh, 1860), viii;
     W F Shene, *Memorials of the Family of Skene of Skene,* NSC (Aberdeen,
     1887), 95. It is possible that Skene gave up the office of mediciner for
     some years, for in 1568 he was evidently referred to merely as a regent
     (Innes, *Fasti,* lxxxv) and in the same year the title page of his tract *Ane*
     Breve Descriptioun of the Pest described him simply as a doctor in medicine.
     Thus the 1571 re-grant of the office to him possibly marks his return
     to office.

21   Anderson, *Officers,* 30.

22   Watt, *Fasti,* 25; SRO, PS 1/63, Register of the Privy Seal, ff.17v–18r.

23   Anderson, *Officers,* 8, 31; Middleton, *Appendix,* 38.

24   *RSS, 1581–4,* no. 354.

25   Henderson, *Marischal,* 24.

26   Anderson, *Officers,* 35; Skene, *Memorials,* 95–6; AUL, MS K 256/34/8,9.
     French, 'Medical teaching', 137 is incorrect in saying that Skene sold his
     manse to the college; and the suggestion that he was only allowed to retain
     office as mediciner through royal pressure (ibid., 135, 140) is rendered
     implausible by the fact that, in the parallel cases of the canonist and the
     civilist, holders of 'abolished' offices were left undisturbed in possession
     of them until they died.

27   Henderson, *Marischal,* 21.

28   Anderson, *Officers,* 45.

29   Walter Stewart's appointment as grammarian is not noted in Anderson,
     Officers: but see *RSS, 1575–80,* no. 992.

30   Anderson, *Officers,* 44, 52.

31   Scott, *Fasti,* 6, 66; Anderson, *Officers,* 93; AUL, MS K 256/10/11, and
     35/18–23; Innes, *Fasti,* 134. Innes served more than once as a baillie
     of Old Aberdeen, and a wynd there still bears his name, A M Munro,
     ed., *Records of Old Aberdeen,* NSC, 2 vols (Aberdeen, 1899–1909), 1,
     34, 37, 41, 59, 113 (hereafter Munro, *Old Aberdeen*).

32   F C Eeles, *King's College Chapel. Its Fittings, Ornaments and Ceremonial in*
     the Sixteenth Century, AUS 136 (Edinburgh, 1956), 173, 207; Anderson,
     Officers, 348. The Latin text of the New Foundation equates the economus
     with the provisor, while the Old Foundation only uses the latter word.
     Cosmo Innes, in summarising the 1549 visitation records, confuses the
     issue by translating the 'provisor' of the Latin text as 'economus', Innes,
     Fasti, table, pp.42, 43, and pp. 263, 266–7.

33   J Anderson, ed., *Calendar of the Laing Charters, 854–1837* (Edinburgh,
     1899), no. 1276; AUL, MS K 256/16/1; Munro, *Old Aberdeen,* 1, 511. In
     1589 Innes is referred to as 'commissour' of the college (Innes, *Fasti,* 134).

In 1616 John Leith, commissary of Aberdeen, calls himself 'conservator of the privileges' of King's (AUL, MS K 281/2/6). These offices appear in neither foundation, and their appearance suggests some confusion about what official dealt with college revenues.

34 Henderson, *Marischal*, 23–4.

35 AUL, MS K 256/22/11: the document has long been missing, but is described in inventories—e.g., AUL, MS K 106, P J Anderson, Inventory of the Writs and Evidents belonging to the University of Aberdeen in the Muniment Room at King's College (1891).

36 AUL, MS K 256/34/15 and 35/13–25; Scott, *Fasti*, 6, 66.

37 Innes, *Fasti*, 139.

38 Kirk, 'New Foundation', 292.

39 *BUK*, iii, 1013; *RPCS, 1604–7*, 123n. James Melville's manuscript corrupts Rait's name into 'Donald Rob', though another manuscript is cited as reading 'David Wait', J Melville, *The Autobiography and Diary of Mr James Melville*, ed. R Pitcairn, Wodrow Society (Edinburgh, 1842), 571; Calderwood, *History*, 6, 280, 326, 440. Rait did not preach at the opening of the assembly, as alleged in Scott, *Fasti*, 7, 364 and Munro, *Old Aberdeen*, 2, 205.

40 *BUK*, 3, 1086.

41 J Stuart, ed., *Selections from the Records of the Kirk Session, Presbytery and Synod of Aberdeen*, SC (Aberdeen, 1846), 66, 173, 183; A I Cameron, ed., *The Warrender Papers*, 2 vols, SHS (Edinburgh, 1931–2), 2, 323, 325, 329.

42 SRO CH 2/1/1, Aberdeen Presbytery Minutes, 1598–1610, 8 August 1600 (hereafter APM).

43 Munro, *Old Aberdeen*, 2, 205; APM, 7 August 1601.

44 Scott, *Fasti*, 6, 22.

45 APM, 2 July 1602, 20 July 1604.

46 APM, 13 July 1604.

47 APM, 27 August 1607.

48 APM, *passim*.

49 Orem, *Old Aberdeen*, 89.

50 Munro, *Old Aberdeen*, 1, 37–8. Innes was also an elder on the kirk session, APM, 19 September 1606, 27 August 1607. Earlier (1585) he had been the 'lector' or reader of the parish, AUL, MS K 256/35/16.

51 Munro, *Old Aberdeen*, 1, 38.

52 Ibid., 1, 51–2; Orem, *Old Aberdeen*, 89.

53 Munro, *Old Aberdeen*, 1, 51–3; Orem, *Old Aberdeen*, 89–90.

54 Munro, *Old Aberdeen*, 1, 42.

55 Innes, *Fasti*, 149–52; P J Anderson, ed., *Roll of Alumni in Arts of the University and King's College of Aberdeen, 1596–1860*, AUS 1 (Aberdeen, 1900), 1–3, 204 (hereafter Anderson, *Roll*). I have taken my figures for entrants from Innes, as Anderson's lists are arranged by classes rather than year of entry (a few students entered at second, third or fourth year levels).

56 L Stone, 'The educational revolution in England, 1560–1640', *Past and Present*, 28 (1964), 41–80 adds to his totals for matriculations an allowance of 20% for Oxford and 30% for Cambridge to take account of under-recording, which gives an indication of how great a problem this can be.

57 *APS*, 2, 87; 3, 14.

58 C Innes, ed., *Munimenta Alme Universitatis Glasuensis: Records of the University of Glasgow from its Foundation till 1727*, Maitland Club, 4 vols (Glasgow, 1854), 3, 64–8 (hereafter Innes, *Munimenta*).

59 D Laing, ed., *A Catalogue of the Graduates in the Faculties of Arts, Divinity and Law of the University of Edinburgh, since its Foundation*, Bannatyne Club (Edinburgh, 1858), 18–25 (hereafter Laing, *Catalogue*).

60 Anderson, *Roll*, 204.

61 Stone, 'Educational revolution', 51.

62 For the Four Nations see W M Alexander, *The Four Nations of Aberdeen University and their European Background*, AUS, 108 (Aberdeen 1934), and R N Smart, 'Some observations on the Provinces of the Scottish Universities, 1560–1850', in G W S Barrow, ed., *The Scottish Tradition. Essays in Honour of Ronald Gordon Cant* (Edinburgh, 1974), 91–106.

63 W D Geddes and W K Leask, eds, *Musa Latina Aberdonensis*, 3 vols, NSC (Aberdeen, 1892–1910), 2, 257–9 (hereafter *Musa Latina*); Anderson, *Officers*, 180.

CHAPTER 4, pp. 61 to 93

1 G F Shand, ed., *Funerals of a Right Reverend Father-in-God, Patrick Forbes of Corse, with a Biographical Memoir*, Spottiswoode Society (Edinburgh, 1845), 224 (hereafter Shand, *Funerals*).

2 W G S Snow, *The Times, Life, and Thought of Patrick Forbes, Bishop of Aberdeen 1618–1635* (London, 1952), 22–31 (hereafter Snow, *Forbes*).

3 *RMS, 1563–1608*, no. 1084.

4 Snow, *Forbes*, 46.

5 Calderwood, *History*, 7, 160–3; Snow, *Forbes*, 46–7; *Fasti*, 6, 22, 319. Forbes and Chalmers may have been related: Gilbert Burnet, *Memoir of the Life and Episcopate of William Bedell, Lord Bishop of Kilmore*, ed. E S Shuckburgh (Cambridge, 1902), preface, says Forbes may have been brought into the ministry after 'having a most terrible calamity on him in his family, which needs not be named'.

6 *Bibliographia Aberdonensis*, 1, 157–8, 161–2.

7 Snow, *Forbes*, 46–68; Shand, *Funerals*, 207–11; Laing, *Original Letters*, 2, 553–4.

8 *RPCS, 1616–19*, 547–9, 602; Snow, *Forbes*, 119; *RMS, 1609–20*, no. 2011; Innes, *Fasti*, 46, 273–5.

9 Laing, *Original Letters*, 2, 633.

10 Gordon, *History*, 2, 156–7.

11 At the time of Alexander Arbuthnot's death in 1583 the college had had sixteen silver spoons—as well as a great silver cup with a cover, AUL MS K 281/2/9.

12 Innes, *Fasti*, 275–5.

13 Ibid., 276–8.

14 SRO, RD 1/288, Register of Deeds, ff. 406r–408r. The list of overseers given in the deed differs in some respects from that in the report of the visitors, Innes, *Fasti*, 277.

15 Anderson, *FAM*, 1, 85; 2, 63n.

16 Innes, *Fasti*, 276–8; Rait, *Universities*, 124–9.

17 D Littlejohn, ed., *Records of the Sheriff Court of Aberdeenshire*, NSC, 3 vols (Aberdeen, 1904–7), 1, 475; 2, 537 (hereafter Littlejohn, *Sheriff Court*).

18 Anderson, *Officers*, 30, 31, 35, 46; R French, 'Medical teaching', 141–2 notes evidence that Dun did some teaching as mediciner.

19 Innes, *Fasti*, 275.

20 See R G Cant, *The College of St Salvator* (Edinburgh, 1950), 172–3 for similar squabbles at St Andrews between active teachers and nominal college officials.

21 Ibid., 278–80.

22 Snow, *Forbes*, 123–4; Laing, *Original Letters*, 2, 634.

23 Patrick Forbes's predecessor, Bishop Alexander Forbes, had also evidently wished to deprive Aidy (Snow, *Forbes*, 123) which suggest that Aidy was not deposed because (unlike Rait) he defied the visitors.

24 Anderson, *Officers*, 97; G D Henderson, 'The influence of Bishop Patrick Forbes', *Religious Life in Seventeenth-Century Scotland* (Cambridge, 1937), 41–2 (hereafter Henderson, 'Forbes').

25 F C Eeles, *King's College Chapel*, AUS, 136 (Edinburgh, 1956), 199.

26 Laing, *Original Letters*, 2, 634.

27 Innes, *Fasti*, 280–3; AUL, MS K 256/23/42.

28 The 1624 contract is summarised in AUL, MS K 281/4/1/21, a 1632 inhibition, Principal Leslie *contra* Andrew and Mr William Rait.

29 Scott, *Fasti*, 6, 18, 66.

30 AUL, MS K 256/18/33; Innes, *Fasti*, 144.

31 Laing, *Original Letters*, 2, 633–4.

32 AUL, MS K 256/35/26; 256/52/4–9.

33 Innes, *Fasti*, 142–3.

34 AUL, MS K 256/34/22; Littlejohn, *Sheriff Court*, 2, 349, 397.

35 AUL, MS K 256/34/17–18.

36 W M Morrison, *The Decisions of the Court of Session* 22 vols (Edinburgh, 1811–16), 10, 7945, 7948.

37 Sir Thomas Hope, *Hope's Major Practicks, 1608–1633*, ed. J A Clyde, Stair Society, 2 vols (Edinburgh, 1937), 1, 23; M P Brown, *Supplement to the Dictionary of Decisions of the Court of Session*, 5 vols (Edinburgh, 1826), 1, 45; AUL MS K 256/1/12; Littlejohn, *Sheriff Court*, 2, 349, 397. For other legal cases concerning college property see SRO, CS

7/487, ff. 74v-77v, 185r-187r, 221v-224v, 361v; CS 7/494, f.329; CS 7/843, ff.81v-83r: I owe these references to John Bannatyne.

38 AUL, MS K 256/44/72.

39 Henderson, 'Forbes', 37–8; Snow, *Forbes*, 125–30; Rait, *Universities*, 129–31.

40 Henderson, 'Forbes', 38–9.

41 Scott, *Fasti*, 7, 369–70; H R Sefton, 'Scotland's greatest theologian', *AUR*, 45 (1973–4), 348–52.

42 Anderson, *Officers*, 314–15; Rait, *Universities*, 118–19; Snow, *Forbes*, 130.

43 Innes, *Fasti*, 283–5.

44 Rait, *Universities*, 35.

45 Wodrow, *Selections*, 98; Rait, *Universities*, 166.

46 Anderson, *Officers*, 32, 35. For the royal letter appointing Gordon see C Rogers, ed., *The Earl of Stirling's Register of Royal Letters relative to the affairs of Scotland and Nova Scotia from 1615 to 1635*, Grampian Club, 2 vols (Edinburgh, 1885), 2, 585 (hereafter *Stirling Register*).

47 Sandilands also agreed to resign if he could not obtain the degree of doctor of canon law—but there is no evidence indicating that he ever did gain the degree. AUL, MS K 36, pp. 7–8; Anderson, *Officers*, 30.

48 Innes, *Fasti*, 394–5.

49 *APS*, 5, 73–5; Innes, *Fasti*, 145–149a; Anderson, *Officers*, 329.

50 *APS*, 5, 73, 75–6.

51 Similar letters were sent to the Archbishop of Glasgow and the Bishop of Edinburgh concerning their own universities, *Stirling Register*, 745–6, 747, 752; Innes, *Fasti*, 393–4.

52 AUL, MS K 281/4/2, appointment of William Leslie as common procurator.

53 AUL, MS K 36, p. 2.

54 W M Alexander, *The Four Nations at Aberdeen University and their European Background*, AUS, 108 (Aberdeen, 1934), 9 (hereafter Alexander, *Four Nations*); Anderson, *Officers*, 8n, 55.

55 Anderson, *Officers*, 68–9.

56 G D Henderson, 'A Benefactor of King's College: Professor Andrew Strachan', *AUR*, 22 (1934–5), 24 offers an alternative explanation: that John Forbes resigned his chair because he was so poorly paid, but returned to it after inheriting the family estates on his father's death, as this solved his financial problems. But there appears to be no evidence to support this conjecture.

57 Innes, *Fasti*, 57.

58 Ibid., 394.

59 Ibid., 396.

60 Henderson, 'Forbes', 39 (copied word for word in Snow, *Forbes*, 134, without acknowledgement) indicates that by this time there was joint teaching of theology by the staff of the two colleges: all postgraduate theology students had to study both at King's and Marischal. But the

evidence cited is unconvincing: nearly a century later a biographer of Archbishop James Sharp (a King's graduate of 1637) said he had studied under the divinity professors of both Aberdeen colleges. See J Buckroyd, *The Life of James Sharp, Archbishop of St Andrews, 1618–1679. A Political Biography* (London, 1987), 11.

61   Innes, *Fasti*, 395; AUL, MS K 36, pp. 5, 8.

62   Innes, *Fasti*, 304–10.

63   Ibid., 399–400, 534.

64   Ibid., 400–1.

65   *Stirling Register*, 2, 779–80; Innes, *Fasti*, 401–3.

66   Innes, *Fasti*, 400, 403; See also AUL MS K 36, p. 22. For Davidson see J Small, 'William Davidson', *Proceedings of the Society of Antiquaries of Scotland*, 10 (1872–4), 265–80.

67   P J Anderson, 'Notes on the University Libraries', *Aberdeen University Calendar, 1893–4* (Aberdeen, 1893), appendices, pp. 78, 89 (hereafter Anderson, 'Libraries').

68   AUL MS K36, pp13–15.

69   Innes, *Fasti*, 396–404; AUL MS K 36, pp. 16–17, 24. Snow, *Forbes*, 131 erroneously states that at this visitation the regents were censured for laxity in teaching. This is a misunderstanding. They were indeed 'censured'—meaning examined as part of the visitation—and their conduct approved.

70   Shand, *Funerals*, 235–51, 359–62, 383–9, 447.

71   Ibid., 224, 231.

72   Innes, *Fasti*, 280, 401, 534–5; Anderson, 'Libraries', 78.

73   Anderson, *Officers*, 73.

74   Ibid., 97–8.

75   G D Henderson, 'The Aberdeen Doctors', *The Burning Bush. Studies in Scottish Church History* (Edinburgh, 1957), 79–82 (hereafter Henderson, 'Aberdeen Doctors'); D Macmillan, *The Aberdeen Doctors. A Notable Group of Scottish Theologians of the First Episcopal Period* (London, 1909), (hereafter Macmillan, *Aberdeen Doctors*); J Forbes, *The First Book of the Irenicum: a contribution to the Theology of Re-Union*, ed. E G Selywn (Cambridge, 1923).

76   Henderson, 'Aberdeen Doctors', 86–7.

77   See *Bibliographia Aberdonensis*, index under Baron.

78   H Kearney, *Scholars*, 89.

79   C Shepherd, 'Philosophy and Science in the Arts Curriculum of the Scottish Universities in the 17th Century' (Unpublished Ph D thesis, University of Edinburgh, 1975), 83; Kearney, *Scholars* 89.

80   G D Henderson, 'A Benefactor of King's College: Professor Andrew Strachan', *AUR*, 22 (1934–5), 25–7 (hereafter Henderson, 'Strachan').

80   Kearney, *Scholars*, 89.

81   Shepherd, 'Philosophy', 290.

82   Kearney, *Scholars*, 89.

83   E S Shuckburgh, ed., *Two Biographies of William Bedell* (Cambridge, 1902),

preface to 'Memoir' by G Burnet; E Hyde, Earl of Clarendon, *The History of the Rebellion and Civil Wars in England*, ed. W D Macray, 6 vols (Oxford, 1888), 1, 110; Henderson, 'Forbes', 36.

84 Henderson, 'Aberdeen Doctors', 81.

85 H R Sefton, 'Scotland's greatest theologian', *AUR*, 45 (1973–4), 348–52.

86 Innes, *Fasti*, xxxvi; W K Leask's more extreme denunciation of Patrick Forbes for reducing King's 'to the position of a church training college for the education of a sect'—the episcopalians—(*Musa Latina*, 2, xv-xvi) is absurd. Indeed the denunciation could be applied much more appropriately to the Melvillians and their presbyterian 'sect' which had abolished the faculties of law and medicine than to Forbes who at least sought to restore them.

87 Anderson, *Officers*, 46–7, 54; *Bibliographia Aberdonensis*, 1, 253; SRO, GD 86/537, Fraser Charters—letters of admission of John Lundie.

88 Anderson, *Officers*, 35–6; *Stirling Register*, 2, 585.

89 *RPCS, 1635–7*, 228–9.

90 French, 'Medical teaching', 148.

91 Anderson, *Officers*, 30, 32; *RMS, 1620–33*, nos. 1007, 1411; Littlejohn, *Sheriff Court*, 2, 311.

92 Anderson, *FAM*, 2, 11.

93 Snow, *Forbes*, 92; J R Pickard, 'A History of King's College Library, Aberdeen, until 1860', 4pts (Typescript in AUL, 1979–84), 35–6.

94 See P J Anderson, *Notes on Academic Theses with Bibliography of Duncan Liddell*, AUS 58 (Aberdeen, 1912); J F K Johnstone, 'The lost Aberdeen theses', *Aberdeen University Library Bulletin*, 2 (1913–15), 739–51; and J F K Johnstone, 'The lost Aberdeen theses', *Aberdeen University Library Bulletin*, 4 (1918–22), 415–23.

95 W L Davidson, 'The university contribution to philosophy', *Studies in the History and Development of the University of Aberdeen. A Quatercentenary Tribute paid by Certain of Her Professors and Her Devoted Sons*, AUS 19 (Aberdeen, 1906), 73–4.

96 Henderson, 'Strachan', 25.

97 *Bibliographia Aberdonensis*, 1, 254. What is supposed to be a description of King's College at this time is contained in David Chalmers, *De Scotorum Fortitudine, Doctrina et Pietate* (Paris, 1631), reprinted in J Robertson, ed., *Collections for a History of the Shires of Aberdeen and Banff* SC (Aberdeen, 1843), 211–14. See W Knight, Collections, vol. 8 (AUL, MS M 116), pp. 3505–8 for an English summary. However, this is not a source to rely on: having described life at King's the author goes on to list (presumably out of excessive local patriotism) *five* other colleges in Aberdeen. As Knight mildly commented, one wonders somewhat at his impudence!

98 Anderson, *Theses*, 4–5; W. Lauder, Panegyricus (AUL, MS K 139—a copy made in 1908).

99 The presence of a printer in Aberdeen may well account for the arrival of the town's first known bookbinder a few years later. Francis van

Hagen, an Englishman of German extraction, provided this service for the colleges and private customers. W S Mitchell, *A History of Scottish Bookbinding, 1432 to 1650*, AUS, 134 (Aberdeen, 1955), 97.

100 Shand, *Funerals*.

101 There are of course exceptions—like George Jamesone, Scotland's most gifted painter of the age, who though an Aberdonian has no traceable connection with Forbes or the colleges, though he painted portraits of James Sandilands (see p. 92 above) and Patrick Dun.

102 Wodrow, *Selections*, 98.

103 Innes, *Fasti*, 149a–149i, from AUL, MS K 286. Payments in kind have been converted into money using the Aberdeenshire fiars prices for 1632, as the prices for 1633–48 inclusive are lacking, D Littlejohn, ed., 'Summary of fiars prices in Aberdeenshire', *Miscellany of the New Spalding Club*, 2 (Aberdeen, 1908), 18–19.

104 AUL, MS K 281/3/3.

105 See Appendix I below, pp. 146–8.

106 SRO, RD 1/545, ff.129v–130v, contract of 20 October 1631 between the college staff and Thomas Merser in Old Aberdeen, appointing Merser provisor for 1631–2. Among his duties were brewing ale within the college and baking oat bread within or outside it, from the college's own meal.

107 Innes, *Fasti*, 456–62.

108 Figures calculated from Laing, *Catalogue*, 25–58; Innes, *Munimenta*, 3, 205; and Anderson, *Roll*, 205. As with student numbers cited in the previous chapter, it must be emphasised that these are very approximate figures, taken from very imperfect records.

109 Contributors to the memorial volume for Patrick Forbes include four Aberdeen students of theology. One can be traced as an arts student at King's in earlier years, one at Marischal: Shand, *Funerals*, 414, 418, 422, 456; Anderson, *Officers*, 185; Anderson, *FAM*, 2, 206.

110 Innes, *Fasti*, 291, 292.

111 Ibid., 275, 280.

112 Gordon, *History*, 2, 156, quoted in Anderson, *Officers*, 328n.

113 SRO, GD 45/14/20, Dalhousie Muniments, transcribed in full in Appendix IV.

CHAPTER 5, pp. 94 to 123

1 Shand, *Funerals*, 447.

2 R Baillie, *Letters and Journals*, ed. D Laing, Bannatyne Club, 3 vols (Edinburgh, 1841–2), 1, 436 (hereafter Baillie, *Letters*); Wodrow, *Selections*, 122.

3 Gordon, *History*, 2, 157.

4 Ibid., 3, 231; Middleton, *Appendix*, 25; Sir T Urquhart, *Works*, Maitland Club (Edinburgh, 1834), 262.

5   AUL, MS K 36, pp. 24, 25–6; AUL, MS K 279/4.
6   Munro, *Old Aberdeen*, 1, 64–5.
7   AUL, MS K 36, pp. 30, 31.
8   *RPCS, 1635–7*, 311–12.
9   BL, MS Add 23112, Register of the Secretary of State for Scotland, f. 46v.
10 *RPCS, 1635–7*, 364.
11 Innes, *Fasti*, 405.
12 AUL, MS K 36, pp. 37, 38; Innes, *Fasti*, 405.
13 AUL, MS K 36, p. 36.
14 Ibid., p. 37.
15 Ibid., pp. 31, 32, 34–5.
16 Ibid., p. 35.
17 *RPCS, 1635–7*, 469.
18 Ibid., 469–70. Leech is recorded in 1636 living in Old Aberdeen with his wife and her two bairns (by a previous marriage?) and servants, Munro, *Old Aberdeen*, 1, 349.
19 Ibid., 478–9, 692. For a draft of a similar commission relating to Glasgow see *RPCS, 1544–1660*, 460–1.
20 Huntly's other two sons entered the college in 1638 and 1642, Anderson, *Officers*, 4; Innes, *Fasti*, 460, 464; J Spalding, *Memorialls of the Trubles in Scotland*, ed. J Stuart, SC, 2 vols (Aberdeen, 1850–1), 2, 216 (hereafter Spalding, *Memorialls*).
21 *Stirling Register*, 2, 599. Had Huntly himself been openly Catholic he would not have been able to send his children to King's: in 1629 nobles suspected of Catholicism were ordered to send their sons to the universities of Edinburgh, Glasgow or St Andrews, *RPCS, 1629–30*, 20–1. Presumably the omission of the Aberdeen colleges reflects a fear that the strength of Catholicism in the area would enable such students to keep in contact with the old faith.
22 *Musa Latina*, 2, 239–40; D Leech, *Philosophia Illachrymans* (Aberdeen, 1637).
23 AUL, MS K 36, p. 41.
24 Ibid., p 42; Innes, *Fasti*, 406–7.
25 AUL, MS K 36, pp. 44, 45; Innes, *Fasti*, 407–8.
26 BL, MS Add 23112, f. 72v. The letter is dated 1 September, but Anderson, *Officers*, 329 misdates it 7 October through misunderstanding a passage in Innes, *Fasti*, 287.
27 Innes, *Fasti*, 408.
28 Ibid., 409; BL, MS Add 23112, ff. 80r, 82r.
29 Innes, *Fasti*, 286.
30 Anderson, *Officers*, 330.
31 The original charter, AUL, K 256/48/3, is endorsed as having been produced before the visitors.
32 Innes, *Fasti*, 286–8.
33 Ibid., 290.

34   Ibid., 291–5.
35   Ibid., 295–303; W Kennedy, *Annals of Aberdeen*, 2 vols (Aberdeen, 1818), 2, 375–7, 439–42.
36   BL, MS Add 23112, f. 84r.
37   Innes, *Fasti*, 411.
38   SRO, GD 45/14/20, Dalhousie Muniments, transcribed in Appendix IV below, pp. 169–71. The letter refers to a 'Mr Leith' as Maule's cousin and a contact between him and the college. This may be David Leech, whose name is often spelled Leitch or Leith. There are references to Maule and the college in Sir T Hope, *Diary*, ed. T Thomson, Bannatyne Club (Edinburgh, 1843), 37, 55.
39   BL, MS Add 23112, f. 85v.
40   Acts, chapter 18, verses 12–17.
41   S Rutherford, *Letters*, ed. A A Bonar, 3rd edn (Edinburgh, 1891), 149, 189, 163, 191, 239, 275, 300, 340, 346, 410. John Forbes was certainly involved in the plan for uniting the Calvinist and Lutheran churches, M C Kitshoff, 'Aspects of Arminianism in Scotland' (Unpublished M Th thesis, University of St Andrews, 1968), 125 (hereafter Kitshoff, 'Arminianism').
42   AUL, MS 635A, Diary or Spiritual Exercises of John Forbes of Corse, 1624–47, p. 81 (hereafter Forbes, Diary). For the general character of this work see G D Henderson, 'A Scottish diary of the seventeenth century', *London Quarterly Review*, 151 (1929), 88–97.
43   BL, MS Add 23112, f. 82r.
44   SRO, GD 406/1/416, 432, 639, Hamilton Muniments; J Forbes, *A Peaceable Warning to the Subjects in Scotland* (Aberdeen, 1638).
45   For general studies of the six doctors see MacMillan, *Aberdeen Doctors*; Henderson, 'Aberdeen Doctors'; and Kitshoff, 'Arminianism'.
46   Kitshoff, 'Arminianism', 124–39, 141.
47   Anderson, *Officers*, 47; D Stevenson, 'The National Covenant: A List of Known Copies', *Records of the Scottish Church History Society* 23, pt 2 (1988), 287–8, no. 11.3—but Lundie's signature indicates that this copy was signed in Aberdeen in July 1638, not April 1639 as indicated in the list.
48   G D Ogilvie, 'The Aberdeen Doctors and the National Covenant', *Papers of the Edinburgh Bibliographical Society*, 11 (1912–20), 73–86.
49   SRO, GD 406/1/433, 664, 764; Forbes, Diary, 88.
50   J Leslie, Earl of Rothes, *A Relation of Proceedings concerning the affairs of the Kirk of Scotland*, ed. D Laing, Bannatyne Club (Edinburgh, 1830), 185–6; SRO, GD 406/1/664, 677, 725.
51   SRO, GD 406/1/446.
52   SRO, GD 406/1/446, 451, 457, 665, 666, 668.
53   Gordon, *History*, 1, 153–5.
54   Innes, *Fasti*, 411–14; Gordon, *History*, 1, 154–5; Baillie, *Letters*, 135.
55   Gordon, *History*, 1, 154, 155, 157; Baillie, *Letters*, 1, 170–1; Spalding, *Memorialls*, 1, 114–15, 121, 139.

56 Baillie, *Letters*, 1, 491–2; A Peterkin, ed., *Records of the Kirk of Scotland, containing the Acts and Proceedings of the General Assemblies* (Edinburgh, 1838), 47 (hereafter Peterkin, *Records*); Gordon, *History*, 1, 224–5n.

57 Innes, *Fasti*, 411–14; Spalding, *Memorialls*, 139–40; J Row, *The History of the Kirk of Scotland*, ed. D Laing, Wodrow Society (Edinburgh, 1842), 506.

58 Anderson, *Officers*, 46–7.

59 Gordon, *History*, 2, 219–21.

60 Spalding, *Memorialls*, 1, 139–40, 147, 151; Gordon, *History*, 2, 225; Forbes, *Diary*, 102.

61 NLS, MS Wodrow, Folio LXIII, no. 77 (f. 215r).

62 Spalding, *Memorialls*, 1, 165–6, 187–8; Forbes, *Diary*, 102.

63 Gordon, *History*, 2, 224–5.

64 Spalding, *Memorialls*, 2, 231–2.

65 Ibid., 1, 166.

66 Peterkin, *Records*, 257, 262; NLS, MS Wodrow, Folio LXIII, no. 63 (f. 128r).

67 SRO, CH 1/1/4, 1639, p. 69.

68 NLS, MS Wodrow, Folio LXIII, no. 77 (f. 215r); Peterkin, *Records*, 209.

69 AUL, MS K 36, p. 52; Spalding, *Memorialls*, 1, 232–3; Gordon, *History*, 3, 225; Innes, *Fasti*, 414–15.

70 AUL, MS K 36, pp. 53, 54–5.

71 Spalding, *Memorialls*, 1, 241. Spalding was a royalist and traditionalist, but his hostility to Sandilands probably derives from the fact that he himself was a student at King's in 1640–4 and had heard the regents complaining about him, D Stevenson, 'Who was John Spalding?', *AUR*, 51 (1985), 107.

72 Innes, *Fasti*, 415–16; Spalding, *Memorialls*, 260–1, 260n; See also AUL, MS K 36, p. 61 for Sandilands' salary.

73 Spalding, *Memorialls*, 1, 257.

74 A bequest by Dr Alexander Reid, who died in 1639, included money intended for a modest increase in regents' stipends, Innes, *Fasti*, 534.

75 Spalding, *Memorialls*, 1, 232–3n; Forbes, *Diary*, 144, 147, 161.

76 Spalding, *Memorialls*, 1, 260 and n, 300–1 and n; Forbes, *Diary*, 223.

77 Spalding, *Memorialls*, 1, 310–13, 318–19; Peterkin, *Records*, 279; Gordon, *History*, 3, 221, 226–7, 256–7; Alexander, *Four Nations*, 9.

78 Gordon, *History*, 3, 231.

79 Spalding, *Memorialls*, 1, 310–11, 312, 313, 318–19; Gordon, *History*, 3, 226–34, 224, 256–7; Forbes, *Diary*, 245–6; Macmillan, *Aberdeen Doctors*, 272–6.

80 Forbes, *Diary*, 284.

81 Spalding, *Memorialls*, 2, 17–18 & n, 57.

82 Anderson, *Officers*, 315.

83 Kearney, *Scholars*, 130–3.

84 AUL, MS K 36, p. 66.

85 Peterkin, *Records*, 293–4.
86 J K Cameron, ed., *The First Book of Discipline* (Edinburgh, 1972), 60, 143–4, 161–2.
87 Innes, *Fasti*, 150–6; *APS*, 5, 475; *RMS, 1634–51*, no. 1012; Anderson, *FAM*, 1, xvi, 255–6. The new revenues due to King's were estimated at 4,000 merks a year—about £220 sterling (Innes, *Fasti*, 536). Spalding puts the total bishopric revenues at 8,000 merks a year, which would have meant King's College's share was 5,333 merks a year (Spalding, *Memorialls*, 2, 85).
88 *RPCS, 1638–43*, 487; Innes, *Fasti*, 156–7.
89 Anderson, *Officers*, 4.
90 Ibid., 25–7. William Guild achieved the uncomfortable distinction of being deposed twice, first by the covenanters in 1649 and then again in 1651 by the country's English conquerors.

Appendix I

Establishments and Salaries under the Old and New Foundations

THE OLD FOUNDATION: THE 1529 CHARTER

The figures set out below are derived from Bishop Dunbar's Charter of 1529 (which confirmed Bishop Elphinstone's second foundation of the college of 1514) and the New Foundation of the 1590s. Obviously they do not tell the full story: the regents had the tuition fees paid by their students; the grammarian would have had his fees as master of the grammar school; and the salary of the provisor is not specified.

I am most grateful to Dr Leslie Macfarlane for helping me with some details of the figures set out below. The totals given for the salaries of the eight prebends include small amounts for providing vestments and undertaking extra duties. They are thus partly intended to cover extra expenses incurred.

Teaching	Principal	£26.13s.4d.
Staff:	Canonist	£26. 6s.8d.
	Civilist	£20
	Mediciner	£13. 6s.8d.
	Grammarian	£13. 6s.8d.
	Subprincipal	£13. 6s.8d.
Postgraduate	6 Students of Theology/	£10 × 6 = £60
Students/	Regents in Arts	
Teachers:	2 Students of Civil Law	£10 × 2 = £20
	1 Student of Canon Law	£8
Undergraduate	12 Arts Students	£8 × 12 = £96
Bursars:	1 Arts Student	£5
Chapel	5 Prebends	£11 × 5 = £55
Staff:	1 Prebend (Cantor)	£14
	1 Prebend (Sacrist)	£15. 6s.8d.
	1 Prebend (Organist)	£12. 6s.8d.
	5 Choristers	£2.13s.4d × 5 = £13. 6s.8d.
	1 Chorister (Bell Ringer)	£4

Fee to member of staff who acted as
             Procurator   £3. 6s.8d.

Total Salaries,   42 staff and bursars: £416. 6s.8d.

To be set aside for maintenance of
             buildings   £40
To be set aside for wax, wine, etc.
             for services   £6.13s.4d.

TOTAL RECURRENT EXPENDITURE SPECIFIED: £463

Sources:
Innes, *Fasti*, 13–17.
F C Eeles, ed., *King's College Chapel, Aberdeen. Its Fittings, Ornaments and Ceremonial in the Sixteenth Century*, AUS 136 (Edinburgh, 1956), 207–31.

THE NEW FOUNDATION
The figures given below take no account of the tuition fees of the regents and the grammar school fees of the grammarian. Provision was made for revising salaries upwards once the college's financial position improved. The two servants were assigned to the principal and subprincipal and were paid by them.

The elements of salaries payable in kind (bolls of oatmeal or barley) have been converted into money according to the earliest surviving fiars prices for Aberdeenshire, those struck in April 1604 for the 1603 crop. The price then struck was £2.13s.4d. a boll for ferme meal: D Littlejohn, ed., 'Summary of Fiars Prices in Aberdeenshire, 1603–19', *Miscellany of the New Spalding Club*, 2 (Aberdeen, 1908), 15.

Teaching Staff:	Principal	£133.6s.8d. + 24 bolls = £197.6s.8d.
	Subprincipal/Regent	£80 + 24 bolls = £144
	3 Regents in Arts	£47.17s.0d. + 16 bolls = £90.10s.4d. × 3 = £271.11s.0d.
	Grammarian	£53. 6s.8d.
Undergraduate Bursars:	12 Bursars	£30 × 12 = £360
Servants:	Economus	£66.13s.4d. + 6 bolls = £82.13s.4d.
	Cook/Gardener	£30
	2 Servants	
Total Salaries	22 staff and bursars:	£1146.17s.8d.

To be set aside for maintenance of
                   buildings   £40

TOTAL RECURRENT EXPENDITURE SPECIFIED: £1186.17s.8d.

Source:
Anderson, *Officers*, 334–48.

Appendix II

The New Foundation

Translation by G Patrick Edwards

As already explained (see pages 88, 90 and 93 above) the original text of the *Nova Fundatio* in the possession of the college was deliberately destroyed in the early seventeenth century, but secretly a copy of it had been made prior to its destruction.

The oldest surviving text, presumably deriving directly or indirectly from this copy, was made by Professor Thomas Gordon (died 1797), and can be found in volume 2 of his collections on King's College, AUL, MS K 35, pp. 181, 183, 187, 191, 195, 199, 203, 207, 211, 211b, 213 (the text is split up in this way through Gordon interleaving it with many 'parallel places' from the foundation charter of Marischal College and a few from the *Nova Erectio* of St Andrews).

A second surviving text is provided by Professor Thomas Knight (died 1844) in volume 5 of his collections on Marischal College, AUL, MS M 113, pp. 1787–1832. Though detailed comparison of these two texts has yet to be undertaken, this would appear to have been copied from Gordon's texts, gaps being left for a few words Knight found illegible.

Finally, there is a late nineteenth century copy which appears to have been made from Knight's text for the use of P J Anderson. Pencil markings made in Knight running together paragraphs probably represent Anderson's instructions to his copyist. The margins of this copy include notes and translations of a few passages, presumably Anderson's work (AUL, MS K 102). The text published (with a short English summary) in Anderson, *Officers*, 335–48 evidently derives from this K 102 version. This is consistent with Anderson's own statement that his transcript is based on Knight's text collated with Gordon's (Anderson, *Officers*, 324).

The text of the New Foundation as it appears in the copies listed above is undated, but it must have been compiled no earlier than March 1587 (as it mentions a gift made to the college that month) and no later than April 1593 (as the foundation charter of Marischal College contains borrowings from it).

For comparison see the *Nova Erectio* of Glasgow, 1577, on which the New Foundation of King's College was based, in J Durkan and J Kirk,

The University of Glasgow, 1451–1577 (Glasgow, 1977), 430–48 (Latin, and English translation); the New Foundation of St Andrews, 1579, in *APS*, 3, 178–82; and the foundation charter of Marischal College in Anderson, *FAM*, 1, 39–77 (Latin, and English translation).

The translation which follows tries to provide a reasonably readable version of the text in modern English: it sticks as closely to the Latin wording as is compatible with this, but in places where a verbatim translation would render the meaning obscure, the general sense of the Latin rather than its literal wording has been conveyed as far as possible.

Sub-headings have been inserted to break up the text and guide the reader through it, though the construction of the document is such that they can only indicate the main subjects dealt with in each section. The division into paragraphs in Knight is similar to that in Gordon, but K 102 and Anderson's published text made many alterations, mainly running together short paragraphs. The paragraphing in the translation that follows is modern, but a double oblique (//) has been placed in the translation at the end of each of Gordon's paragraphs, whether or not this corresponds with the translation's paragraphs.

The translator wishes to thank David Stevenson for his collaboration throughout the preparation of what follows, and for providing the accompanying notes. He is not to blame for any errors or clumsinesses that remain in the translation.

THE NEW FOUNDATION

Introduction
JAMES the Sixth by grace of God King of Scots, to all and sundry who are truly Christians, greeting.

Whereas it belongs to the care of a pious ruler and to the concern of royal office, not only duly to institute and set in order the commonwealth and its parts, but also, if anything among these be changed for the worse by the degeneracy of the time, or be fallen to ruin through negligence, or have lapsed in morals, to bring back the whole of it to its first origin, or to re-establish it in a better condition and to reform it; and whereas this needs to be done diligently in all parts of the commonwealth and most chiefly in that part which pertains to the honourable education of youth, and so is directly the beginning and nursery for the rest, it needs such diligent care and constant work that virtually in the right instituting of this one thing lies the well-being of the commonwealth and its preservation, and in the neglect of the same lies its collapse and death; and whereas it is proper for us to strive for those things above all, since Divine Providence has brought us to the governing of the commonwealth in those very times in which she has willed the light of the Gospel to shine forth upon this Scotland of ours (the dark shadows of popery being driven out), and it behoves us especially to be concerned that so great a benefit should be extended to our posterity, which cannot be brought about more advantageously by any other means than by sound education of that kind and by the right fashioning of youth: we therefore, desirous of extending our royal care and fatherly concern to this so useful and necessary part of our commonwealth, after the reforming and establishment of the Universities of St Andrews and Glasgow, duly carried through and ratified by us with the counsel of the most eminent men, have thought, again with the counsel of the most eminent men, that our King's College of Aberdeen also, no small nursery of our commonwealth in the northern parts of our kingdom in the right establishment of letters and morals, should in part be established and founded now for the first time, and in part be reformed and re-established and altogether truly ordered and established in the best way that it is possible to be done. And although the foundations of this splendid work—laid by our forbears with the counsel of the Bishops of Aberdeen— are not to be regretted, yet since that age tolerated many things which do not conform with the clear light of the Gospel in these our own times, and since the slight and meagre resources, which in those days were determined for sustaining the members of that college in accordance with the standard of the time, in today's inflation of costs can in no way be sufficient to support those same, we have reckoned it a worthwhile reward for our trouble that we can prescribe for this our gymnasium, generously enlarged by us with new revenues, that law which seems best able to serve the glory of God, the well-being of the church, the commonwealth, the collective advantage of our people and, lastly, these enlightened[1] times of ours.

Endowments
First, therefore, so that money and resources should not be lacking to this gymnasium of ours, whatever sources of income have been apportioned and granted by our forbears, by William Elphinstone Bishop of Aberdeen, or by any others before our time, we hold all these as confirmed, we approve and ratify them by our authority, and to the extent that we are able we present them afresh: that is to say, the entire and complete rectories and vicarages of the parish churches of Glenmuick, Abergerny, Slains, Forvie, Aberlethnott and Snaw [Old Aberdeen], with all the teinds of the same, their fruits, profits, rents, emoluments, dues, manses, glebes, kirklands and pertinents of the same whatever, situated in the dioceses of Aberdeen and St Andrews and the sheriffdoms of Aberdeen and Kincardine respectively. Likewise the lands, wholly and severally, of Drumlagair; likewise the lands of Bonakettle, Audiale, Berryhill, Collynie and Andet, and certain crofts situated in Aberdeen; situated in the sherrifdoms of Banff and Aberdeen respectively. // Likewise all the rents following: £20 from the barony of Belhelvie; 19 merks from our royal waters of Banff; £12. 6s. 8d. from the lands of Ord, Monbray, Blairshinnoch and other neighbouring lands of Boyne; £5 from the lands of Udoch; and £4 from Pettie. Likewise the annual rents and feu duties from the lands of the hospital of Saint Germain situated in any place within the bounds of the kingdom of Scotland. Likewise the lands in which the said college is situated, with adjacent gardens and crofts, with the manses and buildings of the canonist, civilist, mediciner

and grammarian, with all other and sundry teinds, annualrents from the land, chaplainries, and any other revenues granted before our time, whether by our forbears, by the bishops of Aberdeen, or by any others, to the aforesaid college, or possessed in any way at all by the said college, as is contained more fully in charters and deeds of gift of the same. // All of which we ratify, approve and confirm for ourselves and our successors in perpetuity.

But because, as we have said, the rents and revenues aforementioned would be not only too modest to sustain the proper number of teachers and students, and were not sufficient to support so great a household in the present expensiveness of all things and inflation of costs, we have by our munificence, on the advice of our counsellors, given, granted, incorporated, and committed in mortmain to the same college, its masters, teachers, and to the students in the same, and to the other members of the same which shall be named hereafter, and moreover by these presents we give, grant, incorporate and commit in mortmain for ever all the rents, fruits, teinds, garbal teinds[2], emoluments, revenues, buildings, lands, gardens, church manses and glebes, their profits and other things of all kinds pertaining to the cathedral church of Old Aberdeen, which is the parish church of St Machar, the rectory and vicarage of the same, and is called the deanery of the cathedral church of Aberdeen. Likewise all teinds, feu duties, annualrents, and revenues of the church of Forvie, which is called the rectory and vicarage of Forvie. Likewise all the teinds, rents, revenues, emoluments, buildings, gardens, lands, manses, glebes and all else which formerly pertained to the Carmelite friars of Banff. Likewise all teinds, rents, revenues, emoluments, buildings, gardens, lands, church manses, glebes and other possessions of the church of Saint Peter, which is called the church of Spital, or succentorship of Aberdeen. Likewise all teinds, rents and revenues of the church of Methlick, which is called the rectory and vicarage of Methlick. Likewise the chaplainries which they call those of Westhall and Folla Rule, and the 300 merks which John Chrystison of the Carmelite friars left to the same college. Likewise all annualrents, fields and buildings pertaining to the chaplainry of Mary Magdalene occupied and possessed through the late Master John Kennedy, and all annualrents which formerly belonged in common to the chaplainry of the said college, with all other lands, buildings, profits, teinds, annualrents, feu duties, rights, jurisdictions, and whatsoever payments which have been made to the aforesaid college, its masters, regents, bursars or members, whether by our forbears or by us, either by agreement of the regents or through our council, or in whatever way, whether by bishops of Aberdeen of earlier time, or that have been up to this time granted, presented or assigned in any way by any others, or whatever the said college or persons on its foundation as heretofore, possess, have possessed or may be able to possess in any way.

All these things we approve to remain in perpetuity, we ratify, and, for ourselves and our successors, we confirm in perpetuity by our royal authority to the same college, and to the members who are to be established within it.//

In order that this generosity of ourselves or of our predecessors may be understood as being responsibly administered, and that these rents gathered together by us for our college may be duly spent to the advantage of the Christian commonwealth, we wish that in this particular all superfluous and unprofitable things which relate either to persons and members of the college or to other offices and duties, be cut out and amputated; and likewise all those things of the past which either do not accord with these times of ours or are not fully in agreement with the clear light of the Gospel (by which now, through the grace of God, our kingdom is illuminated); and that this our college of learned people, now at last reformed and renewed, be instituted for 22 ordinary or resident persons: a gymnasiarch whom they call principal; four regents, of whom the first shall be subprincipal; a teacher of grammar; an economus [steward]; 12 poor students [bursars]; two servants, one the principal's, one the subprincipal's; and a cook; each of whom we wish individually to be diligent in pursuing his own duties, and for their labours to receive honoraria and stipends, whereby they may watch over their offices with greater alacrity. Most importantly, our wish is that all 22 persons (with the exception of the teacher of grammar) are to live collegiately, that is to say, that they are to take their meals and sleep within the bounds of the college together.//

The Principal

The gymnasiarch, whom they call principal, must be first and foremost a godly and upright man, being one to whom the whole college and its several members must be subject; to him we commit ordinary jurisdiction over the individual persons of our college. He must be thoroughly proficient in the Holy Scriptures, well qualified to open the mysteries of the faith and the hidden treasures of the Divine Word, knowledgeable and skilled in languages also, but particularly in Hebrew and Syriac, as professor of which we appoint him (for we desire him to promote the sacred tongue, as is right, among our subjects, so that the fountainheads and mysteries of the Scriptures be more directly opened). Therefore we commit to our said gymnasiarch, in order that, by his diligence, he may provide an example of assiduity to the whole college, that every day[3] he should devote at least one hour to prelecting [lecturing], at the time which shall be most suitable, and every second day by turns he should choose a theological prelection, for expounding the profundities of the Scriptures, and on the intervening days he shall explain the sacred tongue itself [Hebrew] to his audience; and at his prelection we wish all the regents and [the classes] of the two most senior to be present;[4] but on Saturday we allow him to be free from prelections, since he needs to obtain from his hearers an account of the whole week,[5] and effort needs to be given to preparing the sermon for the people of St Machar's parish (for since our college is sustained in part by the teinds and revenues of that church, we have thought it just[6] that those who provide the temporal things should receive the spiritual things, and not be deprived of the bread of life, which is the Word of God); therefore the gymnasiarch shall apply the most diligent care, as far as he shall be able, to the end that he should feed the people then and hold them in the right discipline of life and morals, and on each Sunday exhort them to holiness.

Therefore let him reside in the said college and not move his foot from there for any lengthy excursion, unless he has communicated the matter to the rector of the academy [university], the dean of faculty and his other regent colleagues, and has obtained their permission, for some weighty reason and at the convenience of the said college; and he is not to be absent for more than three days without permission having been obtained.//

As often as the said office of gymnasiarch happens to fall vacant, in whatsoever way, the regents for the time being shall be required to make at once a pronouncement of that vacancy to the electors of the said gymnasiarch, so that they, on being informed, may be able to furnish another serious and well-qualified man who may discharge this high responsibility. The lawful time for this election shall be within 60 days from the declaration of the vacancy in the said office. But if any of the electors named below defer the election of the gymnasiarch, then a majority of them, when the prescribed time of 60 days is complete, shall carry out the election, and this within 40 days after the previous period of 60 days is completed. The examination and election of the said gymnasiarch is to be in the hands of the Prefect or Primarius [Principal] of the New or Theological College in St Andrews University; the Chancellor of the University of Aberdeen, who is the Bishop of Aberdeen; the rector of the university; the dean of faculty; the subprincipal of the college; the three other regents of the same college, on condition that all three of them together have only one vote; the minister of the church of New Aberdeen; and the Gymnasiarch of the College of Edinburgh.

Whoever has been elected by all these, or by a majority of them which includes the chancellor and one of the two said gymnasiarchs of St Andrews and Edinburgh, with their votes agreeing upon the same choice, while the others are absent and do not compear at the appointed day though they have been lawfully informed of it, his election shall be valid. But if neither of the aforesaid two gymnasiarchs shall be present and agreed, let the election be invalid.

This examination, election and admission we wish to proceed by means of a public announcement, posted up by the regents on the doors of the College of Aberdeen and the churches of both the Old and the New Town, notice being given over 30 days at least. In addition the said regents by their announcement are to give notice to those in St Andrews, Glasgow, and Edinburgh, that if any are qualified to undertake the office, they are to be present on the appointed day, on which let the matter be brought to its conclusion not by favour nor by means of parties, but by virtue and excellence in learning.

Let preference be given by the outside electors to anyone found in the bosom of the College of Aberdeen if he be suitable to undertake this duty, when he has filled the office of regent at each level.[7]

In this whole election of a gymnasiarch, and also that of other teachers of the said college, no one is to be able to vote for himself, or canvas a vote for his own election; or if one and the same individual should hold by chance two or more roles among the said electors, our wish in that case is that he should have the right to one vote only. Nor may the right to elect or to exercise votes be allowed to any of the electors unless in solemn fashion he swears beforehand that he will conduct himself with good faith in the whole process of examination and election, without favour or respect to persons.

Since we seek a learned man on whose shoulders the burden of the whole college may rest, and since we entrust to him in addition the charge of the church of St Machar, and he would not be able to undergo the labour nor meet the expense unless he be attracted by honourable rewards, for this reason, by way of sustenance and honorarium for him and his servant, we determine for the time being, according to the level of the rents which the college now has, 24 bolls of oatmeal or barley and 200 merks of Scots money; and when something has accrued to the rents of the college, through detrimental leases being terminated or in any other way, then at the first opportunity let there be added another 24 bolls of oatmeal or barley for the said principal, so that at the harvest he would receive three chalders or 48 bolls, and when these are received in their entirety let there be deducted from the aforesaid sum of 200 merks, from the annual salary of the said principal, 33 merks five asses (or shillings) and six pence, if they are unable otherwise to bear the expenses of the college.

In this way we wish the principal of our college, whom we elect for the whole course of his life, to establish his way of living; and if he be negligent in his office, and if he has not fulfilled whatever is enjoined upon him by this special election, and if he is unwilling to come to his senses again when he has been warned three times by the chancellor, the rector of the university, the dean of faculty, the regents of the college, or the majority of them, but if he is inclined to corrupt ways, let him be deprived of office by those same authorities whom we have appointed to have responsibility for the election.//

The Regents and the Curriculum
We intend to provide four regents as being necessary for the advantage of the gymnasium, who may be in charge of instructing the youth and may assist the principal. One of whom, next after the principal, is called subprincipal, and to him the fourth class is entrusted. He, like the principal, shall remain in that office to the completion of his life's span; on this office see more below.

Of these four regents the one put in charge of the first and lowest class shall profess the teaching of the Greek tongue, with the expounding, in addition, of the easiest and best authors of both languages [Latin and Greek], and he shall accustom them to frequent exercise in writing—in the first six months to Latin composition, and in the remaining months that follow to the writing of Greek.//

The next regent in the following year shall teach his class the rules of invention [collection of material for speeches etc.], disposition [ordering and arrangement of argument], and elocution [public delivery of speech], by as easy a method as he may, and he shall add to these rules the study of their use from the best authors in each language, and he shall give the youths practice in both writing and public speaking, so that they, being equal with regard to their facility in both languages, may emerge more fitted to grasp the rules of philosophy.//

The third regent shall explain the rudiments of arithmetic and geometry, a selection from Aristotle's *Organum Logicum*, together with his books of *Ethics* and *Politics* from the Greek text, to which he shall add also the expounding of Marcus Tullius [Cicero]'s books *On Duties*, for the better shaping of morals and to enrich [knowledge of] the Latin tongue.//

Let these three regents, or any one of them, be elected, as often as a vacancy of this kind occurs, by the chancellor of the university, the rector, the dean of faculty, the principal of the college, the subprincipal, the minister of New Aberdeen, the three regents of the same college (in such a way that all three together have one vote only); or if fewer than all are able to be present together, we wish four from the above-named electors, that is, a sufficient number to cast four votes, to be present as a minimum, and among these four shall be included the principal of the college together with the minister of New Aberdeen; otherwise the election is to be invalid. It shall be permitted to each one of these three [regents] to remain in their office as long as they are assiduous and diligent, provided that they do nothing which would merit depriving them of their authority. To each one of these regents, for their yearly living and salary, as long as the revenues of the college are in their present condition, we assign one chalder of oatmeal, together with £47. 17s. of the coin of our realm. When however there shall be some increase in the college's rents, either when detrimental leases are expired [or in some other way], then we wish there to be added, to each one of these, eight bolls of oatmeal or barley, and that from the total of £47. 17s. there be deducted £7. 17s., so that each one of these three may have, as from that time, for his living and salary, 24 bolls of oatmeal or barley and £40.//

The Subprincipal
The fourth regent, whom we name subprincipal, and who shall last in that office as long as he lives, shall be a godly, modest, and learned man. He shall expound all physiology, and that part of the nature of animals as is chiefly necessary, from the Greek text of Aristotle. He shall also profess geography and astronomy, and in addition general cosmography and the computation of times from the foundation of the world, which subject brings no small light to bear on other disciplines and the knowledge of history; to which, around the end of the year, he shall adjoin the rules of the sacred tongue [Hebrew] together with some practice of them.

His election shall be under the control of the chancellor of the university, the rector, the dean of faculty, the principal of the college, the minister of the church of New Aberdeen, the three regents of the same college (on condition that these three together have only one vote); or, if all of them cannot be present together, we wish that four from the above-named electors, that is as many as hold four votes, be involved as a minimum; and among these four shall be included the principal of the college together with the minister of New Aberdeen, otherwise the election is to be invalid. His election shall be within a month of the day of the vacancy when the public announcement is posted up by the principal upon the doors of the college and on those of the churches of New and Old Aberdeen.

Since we wish that, to the work and labours of this fourth regent who is also called subprincipal, there be added the finishing-touch [*colophon*] of philosophical study, and that the youths, being crowned with the cap of graduation, should hasten more eagerly to studies of greater importance, and moreover since the responsibility for the gymnasium and its care and discipline shall belong to him especially in any absence of the principal or his preoccupation with the administration and care of the church of St Machar, we assign to him and his servant for annual living and salary, as the college rents are at present, 24 bolls of oatmeal and £80 in money of our kingdom of Scotland; but when there be some addition to the college's rents, as detrimental leases come to an end, then there shall be added to him another 24 bolls of oatmeal or barley, and from the aforesaid sum of £80 there shall be subtracted £13. 6s. 8d., so that the aforesaid subprincipal may have as from that time for his annual living and salary three chalders of oatmeal or barley and £66. 13s. 4d.//

Teaching and Organisation of Classes
We wish that these four regents should not (as was formerly the custom in the academies of our realm) change to new professions each year, whereby it came about that, while they professed many subjects, they were found expert in few; but we wish them to exercise themselves in the same profession, so that the youths who climb up, step by step, may be able to find a teacher worthy of their studies and talents. But if it shall be in the interest of the gymnasium, and if it seems good to the gymnasiarch, subprincipal, rector, chancellor, dean of faculty, or to three of these (that is to say the principal, subprincipal and dean of faculty), the three other regents, by their authorisation, are able to exchange their fields of duty between themselves: and these also are to prescribe the authors to be put before the youth in each year, but in such a way that all authors shall be expounded to the students in the languages in which they originally wrote. We wish also that our aforementioned regents should exercise those entrusted to their care in teaching, writing, declaiming, and disputing as diligently as possible in the literary arena, but especially that the students in the two lowest classes be accustomed to daily composition, and that one hour every day at least be devoted to this. Next, after the completion of the first eighteen months, that they should practise all students diligently, each month, in public declamations in both Greek and Latin; and so that their studies may be the more inspired by this worthy rivalry, we wish that all the students be divided into groups of ten, and each month a vote be taken so that the most learned student in each group be placed above all the rest.//

In addition we wish no one to be admitted into the number of students in the first class, unless he shall be deemed worthy of that rank after careful examination, with the dean, principal, subprincipal, three regents, the teachers in both the grammar schools [of New and Old Aberdeen] or one of them, all having sworn to it. And in each year of the course we wish there to be promotions through the steps of advancement, so that students of the first class may progress to the second, those of the second to the third, the third to the fourth, and those of the fourth finally, with their philosophical study completed, be presented with the crown of the master's degree.

In these steps let care be taken to make sure that no one unworthy of promotion should pass to a higher class, but only by due examination by the dean of faculty, principal, subprincipal, the three regents, and the masters of the [grammar] schools of New and Old Aberdeen (or one of them), conducted by them after they have all been sworn to it publicly. But if any one shall be deemed by them unworthy of promotion, he shall remain in the same class as before, until he shall be adjudged, through them, worthy of promotion to a higher class. We wish that these examinations and promotions and the admissions to our College begin each year on the first of October.//

On each Sunday in each class we wish the sacred lesson to be set forth from the New Testament in such a way that at 6 a.m. the teachers should read through to the first class the Gospel of Luke; to the second the Acts of the Apostles; to the third the Epistle of St Paul to the Romans; and to the fourth the Epistle to the Hebrews; and at 4 p.m. each one should examine his own pupils on the same lesson.//

The power of emending and correcting the said regents shall be in the hands of the said principal and subprincipal, with whom also shall be the power to expel the same from the college if, having laid aside their duties and having been warned, as has been said, three times, they have been unwilling to come to their senses again; though only for a known cause, and with the advice being sought of the rector and dean of faculty.//

The Bursars

Having had consideration for poverty and the fact that many are deterred from good letters by lack of means, we have provided in addition twelve poor students whom they call bursars, and to each one of them we allot for his yearly living, from the revenues of the college, £30. We wish to be recommended, because of their poverty, those for whom parents and friends, by their lack of means, are unable to supply food and clothing, and we wish that they may excel in distinction of talent, proficiency in grammar, and good character.//

The election, admission, and collation of the said bursars shall be according to the following form. The principal, or in his absence the subprincipal, by posting a public advertisement at the college doors 20 days before the first of October, shall announce to all those seeking benefit that, on that day, they should present themselves for examination by the rector, dean of faculty, the minister of New Aberdeen, the principal, subprincipal and three regents (to whom we allow one vote together), all being under oath, and those who, after careful examination has been made, are found, because of poverty and learning, most to need that benefit and to be most deserving of it, are to be inscribed in the album of bursars; but regard being paid to that privilege which Bishop William Elphinstone of blessed memory reserved in the first foundation of the College for two poor students of his own surname. Not that it would be right for any other privilege to be left owing to others, whoever they may be, for benefit conferred upon this our college, such as that which is owed to the family and name of Master Robert Maitland, by whose efforts the addition of the deanship was made to our college, for it would be unjust to pass over those who belong to his kin and share his name. Special consideration needs to be given also to those poor students from whose parishes the annual expenses are provided for our college; and indeed, other things being equal, they should be preferred to others.

It shall be the responsibility of the rector, dean, gymnasiarch, regents, and other electors to take care that no rich students be admitted in the place of poor, and that no drones feed from the hive, but to receive into the gymnasium only those who shall be able to serve as an ornament to our country and to be of service to the church. We wish these poor students of ours to be a model of humility and obedience, and through all things to regulate their behaviour in accordance with the wishes of their teachers; and if they fail to do so, we empower the said gymnasiarch and teachers to punish them in accordance with the seriousness of the offence, up to and including their expulsion from the said college if they have deserved it by their wilful behaviour.

They are to be be clothed in long gowns, girt round with a white leather belt extending to four fingers in breadth; and it shall be their task, week by week and in turn, to go round the bedchambers of all sleeping in college at 5 a.m. to rouse the students to their studies, to bring light in winter time, and to fulfil other lesser duties in the hall at the time of dinner or supper (such as placing dishes and courses on the table, and serving water), and to perform such other tasks of that kind which, without detriment to their own studies, may be enjoined on them by the gymnasiarch and other teachers. Moreover, they are to take turns in fulfilling the role of janitors, until, as the revenues of the academy are increased, some definite person may be chosen for that office.

Let their entry to the college be on the first of October, and let them continue in literary studies and be fed at the expense of the gymnasium, as has been said, for four years in all, as this is the length of time we judge to be appropriate for completing the study of philosophy and attaining the wreath [graduating]; and when they have completed the course let new bursars be provided until they in their turn run to the finishing-line.//

The Economus

As economus [steward] and provisor we require a good and energetic man, for whom the well-being of the college is to be the particular concern. At the beginning of his tenure of office he shall give an undertaking that the affairs of the college will be safe and sound and that he will administer them in good faith. In his control shall be the collection of all the revenues and rents of the college, of whatever kind; the appointing of a day for debtors; attendance in court in the name of the college; and the lawful transaction of other business.

It shall be his task, at the proper time, to provide for the college, according to the will of the teachers, in those matters which pertain to subsistence, and to have day to day responsibility for marketing, purchasing those things which pertain to the sustenance of the college; to distribute, at the due time, the fruits and rents of the college, that he has received, to the principal, subprincipal, the three teachers [regents], and likewise to all founded persons, whatever we assign in this foundation of ours, and to pay in good faith at the fixed terms of the year respectively (but having first deducted the cost of the subsistence of the said founded persons) the total sum of money at the two terms of the year, by means of two equal parts at the feast of St Martin [Martinmas] in winter and the feast of Pentecost [Whitsunday].

The harvest he is to distribute[8] each year before the first of March; and he is not to satisfy the principal or subprincipal before the lowest persons on the foundation, [but pay] all without distinction; and let him pay moneys regularly due, sums added, and stipends, according to the proportion of each.

Of all these things he shall be required each week to render account to the principal, subprincipal, and other teachers, lest in any matter the slightest fraud be perpetrated against the founded persons; and they shall also try and punish the economus's negligence and lack of care, if there be any; and in these matters there shall be joined [to them], when the situation demands it,[9] the rector and dean of faculty for their advice; and they are to make prompt provision for a remedy in all matters of loss threatening the college.//

Let the election of the economus be according to the form which we have prescribed for electing the three lower regents, and he shall remain in that office for at least three years. Because it belongs to his duties to make provision at the proper time in regard to those things which pertain to the sustenance of all members of the college, in order that he may be able to fulfil this more conveniently at a just and fair price, our wish is that every year on the first day, that is to say of October, by decision of the rector, dean of faculty, principal, provost and baillies of New and Old Aberdeen, together with the addition of four others from the burgh council of New Aberdeen, are to be estimated and established the prices for provisions for all the founded persons of the college, then also of other residents in the college who are not on the foundation, according to the dearness and cheapness of those things which pertain to sustenance, and at the same time let it be prescribed what is to be the number of courses and dishes, what the measure and quality of drink and of bread, and how it is to be prepared.

We wish the said economus to observe and follow their decision in this matter, and because it is usual for there to be frequent changes in prices, and so that there should be no loss to our college or to the said economus, we wish that three times each year, that is to say on the first days of February, May and August afterwards [following the October meeting] the same economus, by decision of the rector, dean of faculty, principal, masters of the college, with the addition of two citizens, baillies or councillors, of the New Town of Aberdeen, may be able to increase or reduce the measure at the price previously established for provisions according to the dearness and cheapness of things.//

Since our provisor [economus] will need to be occupied by various responsibilities and concerns, we assign and apportion to him by way of salary (in addition to those expenses which he will necessarily incur in order to recover the college's rents, and which it is reasonable to deduct for him in the accounts), in accordance with the present state of the college's rents, six bolls of oatmeal and £66. 13s. 4d.; but when the college's rents increase, with detrimental leases being terminated, for his yearly salary let him receive from the college's rents 16 bolls of oatmeal and £50 in money of our kingdom of Scotland.//

The Grammarian

We wish the teacher of grammar to be a good and learned man, and especially well-read in Latin and Greek literature both in verse and prose: and his election shall be according to that form which we have prescribed in the election of the three regents. Let him not be tied to living in college, but let him live according to his own wish where the more convenient opportunity for living shall be presented to him, whether in college or outside the college's bounds. The gymnasiarch shall provide at the college's expense a convenient school outside the college, for the benefit of the younger pupils committed to his care, together with a bedchamber within the bounds of the college for the said master of the grammar school. To this teacher for annual stipend we assign and account from the rents of the college £50, together with the extra payment of five merks which he enjoyed previously.//

The Cook

Let a suitable cook also be appointed by the principal, subprincipal, regents and provisor [economus], who is to serve by preparing food and cultivating the garden of the gymnasium. To him for his work and subsistence we allot £30; he shall supply vegetables at his own expense[10] for the use of the members of the said college; and he shall take care to see that the garden and walks shall be kept tidy for the use of the masters of the said college; and the remaining produce of the garden he shall be allowed to apply to his own uses.//

College Buildings

To the maintenance of the college (in order that its buildings may be completely safe), each year from the first income of the same we allot at least £40 in money of the kingdom of Scotland, which we order to be put aside in the chest, and when something accrues to the college's rents, as detrimental leases come to an end or by death of the holders of those properties which belong to the college, or in any other way, we wish the first part of this to be spent on further repair and necessary expense by the economus in collecting college revenues and gathering rents. All the remainder is to accrue to the honoraria of the principal, subprincipal, regents and economus in proportion, to be distributed to each yearly by decision of the chancellor, rector, dean of faculty, and the minister of New Aberdeen.//

Discipline

In order that each person in this academy may be more freely attentive to his own duty, we forbid any of the masters to take upon himself any other public office outside the bounds of the college, apart from what we have enjoined in this our foundation and erection, so that none of them may hold either the office of rector or that of dean of faculty.//

If it happen that any of the founded persons marry a wife, we forbid that his wife, daughter or maids should pass their time within the bounds of the college, still less reside there or spend the night there.//

In order that this our gymnasium may flourish all the more in the cultivation of letters and refinement of behaviour, and that this our institution may bring forth more abundant fruits, we wish all the persons on the foundation of our college, as well as the students congregating in it, to be constrained by strict moral discipline. And so that no loss be incurred to either morals or letters by interruption of studies, we wish that all vacations from studies as were formerly customary be utterly abolished. We also forbid that any over-lavish festivities should be held in connection with promotions, to whatever grade of advancement, or that anything be admitted which might in any way either remove or slacken the discipline prescribed in the gymnasium.//

First and foremost however we stipulate that none of those studying, except the teachers, should possess arms of any kind whether designed for inflicting injury or defending against it, such as a cuirass, iron breastplate, helmet, iron gauntlets, sword, dagger, knife, spear, firearms and that kind of weapon, or that he should in any way use them in the college or outside college; but let only small knives and table-knives for cutting food be used. Anyone who contravenes this is to be penalised by the principal or subprincipal or other teachers, for a first offence by the loss and confiscation of the arms; anyone defaulting a second time from the discipline of the gymnasium is to be punished by a beating in the public school; if he violates this rule a third time let him be expelled as being unworthy to belong to the number of students.//

Also, all the aforesaid persons on the foundation are both to eat and to sleep within the bounds of the gymnasium; if any of the bursars shall sleep outside the college without having obtained permission as has been stated, and does not reform when admonished and punished, let him at once be deprived of the benefit of his bursary. The remaining students who enjoy the use of bedchambers within the bounds of the college, are to go to bed and pass the night in these rooms; if they do otherwise then let them be removed from their bedchambers; and those students who take their meals outside college are not to be found out of college except at the appointed hours for taking meals. If they sleep outside [college] they are to come in at 6 a.m. prompt, and not go out earlier than 9 a.m.; and when they have returned from breakfast before 10 a.m., they shall not be allowed to go out before 12 noon; but after dinner those who take their meals in Old Aberdeen are to come back and enter the college at 1 p.m., those taking meals in New [Aberdeen] at 2 p.m.; and they shall remain together there until 6 p.m., unless permission to play has been granted to all; when that happens they shall go out all together and be led out [to the links] and led back in a body by one of the teachers (who will undertake this responsibility week by week); nor shall the time for playing be extended beyond two hours from departure out of the college, so that they may be able to return to their lessons on time; we enjoin this responsibility also on this teacher, that at 5 a.m. and 9 p.m. he is to visit all the bedchambers.//

We wish also that all students shall live peaceably among themselves with the utmost harmony, and that no-one bring hurt upon another by word or deed; that they use Latin or Greek speech, and refrain from dishonourable and shameful language, from curses, oaths and all blasphemous words. At times of worship, sermon, prayers, sacred readings, and interpretation of the Scriptures, which we call prophesying, they are to attend very diligently what is prescribed; finally, in all things which relate to the discipline of the college they are to comply with the regulations which have been approved by the gymnasiarch with the advice of his colleagues, or which will in future be so approved; to whom also we have committed the power of composing and enacting good statutes for preserving the discipline of our gymnasium firm and secure, as occasion shall require and for each new situation.//

Those who, being now advanced to the distinction of the master's degree, nevertheless decide still to live within the gymnasium,[11] are to be under the rules of discipline of the same, and are to render account of their studies to the principal and the rest of his colleagues; but if, living outside the gymnasium they desire only to attend public or private lectures, let them enter and depart with all modesty, and with no bad example, nor let them hinder in any way the studies of the rest, or make themselves a nuisance by causing laughter; if they behave otherwise, let them be excluded from the college.//

Leases
Because hitherto our gymnasium has suffered much loss through detrimental leases, we determine and ordain that no lease or grant of tenure for cultivation or feufarm, whether for a longer or shorter period of years, either of lands or of teinds, or of buildings or of any things whatsoever, is to be valid or approved which does not have the express agreement and consent of the chancellor, rector, dean, principal and regents assembled together, witnessed and approved by the individual signatures of each one, and by the common seal of the said college, together with the subscription of the minister of New Aberdeen; otherwise let the lease be at once invalid.//

Visitations
And so that all these regulations may be more diligently observed, we ordain that this our college is to be visited and reviewed three times each year, to wit, on the first day of February, June and October, by the chancellor, rector, and dean of faculty, so that if anything, whether in teaching or in discipline or in rents, be neglected or wasted, it may be emended and corrected by their admonition and advice.//

Religious Qualifications

Above all let careful inquiry be made concerning profession of faith and religion, and because herein lies the cunning of Satan, that in every way he tries to divert youth from the profession of the Gospel once more to the shadows of popery (from which by the grace of God our kingdom has been set free), we strictly enjoin that each and every person who shall be incorporated into this academy is to put forth a profession of faith—that [Confession of Faith], to be sure, which has been issued and made public, having been sought from the Word of God and transcribed by us in the assemblies of our kingdom—and this at least once a year.

In particular, while they are being admitted to the college, let [their names] be inscribed individually in the album of the university in the presence of the principal, and let them openly profess the pure faith and religion to the rector and, on the occasion of their being promoted to any degree, to the dean of faculty; and let them promise sincerely that they will remain in that profession.//

Fees

Students admitted to the academy are to show themselves to be not only diligent in their studies and upright in morals, but grateful towards their teachers and the public servants of our college; and therefore let each of the students pay a tuition fee [*minerval*] to his own teacher according to the decision and assessment of the teachers, so that the sons of princes and the upper nobility should be required to pay £6; sons of the lower rank of nobility, £4; sons of farmers, ordinary merchants and craftsmen 40s.; from these payments let the poor be altogether free; to the general attendant [*communis apparitor*][12] let each pay 4s. in the year.//

In examinations and promotions let each bring the following to the common chest of the college: at the first grade and the first year's examination, 6s. 8d.; at the second, 13s. 4d.; at the third, 20s.; at the fourth and last, 30s.; provided that poor students are exempted from all these. But as to the question, who are to be regarded as poor students, the teachers' judgment and estimation shall decide.//

The Rector, the Dean of Faculty, and the Four Nations

Because we have placed many responsibilities in this academy of ours on its rector and on the dean of faculty, our will is that these officials should be elected for one year at a time. Let the rector be a serious and godly man, one who reflects upon and is skilled in justice and equity; to him let there belong ordinary jurisdiction over all who are enrolled as [members] of the academy, whom we call subordinate members; let him be involved in the more fully attended assemblies of the academy, especially in elections, according to those things which are prescribed above; and let him be in charge of those proceedings, especially in the absence of the chancellor, and let him conduct, direct and exercise all those matters which the rector of the academy at St Andrews or Glasgow is known to be able or obliged to conduct, direct and exercise by law, custom and usage.

Let him be chosen by all the subordinate members of the academy divided into four nations (in such a way that the diocese of Aberdeen, because of its greater number, be split into two nations, those of Marr and Buchan; let Garioch be joined to Marr, and let the rest of [the diocese], from the River Deveron, go to Buchan; let the rest of the kingdom which lies to the north of the Grampian mountain be contained under the name of the Moray nation; let that lying to the south, beyond the Grampian mountain, be called the Angus nation). Of these nations let there be individual procurators, who are to elect the rector and his assessors. The rector on being elected shall swear that he will use that office faithfully and diligently, and exercise a jurisdiction that is fair to all, without any respect of persons, in good faith; in elections that he will cast his vote with the same good faith from his heart's conviction and to the advantage of the state and the church, and that he will energetically promote the advantages of the academy, provided that he may do so with godliness unimpaired, that he will never knowingly act against them, and lastly that he will adorn and increase this republic of letters.//

Let the dean of faculty be elected by the same meeting, but by the rector, chancellor, gymnasiarch, the four regents and the minister of New Aberdeen, provided that the gymnasiarch and minister of the New Town are always involved in his election. Let him be a godly, well-read man, well-versed not only in the so-called more humane disciplines, but also in all philosophy, one who is to be involved in and in charge of the yearly examinations and promotions, so that he may obtain from the examiners an oath that they will perform these duties faithfully. Let him supervise the doctrine and diligence of the teachers; let him see that the academy shall not, through the neglect of this matter, incur any loss; in elections let him cast a vote that is incorrupt and is for the common good; and, lastly, let him perform all those things which are understood to pertain to the office and duty of the dean of the faculty of liberal arts in the Academy of St Andrews. Let him swear that he will faithfully use that office, and that in promotions and graduations he will pronounce in good faith and without respect of persons, according to the judgments of the assessors and examiners, from the conviction of his own mind, that he will promote the interests of the college and academy, as much as he may do with unimpaired godliness, and that, in fine, he will perform all those things which he understands to be incumbent, by virtue of his office, upon the dean of the Academy of St Andrews, or of any other academy worthy of praise, and which he knows for sure to be in the interests of the commonwealth of Christianity and letters.//

Privileges
Finally our will is that this our College and Academy of Aberdeen should enjoy and delight in all the immunities and privileges which have been granted by our predecessors or by us or others in any way at all to any of the other academies in our kingdom or anywhere else in the world, provided only that the said immunities and privileges do not contradict this erection of ours.

NOTES

1   The text reads *euditis*, which has been assumed to be an error for *eruditis*.

2   Garbal teinds, also known as rectorial, parsonage or great teinds, were the tithes levied on grain.

3   The text states that the principal was only to lecture on alternate days, rather than every day: but it seems likely that the reading of the parallel section of the Glasgow University *Nova Erectio* is to be preferred here, and it indicates that the principal was to lecture every day (except Saturday and Sunday). Anderson, *Officers*, 338; J Durkan and J Kirk, *The University of Glasgow, 1451–1577* (Glasgow, 1977), 433, 442.

4   The text is corrupt at this point, but presumably it was the classes of the two most senior regents who were to attend the principal's lectures. But the stipulation that all regents should be present raises problems: who supervised the two lower classes while their regents were at the lectures?

5   The meaning is that those who have listened to the principal's lectures during the week are to be tested on this work on Saturday.

6   The text reads *exiguum*, but this seems implausible, as if accepted the passage would appear to describe the ministry of St Machar's as 'only a slight burden', which is hardly in keeping with the reformed church's emphasis on the importance of the office. Therefore the reading of the Glasgow *Nova Erectio*, *equum*, 'just' is to be preferred. Anderson, *Officers*, 338; J Durkan and J Kirk, *The University of Glasgow, 1451–1577* (Glasgow, 1977), 433, 442.

7   This is rather obscure, but the meaning is evidently that in order to be eligible for appointment as principal, a regent of the college must have taught the subjects of all four years of the arts course.

8   The 'harvest' is presumably the payment of that part of the salaries which is defined in terms of barley or oatmeal rather than money.

9   The text reads *ubi representaverit*, but the reading of the Marischal College foundation charter, *ubi res postulabit*, has been preferred. Anderson, *Officers*, 343; Anderson, *FAM*, 1, 50.

10   Stipulating that the cook provide vegetables at his own expense must mean at the expense of his own labour—in other words, he is responsible for growing them in the college garden.

11   Who were these students who have already graduated but decide to live within the college? The obvious answer is that the were postgraduate students—above all those staying on to study theology before becoming parish ministers. But if this is the meaning it seems puzzling that it is not made clear. Further confusion is caused by the fact that the parallel passage in the foundation charter of Marischal College talks of these students as those 'not yet promoted to the dignity of Master', Anderson, *FAM*, 1, 73.

12   The 'general attendant' is not listed as a founded person of the college. The Marischal College foundation charter also says he was 'called the beadle', Anderson, *FAM*, 1, 74, In the 1641 King's College 'laws' there is reference again to the *apparitor*, which Cosmo Innes translated as 'beadle', Innes, *Fasti*, 226 and 'The Table', p. 33.

Appendix III

Examination Silver, Chamber Mails and Spoon Silver in 1623–4

A procuration account voucher listing some of the college's income from fees survives in the university archives, AUL, MS K 281/3/3 and its contents are analysed below.

The section dealing with examination silver lists no payments by the 1st class, and two by the 4th class. This may be interpreted as indicating that examination fees relating to the first three years' work were paid at the beginning of the following session, at Michaelmas. Thus the fees shown as paid by the 2nd class were those for the class just commencing its second year of study, and the 4th year class paid twice as payment was exacted at the end of that year, for the exams relating to the fourth year's work, as well as at the beginning. The 'Cruickshank' who received one-eleventh of examination fees was doubtless the sacrist, Alexander Cruikshank (Anderson, *Officers*, 91). A fragment of an account relating to 1626–8 (AUL, MS K 278/1/1) indicates a reduction in the fees of one-eleventh, suggesting that the payments to the sacrist from this source had ceased.

The exam fees exacted were much higher than those laid down in the New Foundation (see Appendix II).

The figures for payment of exam silver indicate a total undergratuate population of 51 undergraduate students, nine of whom (including bursars) were excused payment on grounds of poverty. As some students lived outside college, it would be logical to expect a smaller number to be paying chamber mails (fees for the rooms they occupied in college). Instead the chamber mail account indicates 57 resident students, fully 32 of whom were non-solvent and excused payment (the criteria for being excused payment must have been different for the two types of fee).

Each bursar was supposed to present the college with a silver spoon. In his 1619 visitation Bishop Forbes had complained that in spite of this the college only possessed six such spoons (see page 65 above), but the account suggests that part of the reason for this may have been that the spoons had been commuted into a monetary payment: but that only two students paid in 1623–4 suggests that payment was irregular Of the two students who paid (John Chalmer, David Houston), one appears to have graduated in 1623, the other in 1627 (Anderson,

Officers, 183–4), suggesting payment could either be in the year of enrolment in the college or that of graduation. If bursars were genuinely chosen on the grounds of poverty, £5 was a very substantial sum to find.

Examination Silver, Michaelmas 1623

Total Students	Non-Solvent Students	Solvent Students	Fee	Total Collected
2nd class				
18	3	15	22s.	£16.10s.
3rd class				
14	2	12	33s.	£19. 5s.
4th class				
11	2	9	44s.	£19.16s.
4th class, Lammas 1624				
8	2	6	55s.	£16.10s.

Total collected,	£72. 1s.
Paid to the College,	£65.10s.
Paid to 'Cruikshank',	£6.16s.

One student in the 3rd class paid only 22s. in exam fees.

Chamber Mails, Michaelmas 1623

Total Students	Non-solvent Students	Solvent Students	Fee	Total Collected
1st class				
12	7	5	10s.	£2.10s.
2nd class				
20	12	8	10s.	£4
3rd class				
14	3	11	10s.	£5.10s
4th class				
11	8	3	10s.	£1.10s.

Total	£13.10s.

Spoon Silver, Michaelmas 1623

Two students each paid £5

Total £10

Examination silver	£65.10s.
Chamber mails	13.10s.
Spoon silver	10
TOTAL	£79

Appendix IV

Letter from William Leslie to Patrick Maule of Panmure, 1638

To the Right Honourable the laird of Panmure these

Right Honourable and Worthy Sir,

Please I had express order from the rector and members of King's College of Aberdeen to render you thanks for your late favour towards the said College in purchasing from his majesty a letter [25 May 1638] directed to the Bishop of Aberdeen [Adam Bellenden], whereby his sacred majesty was graciously pleased to command him after exact trial and notice taken of the state of the said college to make a true and just report thereof to his majesty with all possible diligence, and withall carefully to provide that the blessed memory of his majesty's father King James should noways be extinguished or suppressed, neither anything done prejudicial to the said King James his royal foundation and mortifications made by him to the said college, notwithstanding any letters or commissions covertly and cunningly drawn from his majesty's hand of late.

In obedience of the which order and commandment of our rector and members, I, although unfit and unworthy, yet as *delegatus publico nomine*, do render you many and most hearty thanks for that undeserved courtesy, sincerely and sensibly acknowledging your real performance of what you was pleased to promise to the said college, when you got the tack of your teinds of Haltoun. And withall earnestly entreating you to continue your kindness towards that poor distressed house in this most difficult and dangerous time; when as (to speak nothing of the public calamity and confusions of this kingdom) the royal foundation and mortifications of the King's College are undermined, and in all appearance (except his majesty provide speedy remedy) shall be subverted and inverted, by secret and subtle plots and practises, under a fair and specious pretence of reforming abuses.

Worthy Sir, give me leave, according to the order I have from our corporation, to unfold unto you briefly the course of our affairs.

King James of blessed memory was pleased by advice of his council and clergy (as in St Andrews and Glasgow), so in Aberdeen to set down a new royal foundation of this college, whereby all popish corruptions and abuses were abolished; idle and unprofitable members cashiered, a competent number of profitable and necessary members established, new orders for doctrine and discipline fitting the time and country appointed, and the whole rents both old and new of his own mortifications appropriated to the members of his own forsaid royal foundation. Which foundation was first subscribed by his majesty's own hand and by the hands of his commissioners specially deputed for the framing thereof. Secondly being presented to his majesty sitting in full council was authorised and subscribed again by his majesty and council, ordaining the same to have strength and vigour, and to be ratified in the next parliament. Thirdly was ratified and approved by the General Assembly of the Church of Scotland for the time and subscribed by the clerk thereof. Forthly was ratified by an act of the parliament held at Edinburgh anno 1597, as the register of the said parliament bears. And lastly since that time was the only constant rule and directory of the said college for doctrine, discipline, stipends, number of members, and all.

Until in later times about the year 1627 some crafty and corrupt men, hunting after their own preferments, under colour of restoring the decayed members— that is, the cashiered professors of the popish canon law and other such stuff— for making a way to their entry or rather intrusion into the said college, by their subtle suggestions and persuasions so far prevailed with the late Bishop of Aberdeen of happy memory [Patrick Forbes], that he was induced to be a means of destroying of the said royal foundation, and that in secret, without the privity of the members of he college, except only some few that happened to be mere spectators, and without either public authority, or lawful cognition of the cause before any judicatory. Then the old popish foundation was brought out, and according to it the pretended professors of the popish canon law and such other matters were intruded upon the college *manu forte et vi majore*, and provided to fair stipends out of old and new rents, whereas in the meantime the members established by the royal foundation were brought to disgrace and beggery, and slavish subjection to these new usurpers, wherein also they as yet do continue, and I fear shall long or ever continue, except God and his majesty send remedy.

But here behold the work of God. Whereas the utter extinction and abolition of that royal deed was intended, in God's secret providence the destroyer thereof gave express order to one of the masters of the college, who yet survives, to cause draw a just double or copy of the said foundation, word by word, subscriptions and all exactly collated and concorded with the original *in omnibus*. Which double, after the perusal and collating thereof, he delivered in first to the said master, willing him to keep it *in omnem eventum*, and this was done immediately before the burning of the royal deed. Now the truth is, although the said just double since that time hath been and yet is faithfully preserved by him who was entrusted therewith, *tanquam depositum bone fidei*, yet during the said bishop's time, himself being chancellor and his son rector, none durst make the least motion concerning the abolition, or restitution of the royal foundation. But now in this worthy bishop's time, when he was fully informed of the whole passages and proceedings, out of a sincere zeal and respect to King James's honour and his present majesty, he was well content that we should use all honest and lawful means for restoring and setting up again of that royal deed destroyed. To this purpose we laboured divers ways and times to inform his sacred majesty concerning the whole business, humbly begging his majesty's royal support for the reviving of his majesty's father's deed (almost extinguished and buried in the grave of oblivion) and that we might have the benefit of the common law and ordinary course of justice for proving the substantial tenor of the destroyed foundation both by writings and by the depositions of famous witnesses yet living, who were partly framers, partly subscribers of the said foundation, and likewise even by the oaths of those men who were the devisers and contrivers of the destroying thereof. Likeas we have a process already depending before the lords of his majesty's council and session for the said effect, and for obtaining a declarator, that King James's mortifications belong only to the members established by his foundation, unto which his mortifications have a special relation. In the meantime these usurpers and intruders, over-leaping the lords of his majesty's general committee for visitation of all the colleges in the kingdom, by moyen of a great nobleman (who, we hope, is not unknown to you) purchased a power from his majesty directed to some lords and bishops for visiting of our college in April last. Which visitation holding, and they finding that the power was not ample enough for the utter abolishing of the royal foundation, and bearing down the maintainers thereof, immediately after [by] the same moyen and mean have purchased another most ample commission under the great seal for final accomplishing of all their designs, in maugre [ill will, spite] of us, who plead for the king's honour and the well of his college; and his commission, as we believe, is already passed the seals. We foreseeing and fearing this tempest to come upon us, wrote to sundry worthies about court, and especially to yourself by your cousin Mr Leith our good friend and colleague, who lately delivered to us from you his majesty's letter to the Bishop of Aberdeen, whereby we gladly understand his majesty's gracious and royal pleasure concerning his father's foundation.

Worthy Sir, our earnest request to you is, that out of your goodness you will be pleased to represent again to his majesty the whole case of his college as it now stands, and to obtain [for] us another letter to second the first, that his commission may be stopped or suspended, until we may have just audience before the lords of the session which is the sum of our wishes. By so doing you shall oblige the present members and their successors to be daily orators unto the almighty God for continuance and increase of all earthly and heavenly blessings upon you and all yours, besides any other service that happily upon occasion they may do you. Now Sir, let me beg this favour of you to myself, that you will pardon both my presumption and prolixity. It may please you take this paper not only for a letter, but likewise for an information. I promised to be brief, but an earnest desire of particular expression hath miscarried me. The God of heaven bless you, and make you a good instrument to succour his afflicted.

Your servant at all power

King's College of Aberdeen 2 July 1638.   Mr Willesly. Principal.

Source:
SRO, GD.45/14/20, Dalhousie Muniments

Spelling, capitalisation and punctuation modernised. Leslie frequently runs his abbreviated Christian name and surname together in his signature.

Bibliographical Note

As the footnotes demonstrate, much of the evidence used in this study has been gleaned from scattered references in a wide range of sources relating to the general history of the period, and it would not be useful to try to cite them again here. But there are two core collections of published sources central to the college's history:

C Innes, ed., *Fasti Aberdonensis. Selections from the Records of the University and King's College of Aberdeen*, SC (Aberdeen, 1854).

P J Anderson, *Officers and Graduates of the University and King's College of Aberdeen*, NSC (Aberdeen, 1893).

Without the labours of these dedicated editors the work of the college historian would be difficult indeed.

The foundation and early history of the college are narrated and analysed in detail in:

L J Macfarlane, *William Elphinstone and the Kingdom of Scotland, 1451–1514. The Struggle for Order* (Aberdeen, 1985), chapter 7.

The middle decades of the sixteenth century, especially the impact of Reformation, have inspired a number of articles, references to which can be found in the notes to chapter 1. But the period from about 1580 to 1619 has received very little detailed attention from historians, though a study of the founding of Marischal College throws much incidental light on the state of King's:

G D Henderson, *The Founding of Marischal College, Aberdeen*, AUS 123 (Aberdeen, 1947).

For the period that follows the work of Patrick Forbes and the emergence of the Aberdeen Doctors has interested a number of church historians: see references in the notes to chapters 4 and 5.

In putting the college in a wider context of the development of Scotland's universities:

J Kirk, 'The New Foundation', in J Durkan and J Kirk, *The University of Glasgow, 1451–1577* (Glasgow, 1977)

is very valuable. Again the later part of the period is neglected, but there are useful insights in:

R G Cant, 'The Scottish Universities in the Seventeenth Century', *AUR*, 43 (1969–70), 223–33.

For the British context see:

H Kearney, *Scholars and Gentlemen. Universities and Society in Pre-Industrial Britain, 1500–1700* (London, 1970).

Index

Unless otherwise stated, all subject entries refer to King's College and/or Aberdeen University, as do all offices noted as held by individuals. AU = Aberdeen University; KC = King's College; MC = Marischal College

Aberdeen (New Aberdeen), burgh of 2, 8–9, 37; friaries 8; grammar school 67; ministers 107; provosts 17, 37

Aberdeen, bishops of 36, 70; *see also* Bellenden, Adam; Blackburn, Peter; Cunningham, David; Dunbar, Gavin; Elphinstone, William; Forbes, Alexander; Forbes, Patrick; *and* Gordon, William

Aberdeen, cathedral *see* St Machar's Cathedral

Aberdeen, deanery 28, 39, 53, 63, 65, 70, 152, 159

Aberdeen, diocese (bishopric) 14, 34, 48, 59, 122, 145, 165

Aberdeen, Old *see* Old Aberdeen

Aberdeen, presbytery 53–4

Aberdeen, synod 53, 71

Aberdeen, university 26, 36–7, 67–8, 76, 83, 122–3; Caroline University 1, 2, 120, 122

Aberdeen Doctors 4, 5, 105–12, 115, 117

Abergerny 151

Aberlethnott 151

academic year 77, 158, 159

Adamson, Patrick, Archbishop of St Andrews 35

Aidy (Adie), Andrew, principal, MC 69, 137

anatomy 82–3

Anderson, Alexander, principal 8–10, 15, 17–19, 52, 127

Anderson, Andrew, regent 17

Anderson, P J 149, 150

Anderson, William, canonist 67, 68

Andet 151

Angus (Forfarshire) 8, 59, 165

Arbuthnot, Alexander, principal 5, 25–30, 32, 33, 35, 51, 52, 131, 137

Arbuthnot, laird 27

Arbuthnot, parish 26

archery 6, 126

Aristotle, Aristotelianism 2, 21, 23, 42, 46, 51, 59, 81, 85, 119, 156

arithmetic *see* mathematics

Arminianism 105, 107, 110, 117

arts, arts faculty 17, 24, 44, 48, 51, 68; curriculum 4, 42, 44–6, 51, 155–6; deans 26

astrolobe 78

astronomy 12–13, 46, 156

Audaile 151

Banff 151; Carmelite Friary 28, 152

banquets 71–2

Baron, Robert, dean of divinity 75, 81, 85, 107, 110, 112

beadle *see* general attendant

Belhelvie 151

Bellenden, William, Bishop of Aberdeen 80, 94–5, 100, 104, 116, 169

Berryhill 151

Bible 21, 28; New Testament 46, 158

Bisset, John, principal 13

Black Acts 33

Blackburn, Peter, Bishop of Aberdeen 33, 35, 53, 55
Blairshinnoch 151
Bologna, university 78
Bonakettle 151
bookbinder 140–1
Bourges, university 26
Boyne 151
buildings 2, 3, 12, 64–5, 67, 76–7, 87, 95, 120–2, 147–8, 161
bursars 13, 58, 65, 80, 146, 147, 158–9, 167, 168

Calvin, John 16
Calvinism 21, 106, 107, 110, 119, 143
Cambridge, university 26, 136
canonist, canon law, canon law faculty 4, 13, 17, 18, 28, 47–9, 51, 67–8, 102, 114, 116–17, 129, 138, 146
canonist's manse 10, 70
Canterbury, Archbishop of see Laud, William
cantor 72–3, 116, 146
Caroline University see under Aberdeen, university
cathedral chapters 39
Catholics, Catholicism 2, 4, 7–10, 12–15, 17–19, 21–7, 30, 31, 37, 49, 51–3, 59, 61–3, 68, 80, 87, 97, 105–7, 141, 150
Chalmer, John 167
Chalmers, David 140
Chalmers, John, subprincipal 52, 54, 62–3, 136
chamber mails 167–8
chancellors, AU 8, 18, 26, 64, 70, 72, 76, 77, 123
chapel 13, 14, 15, 24, 48, 54, 76
chaplaincies 28
chaplains' chambers 70
Charles I 73, 75, 78, 94–5, 99–112 passim, 115, 120, 122
charters 76, 79, 99, 152
Cheyne of Arnage, James 12
Cheyne, Alexander, canonist 17, 18, 28, 49, 129
choristers 48, 146
Chrystisone, John 152
Cicero, Marcus Tullius 46, 156
civilist, civil law, civil law faculty 4, 28, 47–9, 51, 67, 68, 104, 116, 117, 146
civilist's croft 70
civilist's manse 10
classes 45–6, 47, 58, 75–6, 155–8, 166–8
clerk 74, 80
clerk register 38
College Bounds 54, 55
College Court 54–5
colleges of arts 51
Collynie 151
common procurators 50, 55, 65, 67, 147
commissions, commissioners 41, 100; (1568) 15; (1578) 30, 32; (1581) 30, 32; (1582–3) 30–4; (1584) 34; (1593) 35, 45; (1597) 37, 38; (1619) 63, 64, 69; (1636) 95–8; (1637) 97; (1638) 100; see also visitations
Confession of Faith (1560) 7, 17, 18, 164
convention of estates 127
cook/gardener 147, 161
Copernicus 81
Corrichie, battle of 10, 12
Corse 61
cosmography 46, 156
Counter-Reformation 52, 62, 81, 105
covenanters 1, 4, 94, 105–23 passim, 145
Craig, Sir Thomas 1
Crawford, Countess of 26
Cruikshank, Alexander, sacrist 167
Cunningham, David, Bishop of Aberdeen 32, 34, 35, 38, 48
curriculum see teaching

daily routines 51, 162–3
Davidson, Alexander 133
Davidson, William 78, 79
deans of faculties 67, 74–6, 83, 123, 164–5; see also under individual faculties
degrees 72; BD 82; DD 69, 71, 80, 83, 105; LLD 80, 83, 138; MA 18, 44 158; MD 80
Deveron, river 165
discipline 12, 33, 35, 54–6, 58–9, 162–3

Discipline, First Book of 14, 37, 48, 122
Discipline, Second Book of 29
divinity *see* theology
Douai, college 12
Douglas, James, 4th Earl of Morton 29, 31
dress 73, 75, 76, 78, 159
Dublin, university 81
Dun, Patrick, mediciner, dean of medicine 67–9, 75, 82, 141
Dunbar, Gavin, Bishop of Aberdeen 99, 100, 122, 146
Dunbar, Robert, regent 59
Dundee 35

economus (steward) 50–1, 134, 146, 149, 159–61
Edinburgh 9, 10, 18, 35, 85
Edinburgh, university 39, 51, 56, 90, 104, 138, 141
Elgin, cathedral 8, 15
Ellon 99
Elphinstone, Bishop William 23, 38, 39, 47, 48, 51, 60, 115, 146, 151, 158
Elphinstone, James, 1st Lord Balmerino 37, 38
Elphinstone, John, 2nd Lord Balmerino 114–15
endowments *see* revenues
episcopalians, episcopalianism 31, 39, 53, 87, 106, 114
Erskine of Dun, John 17, 25
establishment (staffing) 4, 12, 13, 17, 47–51, 64, 67–73, 75–6, 83, 96, 128, 146–65 *passim*; 1569 purge, 17–24, 27, 49, 67
ethics 46, 156
examination fees (exam or promotion silver) 57, 65, 117, 164, 167–8

faculties 4, 18, 49, 51, 68, 74–6, 88, 123, 164–5, *and see under individual faculties*
fees 90; *see also* chamber mails; examination fees; spoon silver; *and* tuition fees
fiars prices 147
finance (property, revenues, salaries) 10, 30, 33, 35, 52, 63–80 *passim*, 87–8, 90, 95–7, 99, 104, 117–18,

146–8, 151–65 *passim*, 170; alienation of 13, 14, 52; grants of 2, 5, 28, 39, 52, 65, 85, 122, 123, 145; inadequacy of revenues 4, 5, 25, 27, 28, 37, 39, 41–2, 47–9, 52, 60, 72–3, 77, 88, 96, 102, 120, 138
Five Articles of Perth 80
Folla Rule 152
Forbes of Corse, Patrick, Bishop of Abereen 2, 4, 5, 10, 40, 41, 60–95 *passim*, 99, 102, 105–7, 114–15, 117, 119, 122–3, 136, 140–1, 170; memorial volume 79–80, 84–6, 89, 141; portrait 84
Forbes of Craigievar, William 71
Forbes, Alexander, Bishop of Aberdeen 137
Forbes, Professor John 4, 5, 10, 62, 71, 74–5, 106–12 *passim*, 118–19, 138, 143
Forbes, William, regent, dean of arts 67
Forvie 26, 28, 151, 152
Four Nations, the 58–9, 74, 118, 165
France, French 9, 18, 26, 51
Fraser, Simon, Master of Lovat 6
Fraser, Sir Alexander 132
Fraser, James 132
Fraserburgh 132

Gallio, Junius 107
Galloway, Andrew, subprincipal 17, 18
garden 10, 151
gardener *see* cook/gardener
Gardyne, Gilbert, regent 12, 16, 127–8
general assembly of the Church of Scotland 27, 33, 34, 170; (1560) 127; (1563) 15; (1565) 15; (1567) 15; (1568) 15; (1570) 27; (1574) 29; (1578) 29; (1579) 30; (1582) 30, 31; (1583) 31–2, 37, 42; (1593) 35, 37; (1605) 53; (1610) 53; (1616) 132; (1638) 112–17 *passim*; (1639) 116; (1640) 118–19; (1641) 120
Garioch 165
general attendant (beadle) 57, 164
Geneva 28
geography 46, 156
geometry 156

Glasgow, university 2, 12, 14–15, 29, 31, 35, 45, 47, 48, 56, 61, 73, 90, 138, 141; *Nova Erectio* 29, 35, 51, 131, 149, 151
Glasgow Assembly *see* general assembly (1638)
Glenmuik 151
globes 78, 80
Gordon of Straloch, Robert 91
Gordon, George, 4th Earl of Huntly 8, 9, 10, 14
Gordon, George, 5th Earl of Huntly 15, 17, 27
Gordon, George, 6th Earl and 1st Marquis of Huntly 37, 53, 63
Gordon, George, 7th Earl and 2nd Marquis of Huntly 97, 100, 102, 115, 123, 141
Gordon, James, minister of Rothiemay 2, 10, 38, 91, 118, 120
Gordon, Professor Thomas 149, 150
Gordon, William, Bishop of Aberdeen 8, 13, 14, 18, 26, 48
Gordon, William, mediciner 10, 72, 75–9, 82, 95–100, 102, 104, 114, 117, 118
Gordon earls and marquises of Huntly 37
Gordons 10
Gospel 150, 151, 153
Gowrie, Earl of *see* Ruthven, William
graduation 6, 28, 72, 85, 86, 158, 159
Graham, James, 5th Earl and 1st Marquis of Montrose 115
grammarian (humanist), grammar 25, 47, 50, 67, 68, 79, 82, 114, 146, 147, 161; *see also* Latin
grammarian's (humanist's) manse 10
Greece, ancient 23
Greek 44–6, 58, 155, 157, 163
Guild, William, principal, rector 110, 112, 117–20, 122, 145
Guthrie, John, Bishop of Moray 61, 80
Guthrie, Patrick, subprincipal 64

Hagen, Francis van 140–1
Hay, George 20–7, 30, 42, 44
Hay, Nicholas, civilist 17, 49
Hebrew 25, 26, 28, 44, 46, 65, 79, 100, 153, 156

Heidelberg, university 71
Henderson, G D 36, 133
Heriot, Adam, minister of Aberdeen 15
history 46, 156
Hope of Craighall, Sir Thomas 78
Houston, David 167
Howie, Robert 45
humanism 23, 24, 26
humanist's manse *see* grammarian's manse
humanists *see* grammarians
Huntly, Earls and Marquises of *see* Gordon, George
Huntly's House 10

Innes, Beroald, economus 50, 52, 54, 134
Innes, Patrick, sacrist 110

James VI, King of Scots 7, 27, 30–6, 38–9, 41, 52, 63, 69, 91, 104, 150, 169, 170
Jamesone, George 92, 141
janitors (porters) 58, 65, 159
Johnston, Arthur, rector 97, 99, 100, 101
Johnston, John 45, 133
jurisdiction 54–5, 77, 78

Keith 62
Keith, George, 4th Earl Marischal 30–2, 35–7, 68, 132
Kennedy, John, canonist 13, 152
Ker, Professor John 123, 131
Kincardineshire *see* Mearns
King Charles's University *see* Aberdeen, university
King's Covenant 115
Kinkell 18
Knight, Professor William 140, 149, 150
Knox, John 9, 19, 26, 127

Latin 45, 46, 58, 155, 157, 163
Laud, William, Archbishop of Canterbury 78
Lauder, William 85
law, law faculty 25, 27, 28, 44, 83, 88, 96, 100; dean of 75; *see also* canonist *and* civilist

laws (regulations) 79, 96
Lawson, James, subprincipal 25, 26, 28
Leech, David, subprincipal, dean of arts 59, 79, 81, 96–7, 99, 102–3, 143
Leith (Leech?), Mr 143, 171
Leith, John 135
Leith, John, rector 67
Leslie, Andrew, canonist 129
Leslie, John, canonist, Bishop of Ross 9, 127
Leslie, William, principal 5, 44–5, 75, 78–9, 81, 91–105 passim, 110, 114, 116–19, 169–71
librarian 78
library (books) 13–14, 43, 72, 78–80, 83, 85, 120, 122, 127, 133; device 89
Lindsay of Menmuir, John 37, 38
literature, literary studies 20, 23
logic 42, 46
Logie Buchan 25, 26
Lords of the Congregation 8, 9
Lumsdem of Clova, Robert, rector 130
Lunan, Alexander, regent 66, 81
Lundie, John, grammarian 75, 79, 82, 94, 110, 114–15, 117, 143
Lutheranism 107, 143

Maitland, Robert, dean of Aberdeen 159
Marischal College, Aberdeen 5, 35–7, 39, 45, 51, 56, 57, 75–6, 82–3, 90, 104, 122–3, 131–2, 138, 149–50; and Bp Forbes 62–3, 68–9, 83, 85
Marischal, Earls see Keith, George and William
Marr 59, 165
Mary Magdalene, chaplaincy of (St Nicholas Church, Aberdeen) 152
Mary Queen of Scots 7–10, 13, 15, 27; protects KC 12
Maule of Panmure, Patrick 104–5, 143, 169
mathematics (arithmetic) 27, 46, 156
Maxwell, John, Bishop of Ross 78
meals 57, 58, 159
Mearns (Kincardineshire) 8, 27, 123
mediciner, medicine, medical faculty 4, 18, 25, 27, 44, 47–9, 51, 67, 68,

82–3, 88, 96, 100, 102, 104, 118, 146; dean of 75
mediciner's manse 10, 49
Melville, Andrew 2, 28–33, 35–6, 38, 42, 44, 47–8, 52–3, 61–2, 71, 106
Melville, James 29, 135
Melvillians see presbyterians
Mercer, Robert 133
Mercer, Robert, regent 45, 133
Merser, Thomas, clerk, provisor 80, 141
Methlick 28, 32, 152
Monbray 151
Montrose 61
Montrose, Earl of see Graham, James
Monykebuck see New Machar
Moray 59, 165
Moray, Earl of see Stewart, James
Mortlach 18
Morton, Earl of see Douglas, James
Mowat, Roger, civilist 73, 75, 83, 102, 117
musician's manse 10

National Covenant 100, 105, 108, 110, 115, 116, 118, 119, 143
natural history 46, 156
neo-scholasticism 2, 81, 119
New Aberdeen see Aberdeen
New Foundation (Nova Fundatio), AU 2, 4, 5, 29–60 passim, 94–105 passim, 108, 112, 114–23, 131, 169–71; Bp Forbes and 64–93 passim; text 32, 45, 133, 149–65; text destroyed 88, 90–1, 93, 99–100, 102, 114, 147–9, 170
New Machar (Monykebuck) 67, 70, 90, 95
Nicolson, Thomas, civilist 67–9
Norie, Duncan, regent 17
North East Scotland 2, 7–15, 17–19, 25, 27, 37, 61, 83, 85, 105, 107, 115–16, 123

Ogilvie, Robert, regent 78
Ogston, Thomas, regent 17, 18, 28
Old Aberdeen, burgh 8, 54–5; bishop's palace 8, 10, 78; grammar school 10, 12, 47, 50, 53, 161 ; map 11; music school 72, 95; parish see Old Machar

Old Foundation, AU 2, 4, 5, 18, 29, 32, 34, 39, 41, 47, 48, 50–1, 94–105 *passim*, 108, 114, 146–7; Bp Forbes and 64–5, 67–79, 93, 105, 114

Old Machar (Old Aberdeen; St Machar; Snaw), parish 28, 53–4, 62–3, 65, 70, 79, 90, 151–3; *see also* St Machar's Cathedral

Ord 151

organist 146

Oxford, university 81, 83, 136

Paris, university 26, 78, 79

parish ministry, ministers 4, 5, 19, 27–9, 44, 46–8, 59, 62, 63, 71, 72, 74, 83

Parliament, Scottish 34, 96; (1578) 29, 30; (1581) 30; (1583) 33; (1584) 34; (1597) 37–9, 104, 170; (1617) 39, 40, 73, 104, 132; (1633) 73; (1641) 120, 122

Pettie 151

philosophy 21, 27, 42, 44, 46, 51, 59, 97, 100, 102–3, 154, 158–9

physiology 46, 156

play *see* recreation

poetry 27, 82, 97

politics 46, 156

prebends 48, 146

presbyterians, presbyterianism (Melvillianism) 31–5, 37–9, 41–2, 45, 51–2, 60–1, 106, 114, 132

principals 5, 36–7, 39, 123, 146, 147, 153–5, 166

printing 66, 77, 83, 108

Privy Council, Scottish 15, 17, 30, 35, 95–7, 99, 122, 170

professors 45–6, 64, 71, 75, 97, 119

Protestantism, need for unity 4, 61–2, 80–1, 87, 106–7

provisor 50, 134, 141, 159

Ptolemy 81

quadrant 78

Raban, Edward 66, 83, 85, 108

Rait, David, principal 5, 14, 35–8, 43–4, 50–5, 131, 133, 135; Bp Forbes and 61–72 *passim*, 78, 80, 85, 90; as minister 53–4, 60

Rait, James, regent 133

Rait, William 43, 44, 133

Rait, William, regent, principal 133

Ramism 42, 44, 52, 81, 119

Ramus, Peter (Ramée, Pierre de la) 2, 42–5, 119

recreations (play, sport) 6, 57, 126, 162–3

rectors 26, 32, 67, 74, 76, 79, 83, 123, 130, 164–5; assessors 75, 83

regents 17, 18, 25, 26, 33, 46–7, 50, 57–9, 71–2, 78, 96–7, 104, 114, 117–19, 146–7, 155–8, 166

regenting 47, 119

regulations *see* laws

Reid, Alexander, clerk 74

Reid, Dr Alexander 78, 80, 85, 86

religious education 46, 156, 163

rhetoric 82

Rome, ancient 23

Ross, Alexander, rector 110

Ross, bishops of *see* Leslie, John *and* Maxwell, John

Ross, Gilbert, cantor 10, 72–3, 75, 95, 96, 102

royalists 115, 123

Rutherford, Samuel 107

Ruthven Raid 31–3, 61

Ruthven William, 1st Earl of Gowrie 33

sacrist 17, 146, 167

St Andrews 30, 32, 33

St Andrews, archbishops of *see* Adamson, Patrick *and* Spottiswood, John

St Andrews, university 2, 12, 14–15, 25, 29–30, 38–9, 45, 56, 61–2, 66, 71, 73, 83, 104, 141, 149–51; St Leonard's College 6; St Mary's (New) College 26, 30, 45; New Foundation 30

St Germain, hospital 151

St Machar's Cathedral (Aberdeen Cathedral) 8, 10, 14, 15, 39, 53, 152; *see also* Old Machar

Sandilands, James, elder, canonist 72, 83, 138; portrait 92, 141

Sandilands, James, younger, canonist, civilist 72, 75, 83, 95, 99, 102, 104, 116–18

scholasticism 21, 23, 42, 81; *see also* neo-scholasticism
scientific instruments 78, 80, 85
Scroggie, Alexander elder, rector 110
Scroggie, Alexander younger, regent 116, 117
Sedan, university 71
servants 147, 153
Session, Court of 10, 70, 77, 105, 114
Sharp, James, Archbishop of St Andrews 139
Sibbald, James 75, 110, 112, 117
silver arrow 6, 126
Skene, Gilbert, mediciner 13, 17, 49, 134
Slains 151
Smeaton, Thomas 31–2
Snaw *see* Old Machar
Spalding, John 144
Spital 28, 152
spoon silver 65, 137, 167–8
sport *see* recreation
Spottiswood, John, Archbishop of St Andrews 27
Stewart, James, Earl of Moray 15, 17, 20–1, 25, 27, 41, 42, 60
Stewart, Theophilus, grammarian 12, 17, 50
Strachan, Andrew, professor of theology 80, 81–3, 85–6
Stuart, Walter, principal 5, 28, 33, 35, 43, 44, 50–2
students; admission 56–7, 75, 158, 163; numbers 5, 12, 18, 55–6, 90, 135–6, 141
students of canon law 47, 146
students of civil law 47, 146
students of theology *see* regents
subprincipal 33, 46, 47, 54, 146–7, 155–7

Syriac 153

Talon, Omer (Talaeus, Audomarus) 44
Tartaret (Tartaretus), Petrus 21, 23
teaching 57–8, 64–5, 70–2, 85, 139; content 42, 44–6, 51, 155–6; methods 42, 46–7, 51, 71–2, 119, 157–8
theology (divinity), theology faculty 4, 17, 24, 26, 27, 42, 44, 46–8, 51, 52, 82, 105–7, 138; Aberdeen school 4, 80–1, 94; dean 75; chair 4, 70–2, 108
theses 58, 66, 81, 85
Thirds of Benefices 10
tuition fees 57, 164
Tullynestle 18
Turriff, grammar school 18
Tyrie 18

Udny, Peter, subprincipal 53
Udoch 151
universities, Scottish 2, 14–15, 29–30, 38, 39, 51, 56, 90, 94–6

visitations 1, 41, 74, 79, 163; (1549) 12, 18; (1569) 17; (1593) 37, 45; (1616) 132; (1619) 63–70, 75, 80, 91, 137; (1623) 70, 91; (1628) 71–2; (1634) 74–5, 78, 139; (1635) 95; (1636) 95; (1637) 96–7, 99; (1638) 100, 102, 104, 114, 171; (1639) 115–17; (1640) 118; (1641) 122; *see also* commissions

Wedderburne, David, grammarian 67–8, 82
Westhall 152
Wodrow, Robert 33, 87
Wright, Alexander, sacrist 17